To Guy,

TONY COTTEE

WEST HAM:
THE INSIDE STORY

Happy 50th .....
You Old Git !!

Best. Wishes

Tony Cottee

First published in England in September 2012 by

Philip Evans Sports Media

©Copyright Tony Cottee and Philip Evans

Printed by Advantage Digital Print

Distributed by Gardners Books Ltd

Set in Palatino

ISBN 978-0-9565961-5-4

This book is dedicated to my three fantastic children,
Chloe, Matt and Billy

Acknowledgements

This book would not have been written and produced without the help of numerous people and I would especially like to thank Tony McDonald and Philip Evans.

My publisher and I would also like to acknowledge and thank Danny Francis and Tony Hogg for their valuable input.

Design: Mark Taylor

Cover design: Mark Taylor
Cover photography: Football World

Contents

Introduction

S INCE that defining day in my life, July 11, 2001 – the date I retired from professional football – two questions have been consistently thrown at me:

1. Don't you wish you were born 10 years later?
2. Weren't you involved in a consortium to buy West Ham United?

The first question is an easy one to answer – it's obviously 'yes!' In fact, I could have become rich over the last 10 years given the amount of people who have actually asked this one and, in some cases, taken great pleasure in saying it!

Would I change my wonderful career in terms of the era I played in? Absolutely not. The 80s and 90s were a great time to be a player and we enjoyed ourselves on and off the pitch. Most of my playing career was covered in my first autobiography, *Claret & Blues*, which came out towards the end of 1995, but this follow-up spans my last five-and-a-half seasons as a player and mainly the period since then.

Would I like to have earned the money they get today? Of course I would. Any ex-player who says otherwise is telling porkies.

But the point is, we can't change when we were born, and I wouldn't want to, but it's a very easy answer to the original question.

The second question is put to me as many times as the first but the difference is, when people ask about the consortium I put together between 2004 and '06 to mount a takeover bid at West Ham, they don't actually seem to believe it ever happened. I suspect they think I simply put my name to a project that was dreamt up by the *News of the World*.

That's particularly annoying, because I worked my socks off throughout that period to find the right people to buy my beloved Hammers, yet all I usually get in return is sarcasm and that knowing nod when someone looks at you as if to say "yeah, right."

The truth of the matter is that I DID find someone to buy the club and, through no fault of my own, was not allowed to be a part of what should have been a glorious era for everyone involved. I put in hundreds of hours and flew around Europe to try and achieve my goal. I spoke to foreign businessmen and local entrepreneurs in my relentless pursuit to bring the right owners in.

I spoke about my plans to David Sullivan and David Gold *before* they eventually bought the club in January 2010.

I had arguments with Eggert Magnusson, who, but for me, would never have become chairman and CEO of WHUFC, and his predecessor Terry Brown, whose bitterness led to me being sacked by the club.

I spoke to a Middle East businessman who promised the world and delivered nothing.

And I had West Ham fans from all around the world contacting me with advice and help to try and put the club back where it belongs.

I felt like I spoke to just about everyone on the planet in my quest to turn the dream into reality but all I ever get as a follow-up to my answer to question 2 is: "Yeah right, course you did."

The main reason for writing this book is to put the record straight and, more importantly from a historical point of view, I want to explain how a group of Icelandics ended up owning one of the most famous clubs in English football. So much has happened since I retired as a player but at last I have this chance to explain the full story behind the takeovers.

My great friend in football, Tony Gale, typically refers to me in one of his many speeches: "Tony once tried to buy West Ham for £100m but he ended up £99m short!"

He says it in a way that only Galey can. But the truth is, I got much, much closer to my financial target than that, I can promise you.

Here is the inside story of what *really* happened at West Ham...

Tony Cottee
September 2012

1

West Ham till I die

WHENEVER people approach me for a chat about West Ham, it sometimes disappoints me a little if they seem surprised by my passion for the Hammers, as if my interest in the club simply has its roots in the fact that I happened to play a lot of games for them in two spells spanning the 80s and early 90s. First and foremost, I tell them I was a supporter of my local club before I became a player and now I've reverted to being a fan.

I was at Wembley among the 100,000 or so who watched the 1980 FA Cup Final and the League Cup Final the following year. And 31 years later, I was just as excited to be back at the national stadium to cheer West Ham to victory over Blackpool in the 2012 Championship Play-off Final that secured promotion to the Premier League.

There was never any question where my football allegiance would lie. Born at Forest Gate Hospital in July 1965, almost a year to the day before Bobby Moore lifted the World Cup, and brought up in Essex from where the club has traditionally drawn most of its fans, I really had no choice but to support the Hammers. I saw my first match at Upton Park in March 1972 – we beat Nottingham Forest, 4-2, in a thriller and my boyhood hero 'Pop' Robson scored twice.

What I regard as the second half of my 19-year playing career began back at the club where it had all started for me as an associate schoolboy.

After seven seasons with Everton, I enjoyed the two years of my second spell at the club and it was always my intention to retire as a player at West Ham. Even though

In one of the West Ham corporate hospitality lounges with my boyhood hero 'Pop' Robson, who scored twice in the first game I ever watched at Upton Park.

I'd lost a yard or two of pace, I was pleased to finish 1994-95 and 1995-96 as the club's leading scorer, albeit an honour I shared with Julian Dicks in my second season back.

The distinction of being top scorer was always a prime target that stayed with me throughout my career. To be honest, when Frank McAvennie pipped me to become the leading scorer in 1985-86, West Ham's best ever league campaign, I was livid. Although delighted for Frank that he'd scored 26 first division goals in that memorable season, I felt I'd let myself down by falling six short of his tally. When Peter Beardsley outscored me at Everton in 1991-92, the only time in my six full seasons on Merseyside that I didn't finish the campaign as Toffees' top goal-getter, the blow was softened by the fact that I was injured for a chunk of the season.

My 13 goals in 1994-95 undoubtedly played a key part in keeping West Ham in the Premier League. I was in and out of the team a bit more in my second season back and, as manager Harry Redknapp began to experiment with his foreign legion at Upton Park, I sensed my days were numbered at the start of 1996-97. By then, 'H' had brought in the experienced Portuguese playmaker Paulo Futre plus Florin Raducioui and Ilie Dumitrescu, who had both impressed for Romania in the Euro 96 finals.

Things certainly changed in my second stint at West Ham. There were two dressing rooms at the Chadwell Heath training ground and, for some reason, most of the British lads had ended up in the room on the left as you walked along the corridor, whereas I usually got changed in the one on the right. Many of the players who shared the dressing room with me in my first spell had left the club, which meant I was the only Brit left in a room full of foreigners.

Happy days with Frank McAvennie in 1985-86.

Obviously, I couldn't make out what they were saying to each other and they couldn't understand me either. In the end I thought, 'sod this, I'm going next door', so I packed up my gear and decamped to the other changing room, where all the other British players had created a really good team spirit. There was Dicksie, John Moncur, Ian Bishop, Don Hutchison, Steve Potts, Kenny Brown and Keith Rowland – all good lads and honest pros.

We had some real characters at the club then but, as I say, Harry was experimenting at the start of my third season. It didn't help my cause when I picked up an Achilles injury while running in Hainault Forest in pre-season. It wouldn't happen now. Premier League players aren't asked to undertake the long runs that we did, although none of us knew any different back then. Nowadays, players probably run no more than 400 yards at any given time in pre-season, whereas in our day the manager and his coaching staff just sent us off into the forest and told us to run five or six miles, to build up stamina before the season got underway.

No sooner had I recovered from the Achilles strain than I tweaked my calf muscle in pre-season and had persistent problems with it from then until I finally retired from playing five years later.

Even though I was still the best finisher at the club, it's fair to say that, with all the newcomers arriving – either on permanent deals or short-term loans, in the days before the transfer window – I'd slipped down the pecking order and was fourth or fifth choice striker. If I was not wanted by a club, my philosophy had always been to go somewhere where I was needed and appreciated. I never saw any merit in hanging around just for the sake of picking up my wages, which is what too many lazy players are content to do. Where's the purpose and ambition in that? I wanted to play.

But the truth is, I really didn't want to leave West Ham for a second time. It was always my intention to play on in the claret and blue for another five or six seasons and end my playing days at Upton Park.

A big incentive for me to stay was the chance to overhaul Scottish international John Dick and pre-war winger Jimmy Ruffell, who are tied third in the club's all-time scoring records with 166 goals – behind Vic Watson (326) and Geoff Hurst (252). I was never going to catch Sir Geoff but to have moved above Johnny and Jimmy into third spot would have been a fantastic personal landmark. Those who know how diligently I maintained my scrapbooks and kept statistical records from my early playing days will understand when I say what a big carrot this was for me to stay at Upton

On the ball against Manchester United in my second spell with the Hammers.

Park for the rest of my career...and score the 21 goals I needed to overhaul Dick and Ruffell.

Unfortunately, it wasn't to be and in October 1996 it was time to move on again. But no matter what, I will forever remain West Ham Till I Die.

West Ham United leading goalscorers
The top 10 goalscorers, including all official first team league and cup matches

Pos	Player	Seasons with club	Games	Goals	Gls per game ratio
1	Vic Watson	1920-35	505	326	65%
2	Geoff Hurst	1959-72	502	252	50%
3	John Dick	1953-63	351	166	47%
4	Jimmy Ruffell	1921-37	548	166	30%
5	Tony Cottee	1983-88 & 1994-96	336	146	43%
6	Johnny Byrne	1961-67	190	107	52%
7	Bryan 'Pop' Robson	1971-74 & 1976-79	254	104	41%
8	Trevor Brooking	1967-84	636	102	16%
9	Martin Peters	1962-70	364	100	27%
10	Malcolm Musgrove	1953-63	301	89	32%

2

Feeling the heat

THE only time I'd previously been linked with a possible move to a foreign club came in the summer of 1988, when I chose Everton instead of Arsenal. Fiorentina, who were among the top clubs in Italy at the time, also expressed an interest in signing me from West Ham but nothing came of it.

When I left West Ham for the second time, in October 1996, unfortunately it was not to play for one of the giants of *Serie A* or Spain's *La Liga*, which would have been great. Instead, my destination was that well-known hotbed of world football...Malaysia!

It hadn't crossed my mind that I'd soon be heading to an exotic Far East location when Harry Redknapp called me into his office one day after training at Chadwell Heath. He sat me down and then started laughing. "Are you all right, H – what's up?' The players hardly ever called him by his first name. It was usually 'H'.

"You won't believe this," he said. "I've had an agent on the phone who wants you to go and play in Malaysia."

At this point I also started laughing. "Yeah, all right, H, what is it...April Fool's Day?"

"No, I'm serious," he continued.

Harry Redknapp's foreign revolution reduced my first team chances.

I told him that while I wanted to stay at West Ham, I'd be prepared to discuss the offer with the agent concerned – a company that involved the former Manchester United player Scott McGarvey – to at least hear what he had to say. Nothing materialised for a couple of weeks and I'd made up my mind to stay at Upton Park and battle for my place when another agent, former Leyton Orient midfielder Barry Silkman, became involved and made the deal happen.

The Malaysian club turned out to be Selangor, who were a major force in what was the equivalent of our Premier League. They were permitted only three overseas players and saw me as a replacement for Dave Mitchell, the former Glasgow Rangers striker who had proved quite a star in those parts. Selangor's original target was Niall Quinn but he turned them down for family reasons, although when I phoned him to ask what he thought of the club, he advised me to speak to them.

Selangor paid for my then wife Lorraine and I to fly to Kuala Lumpur and as well as being given a tour of the football club, the trip also gave us the chance to weigh up the capital city and decide if it was right for us and our daughter Chloe, who was about to start school. I'd previously been to Malaysia twice with Everton and all I could remember about the place was the intense heat and humidity, which made playing football very uncomfortable.

Selangor's English manager Ken Worden was there to meet and greet us on arrival in KL and after showing us around the club's training ground and stadium, we were dropped off at a hotel in the centre of a place called Shah Alam. What we didn't realise until later that night was that the hotel was immediately next door to the biggest mosque in the southern hemisphere. Being in no way religious, I hadn't given any thought to how this could impact on us, until we first heard the call to prayer at 10.00pm. Lorraine and I were jetlagged from the 14-hour flight and felt shattered by the time we got to bed. Some hope we had of getting much sleep, though. The sound of wailing woke us up every four hours! I wasn't happy.

The next day Ken and his wife took us to the outskirts of Kuala Lumpur to view possible living accommodation. Selangor owned a number of reasonable apartments but we fancied something a bit more luxurious. KL is a city like many others, fluctuating from areas of extreme poverty to total luxury, and it was important we found the right accommodation.

We also looked at a possible school for Chloe and found an ideal one with its own outdoor pool and we knew she would adapt without a problem. But there was so much to take in over a whirlwind weekend that we were a bit taken aback when Ken said the club would need a decision from me, there and then, on whether I would accept their offer.

The financial terms were good – a two-year deal worth around £200,000 net per year, plus other benefits, which was vastly more than I'd been getting at West Ham – so I had to give it serious consideration. It was a fantastic deal for me, although I still can't get my head around the fact that some players now earn that much in a week!

From a football point of view, it was a big move. I'd spent my career in the top flight and I'll admit it was a disappointment that no English Premier League clubs had shown any interest in signing me. Newspapers linked me with QPR and Southend United but, having been West Ham's top scorer for the previous two seasons, I thought one or two Premier clubs would have expressed an interest. OK, I'd just turned 31 and had lost some of my pace, but I had matured into a better all round player compared to my younger days and felt I still had something to offer at the highest level.

On the other hand, I had to weigh up the fact that I was no longer in West Ham's first team and the move to Malaysia offered an exciting new adventure. At least I'd be earning very good money and when my two-year contract was up, I expected our family to return home to England and I'd see out my playing days at a local lower league club.

Record signing

By the time Ken arrived to drive us to the airport for the flight back to London, we decided to take the plunge and give it a go. I gave him my word that I'd sign for Selangor and all the actual paperwork was later concluded by fax. The most the club had ever paid for a player was £100,000 for Dave Mitchell but I cost them a new record fee of £750,000.

Once I knew I'd be leaving West Ham for the last time, I borrowed the *Hammers News Magazine* executive box at the Boleyn Ground for a night and watched the 1-1 draw with Derby County from there, in the company of family and friends. The fans soon noticed me sitting behind them at the back of the Bobby Moore Stand and started singing my name. The sound of *There's Only One Tony Cottee* echoing round that end of the stadium only added to what was an emotional occasion for me. It was the end of an era. I never thought I'd get the chance to play at Upton Park again.

The football and climate in Malaysia took some getting used to and, in truth, I never did come to terms with it. Although I'd been to Malaysia and agreed to join them in November 1996, their season didn't start until the following April...and by then they had appointed a new manager. Ken Worden later explained that he signed me because he'd wanted to leave a legacy at Selangor, although it's incredible to think that he did so despite knowing he would be gone even before I made my debut.

Dato Aini, the wealthy owner who bankrolled the club and proclaimed that Selangor were 'the Manchester United of Malaysia', replaced Ken with Steve Wicks, the former Chelsea and QPR centre-half. Dato was keen to try and keep me happy and thought the appointment of an English manager would go a long way to achieving that aim. I'd played against Steve and had known him from the early 90s when he worked for First Artist, the agency run by John and Phil Smith, who handled my move to Everton in 1988.

Once he got the job, Steve arranged a mini pre-season tour that involved three matches in England, against non-league Wokingham and reserve teams from Reading and Arsenal, who included Ian Wright. It was a beautifully crisp spring evening at Wokingham, probably around 45 degrees and perfect weather conditions for football, so I was amazed to see most of my new team-mates come out wearing long-sleeved shirts, gloves and tracksuit bottoms! In Kuala Lumpur they were used to playing in temperatures of around 90 degrees fahrenheit and, worse, 90% humidity. For me it was almost unbearable. The other two foreigners in the team, a lad called Chris and another named Mehmet, came from South Africa and Australia respectively and they both adapted better than I did to these stifling conditions.

Football wise, I didn't enjoy it and not just because I missed a penalty on my debut in the Malaysian equivalent of the Community Shield. Despite our 2-0 win in front of a crowd of 35,000 and live TV cameras, the press had a field day wondering how the club's expensive new record signing could possibly fail to score from 12 yards – I never enjoyed taking penalties. English is their second language, so I could read the match reports in the Malaysian papers and they slaughtered me.

At least they couldn't accuse me of not working hard enough. As we sat in the dressing room listening to the manager's half-time team-talk, I noticed a huge pool of water had suddenly appeared at my feet. I thought I must have accidentally kicked over a bottle of water until I realised it was sweat dripping from my body. I quickly realised I'd made a mistake in signing for a Malaysian team as things went from bad to worse, on and off the field.

The best part about signing for Selangor was the five-week family holiday we enjoyed between signing and the start of pre-season training, which saw us spend the Christmas and New Year period in Australia. For the first time in my career I wasn't playing on Boxing Day and it was a rare pleasure to spend part of that day sitting in the sun at the Melbourne Cricket Ground, watching the Australia v West Indies Test. We celebrated the start of 1997 in Sydney Harbour, marvelling at the spectacular firework display.

Chloe and me in Malaysia.
Happily, she avoided a deadly virus.

Paranoid about Chloe

Back in Malaysia, we rented a beautiful three-bedroom apartment overlooking a valley but the view, and our lifestyle, became irrelevant when we feared that Chloe could contract the coxsackie virus, an infection commonly spread among children under the age of six in tropical climates and which was sweeping the country at the time. I'd previously suffered food poisoning after eating prawns but soon got over it but this was something else. The virus had already killed a number of young children and, as parents, we became paranoid about our daughter's health, although thankfully she managed to avoid any illness.

When Lorraine fell pregnant in June '97, we decided it would be best for her and Chloe to return to England while I saw out the rest of my first season in Malaysia alone.

I hated having to look after myself for six weeks – the longest Lorraine and I had been apart since we were married in June 1989. The fact that she was by then expecting twins gave me a convenient excuse to hasten my own departure from Malaysia.

Despite scoring 14 goals for Selangor, who finished fourth in the table and won the League Cup at the expense of Kedah, I knew I didn't want to stay for a second season. Instead of living up to expectations as the team's star performer, the unremitting heat and humidity reduced me to an average player. My team-mates couldn't handle the British weather and I couldn't adapt to their climate.

My unease came to a head when we suffered a 3-2 home defeat by the team at the bottom of the league, thanks to a dodgy own goal, having held a two-goal lead at half-time. One of the goals we conceded was absolutely ridiculous. The 7,000 crowd – well down on early season attendances – vented their anger by throwing full plastic bottles of water down onto the pitch and gave us a torrent of abuse at the final whistle. It was easy to understand their feelings and I, too, had cause to question the integrity of one or two of my team-mates as we lost in, shall we say, highly dubious circumstances.

Cash in brown envelopes

Some of what went on out there was surreal. In one game, four players were sent off for fighting. After home matches, if we'd won the Selangor owner would come into the dressing room and hand each player a brown envelope containing some readies! Not a lot – around £100 each – but it was a nice little bonus. One day, as we were about to kick off, I noticed a huge mushroom the size of a soup bowl growing on the pitch, so I booted it off the field! To minimise the debilitating effect of soaring temperatures, we didn't start training until 5.00pm each day and would train at the 80,000-capacity Shah Alam stadium under floodlights.

The Malaysian season is split into three parts. They play from April to June, then take a three-week break before resuming from the end of June until August. The third, and final, part of the season runs from September until November, when they stage their major cup competition.

It wasn't just the football that got me down. I couldn't get to grips with the culture either. On one away trip, I shared a hotel room with our captain, a devout Muslim, who woke me up at 1.00am and then again at five o'clock in the morning when he got up to pray again. He was a nice fella and while I respected his religious beliefs, the lack of sleep did nothing to help my preparation for the following day's game.

Car insurance and a phone conversation with Steve Walford led to a new adventure with Leicester.

I expressed my dissatisfaction with Malaysian football to Hugh Southon, a journalist friend from England, but when the interview I did appeared in the English press my comments had been sensationalised. By the time it was translated for the Malaysian media, it appeared that I'd been slagging off the club and my team-mates, especially when I questioned the honesty of our disastrous 3-2 defeat by the bottom side. The coverage did nothing to enhance my popularity at Selangor and at the start of August 1997 I told Steve Wicks that I'd had enough and wanted to go home.

He understood my feelings and agreed to release me. In fact, after being misquoted in the Malaysian press, I was actually advised that I wouldn't be welcome back there anyway. It was then just a case of waiting to see if an English club would buy me.

Coming home

It's uncanny how an unexpected sequence of events can sometime change the course of your life and so it was when my dad, Clive, arranged to insure a car for Leicester City's assistant manager Steve Walford. We'd known 'Wally' for years, since we were team-mates at West Ham, and Dad – who owned Chase Insurance Brokers in Brentwood at the time – happened to mention in conversation with Steve that I was looking to return from Malaysia. Leicester were in the Premier League, had just beaten Middlesbrough in the League Cup Final and qualified for the UEFA Cup under Martin O'Neill. Although I spoke to Wally on the phone, I didn't believe anything would come of it. If no Premier League club wanted me before I left West Ham to go and play in Malaysia, why would anyone want me on my return to England?

But Leicester's interest turned out to be genuine. In August 1997, I drove up to meet Martin O'Neill and Wally at that most glamorous of locations, the Watford Gap services on the M1, and agreed to start what would be a wonderful new adventure.

3

The O'Neill Factor

ALL the Leicester City players had their heads bowed, eyes fixed firmly on the dressing room floor, as Martin O'Neill delivered his damning post-mortem just moments after our pitiful performance in the third round of the League Cup at Grimsby in October 1997.

O'Neill never minced his words in these situations. As holders of the trophy, we had slumped to an embarrassingly abysmal 3-1 defeat to second division minnows (the equivalent of League One today) that we should have beaten out of sight. Two months after joining Leicester, it was my first start for them and I knew I'd had a poor game.

As a sub or squad member in the previous eight weeks or so, I'd watched at close quarters how volatile our manager could be, both in the dressing room and on the sidelines. I was amazed how intense and animated he became during matches, how he would rant and rave at everyone, and yet at half-time or at the end of the game still remain calm and composed and speak a lot of sense. But if someone upset him or got something badly wrong, he would give them the most vicious bollocking I've ever seen a manager dish out. He didn't care for reputations – we were all treated as equals – and at times he would not hesitate to rip into his players.

At Grimsby, he verbally caned each player in turn, starting with our keeper Kasey Keller before working his way around the whole team. Eventually, he got around to me: "Tony, how much did I pay for you?"

Martin O'Neill doesn't take any nonsense from anyone.

"Five hundred thousand pounds, boss," I replied sheepishly, bracing myself for a put-down comment that I knew was heading my way.

O'Neill glared back at me and snapped: "Well, that was f****** 500,000 pounds too much!

"You're not fit, you're not mobile and from what I saw tonight, you're no good."

I couldn't argue with him – I was as poor as anyone in a blue shirt that gloomy night on the North-East Lincolnshire coast – and he was fully entitled to lambast the players in front of each other. As I learned in my three mostly very enjoyable seasons with Leicester, Martin O'Neill was usually right and I have nothing but respect and admiration for him as one of the finest managers in recent history.

When I met him for the first time at Watford Gap services to agree my initial two-year contract, a good offer written down on the back of a paper napkin, Martin made it clear then that he wanted me to move up from Essex and base myself much nearer the club. He didn't actually insist on it, though, and because Lorraine was expecting Matt and Billy, and Chloe was about to start at a new school, I continued to live in Essex. It meant driving up to the East Midlands each day for training – a minimum two-hour journey each way from my Chigwell home if there were no traffic delays.

This wouldn't normally have been a problem to me but having to meet two of my team-mates at the Toddington service area on the M1, before we got into one car and continued the drive north, had its drawbacks. Things went quite smoothly when I travelled up with Gary Parker in my first season but after he retired from football, in my two subsequent seasons with the Foxes I had a couple of less reliable companions in Frank Sinclair and Andrew Impey.

They are both great blokes but, true to their Caribbean roots, they could be a bit too laid-back at times, as I found out to my cost on several occasions. Inevitably, most mornings I'd be in the car park at Toddington by nine

Frank Sinclair and Andy Impey, my laid-back companions who caused some fun and games on the way to training.

o'clock, anxiously looking at my watch while waiting for either, or both, of them to pull in. With each of us coming from different directions, the potential for at least one of us to be late for our rendezvous was obvious and resulted in more than a few mad 95mph dashes up the motorway in order to arrive for training just in the nick of time. The three of us had some laughs but, of course, there were occasions when we didn't quite make it and the manager was quite rightly unimpressed.

Martin was never happy about me choosing to commute and he also had this thing about wanting everybody to travel back together on the bus to Leicester after every away game, before collecting their car and driving off home. You were only allowed two 'stop-overs' each during that first season but, bearing in mind there were six London clubs in the top flight at the time, it was a policy that didn't suit me. Having to go back to the Midlands with the rest of the team made no sense – it would have been far easier and saved me a lot of time and motorway travel if I'd been allowed to make my own way home after all our away games played in the capital – but it was Martin's way of getting across his point that we should all live in and round Leicester. Of course, he was right.

In my second and third seasons with Leicester, after I became a first team regular and was scoring goals, he mellowed a bit and allowed me to get off the bus at Toddington, which effectively halved the length of my drive back to Essex.

Playing in Europe

I signed for Leicester at the same time as Robbie Savage and goalkeeper Peggy Arphexad. Having qualified for the UEFA Cup, Martin had to name a squad of 25, so I became his fifth striker alongside Emile Heskey, Ian Marshall, Steve Claridge (who soon left to join Wolves) and Graham Fenton.

I was left out of our first three games of the season despite expecting to be involved. Well, I did expect to play until Martin came into the dressing room at five minutes before two o'clock, just as he always did, read out the team and the subs before walking out again. To my dismay, I didn't even make the bench.

I think he was trying to tell me something and, looking back, I now accept that when I first joined Leicester I wasn't anywhere near fit enough to play at Premier League level. I'd missed a season of English football and although I'd completed a long pre-season in Malaysia, you couldn't compare it to the build up they have in England.

I made my debut as a sub in the 3-3 home draw with Arsenal on August 27, a game made memorable by a fantastic individual goal from Dennis Bergkamp – one of three brilliant strikes the Dutchman scored that night. The only impact I had on proceedings came at the final whistle when I had to separate our captain Steve Walsh and Ian Wright, who were having a head-to-head over something.

In September I finally achieved an ambition to play in Europe, when I appeared as a sub in the 2-1 home UEFA Cup defeat by Atletico Madrid and felt a little deflated to be an unused sub in the first leg in the Spanish capital. We were knocked out of the competition, 4-1 on aggregate, but at least I'd played a very small part in the club's first European home tie since their participation in the 1961-62 European Cup Winners' Cup.

I had to be very patient and because I wasn't getting in the starting line-up, soon after the Grimsby debacle Martin sent me out on loan to Birmingham City for a month to improve my fitness. I enjoyed playing with a good set of lads at St. Andrew's under Blues' manager Trevor Francis.

My brief spell with Birmingham involved slightly more commuting and I used to travel up by car with Paul Furlong, Nicky Forster and Martin Grainger. Quite often the four of us would stop at the mobile takeaway unit, at the top of the road leading to the Blues' training ground, to devour a bacon sandwich! So much for Arsene Wenger's ground-breaking healthy diet that revolutionised English football in the late 90s and is now part and parcel of our game. Well, his philosophy hadn't quite reached as far as Birmingham in those days.

I played five games in five weeks for the Blues, scoring one goal (at Port Vale), but I enjoyed my first taste of first division (now the Championship) football and started to recapture my sharpness. There were some well known

faces around St. Andrew's at that time – Steve Bruce was a fellow old pro coming to the end of his playing career, while the outstanding youth prospect was striker Andy Johnson. They were a big club on the up and if Trevor Francis had tried to sign me from Leicester, I would have jumped at the move. But I had just agreed to stay with them for a second month in December '97 when Leicester recalled me to ease their injury problems.

Twin celebration

My hopes of finally getting a run in the starting line-up were dashed when I spent more time warming the bench. The only excitement I saw over that Christmas/New Year period was the birth – by Caesarean section – of my twin sons, Billy and Matt, on December 27. It

I enjoyed my brief spell on loan to Birmingham.   was one of the happiest, most momentous days of my life and to celebrate I scored my first goal for the Foxes in a 4-0 FA Cup third round victory at home against Northampton Town.

Then came another turning point just before a reserve game at Notts County, when Martin O'Neill boarded the team bus in the car park at Filbert Street and called me to the front for a brief chat. I wondered what I could possibly have done to upset him as he led me off the coach and showed me into his office at the ground but I needn't have worried. He sat me down, said that he understood how difficult it had been for me so far and promised that if I played well at Meadow Lane, he'd play me in the first team the following Saturday. As our next game was at Old Trafford, it was just the encouragement I needed.

After scoring our goal in the reserves' 1-1 draw at Notts County the gaffer kept his word to start me against Man U on January 31. Martin had basically assembled a team of misfits – players who had been too easily discarded by other clubs or were unwanted by the so-called 'big clubs' – and he deserved great credit for getting the very best out of them.

Neil Lennon and Robbie Savage both started at Crewe Alexandra; Matt Elliott came from Oxford United; Steve Guppy was signed from Wycombe Wanderers; Ian Marshall and Steve Claridge had both done the rounds; and Muzzy Izzett was going nowhere in Chelsea's reserves. No-one other than Leicester wanted me on my return from Malaysia but Martin O'Neill took a chance on all of us and got his reward.

We're a shambles

Of all the clubs I've played for, the team spirit we had at Leicester was the best. Stevie Walford used to put on little warm-up sessions on the pitch before each game, which invariably ended up in a chaotic mess, with balls flying everywhere and players bumping into each other and generally not doing what was expected of them. It became a bit of a standing joke among us. We even called this pre-match warm-up 'The Shambles', because that's what it was. When we went out onto the pitch at Old Trafford prior to this particular game, we all asked Wally to do the usual Shambles and, knowing it was done to boost team spirit and banter between the lads, he agreed.

We stood around in a circle and when he called a player's name, that person had to go into the middle of the circle and perform an exercise while on the move. Instead of simply doing a basic groin or hamstring stretch, we'd all do something absolutely stupid. Whatever the player in the centre did, we all had to follow his lead.

I did the 'Mick Channon', imitating his famous windmill goal celebration. Matt Elliott did his impersonation of Balou from *Jungle Book*, jumping with his legs tucked behind him. Muzzy laid down on his front and did the 'caterpillar'. We all looked ridiculous and the Man U fans must have been thinking to themselves, 'look at this shower of shit!' that has turned up to play in the Theatre of Dreams. Of all the Shambles warm-ups we ever did, this was easily the worst ever but it was a laugh and had the effect of further galvanising the team.

Martin delivered a rousing speech before that match at Old Trafford and this is where he's head and shoulders above anybody else I've ever seen in terms of motivating players. He never used to say too much about our opponents. He'd concentrate on getting the maximum he could from his men. In my case, he used to make me feel six feet tall, which takes some doing!

My time with Leicester produced several personal career highlights. When I put one past Peter Schmeichel in the second half to clinch a shock 1-0 victory, it was the first time I'd ever scored at Old Trafford in 14 years of trying. At the time I joined Leicester, the only other top flight grounds I hadn't scored at were Elland Road and Anfield but by the time I left the Foxes I'd put that right and scored at all three.

There were about 8,000 Leicester fans in Manchester to see us pull off a sensational win and some of them still come up to me now and say 'I was there'. The events of that day also convinced me that I had a right to call myself a Premier League player again.

Unlike many modern managers, Martin didn't scribble notes for himself to refer back to or complicate things with fancy tactics or instructions. It was all in his head. He instinctively knew which players to gently cajole and those he had to be tougher with.

He certainly got the best out of Emile Heskey. He really buttered him up and gave him all the love in the world, telling him: "Use your pace to beat four players. Emile, you're a fantastic player, so now just believe how good you really are. On your day, you're unplayable, you're world class, son..."

And when Emile went out onto the pitch with Martin's words of inspiration still ringing in his ears, he really did believe.

Winger Stevie Guppy was also given the kid-glove treatment, because he too had a fragile temperament that needed to be handled with care.

But Martin would adopt a totally different approach to gee-up Neil Lennon, our Northern Ireland international midfielder and now the boss of Celtic. He would give his fellow countryman a bit of a bollocking: "Come on, Lennie," Martin would say, trying to inspire him to new heights. If 'Lennie' had played a good first half, making 20 quality passes but misplacing just one, the Gaffer would pick up on the one poor pass and ask him: "What were you doing?" Lennie would flare up at him but then go out and prove a point by playing a near perfect second half. O'Neill's psychology worked a treat.

Skipper Steve Walsh, who became a good mate of mine, was another who needed to be wound up before a game, and Martin knew how to press all the right buttons.

I remember once he had words with Robbie Savage after 'Sav' had collected the ball from our defence and then attempted to spray an ambitious long, diagonal pass to the far wing, which was intercepted by one of their defenders. At half-time, Martin asked him: "What were you thinking of there?" Sav tried to explain what he'd had in mind but the manager just said: "No. When you get the ball from our back four, you pass it 10 yards to someone who can play."

Again, it was his way of telling us to do the things we were good at. We had Muzzy, our most creative player, to spray passes around in midfield, so Robbie knew he had to keep it simple and play within his limitations.

As far as I was concerned, Martin would just keep it simple with comments like: "Stay close to Emile, feed off each other and go and get us a goal. Do what you're good at."

Martin got to know his players really well and once you became part of his team, he made you feel indestructible. If his team was on a winning streak, he wouldn't change it unless forced to do so by injuries or suspensions. Once you were in, it was your place to lose.

If you were injured during the week, he would walk straight past you at the training ground. He wouldn't even say 'hello' or anything. In his eyes, you were no good to him at that moment. He had his own individual style of managing and his philosophy was completely different to the more fatherly, old school approach I'd been used to at West Ham under John Lyall.

Fear factor

There was undoubtedly a fear factor with Martin – a lot of players were scared of him – and that's something a lot of the most successful managers have. Brian Clough, who managed Martin as a player at Nottingham Forest, George Graham and Sir Alex Ferguson spring to mind. I don't think it does any harm for players to be a bit fearful of their manager.

We didn't see much of Martin on the training ground – he was content to leave that to his two assistants, Wally and John Robertson – but sometimes he would appear with just five minutes to go and watch what was happening.

I recall him joining in a five-a-side once with near disastrous consequences for both him and me. I was having a laugh with Ian Marshall and jokingly said to him: 'Watch this, I'm going to take out the gaffer!' As I attempted to execute a slide-tackle – I use the term 'tackle' very loosely, as I didn't make too many! – Martin fell down and over me into a crumpled heap. I thought my joke had backfired when he was clutching his knee in obvious pain – Marshie and the rest of the lads were pissing themselves laughing but I feared that I might have ruptured the manager's cruciate ligaments.

It was with great relief when, after a couple of minutes, Martin got to his feet and explained that there was nothing to worry about. Apparently, he'd suffered a long-term knee problem that soon became bearable again despite my challenge on him. I think that was the last tackle I made in training!

During the period when I wasn't being picked, it frustrated me even more to think that the manager was hardly ever around to see what I did in practice matches and training in general. Then again, I found it hard to believe how one minute he'd be so demonstrative on the touchline, leaping up and down, waving his arms and tearing his hair out, and yet the next he was delivering the most coherent, intelligent half-time speech imaginable.

It was in the dressing room immediately before a game and during half-time that Martin really earned his money as a top manager. After reading

Martin O'Neill and John Robertson, who liked to turn it on in the five-a-sides.

the team-sheet and subs at 1.55pm, he wouldn't rejoin us until about 2.45 or even 10 minutes before kick-off. But what he said in those few minutes between our pre-match warm-up and kick-off had much more impact than a lot of the waffle many managers spout for 20 minutes. He was very concise and to the point, a very intelligent man. It didn't surprise me when I heard that his hobby was studying law.

He wouldn't come in the dressing room immediately after the final whistle. He'd let us all settle down while he had a quick chat with Wally and Robbo and then, depending on how things had gone in the game, he'd carefully consider what he needed to say and how to put his message across.

Martin O'Neill isn't a coach and doesn't profess to be – at Leicester, he had Steve Walford and John Robertson to do that for him. Robbo was like a middle-man who the players would go to if they had a problem. And if Martin wanted to have words with a player, he'd ask Robbo to bring that person to him. Robbo left the coaching to Wally, although he loved to join in the five-a-sides, where he'd still show flashes of the brilliance that made him one of Nottingham Forest's European Cup-winning legends in the late 70s.

But of all the managers I've played for, and there have been some very good ones, including John Lyall, Howard Kendall, Colin Harvey and Harry Redknapp, Martin O'Neill was the best at motivating his players before kick-off and at half-time. After he left Leicester in 2000, he enjoyed success with Celtic and Aston Villa and Sunderland certainly did themselves a power of good when they brought him out of self-imposed exile in December 2011. He should have been West Ham's manager almost a year before then but that's another story and something I'll cover later in the book.

Stickler for discipline

I was also disappointed when Martin didn't get the England job in 2006 and the FA, in their wisdom, gave it to Steve McClaren instead. Martin doesn't suffer fools and there is no scope for egos. No matter which players step out of line, he will tell them to their face and act immediately. He's a stickler for discipline.

I recall the time, in March 2000, when he came down hard on Frank Sinclair, Andy Impey and myself after we'd arrived 15 minutes late for training due to roadworks. There were only about five minutes of the session to go when Martin emerged with his stopwatch in hand. While all the other players trooped off towards the dressing rooms, he told us three latecomers to stay behind, before ordering us to run to a tree and back again inside 45 seconds. Then he told us to do the same again. I became so angry, I smacked a ball onto the roof of a nearby garage.

Martin called me into his office and demanded to know why we had arrived late for training. I explained about it all being down to roadworks on the M1 but he wasn't interested in reasons or excuses. All he said by way of response was "leave earlier." I kept protesting my innocence but he just repeated the words: "Leave earlier."

I wasn't impressed when he fined me, Sinclair and Impey £400 each but it must have done the trick, because we were never late for training again. And the next day I scored after two minutes in our 2-0 win at Liverpool, so how's that for man-management?

There aren't many, if any, managers around who would have got the results with Leicester City that Martin O'Neill did in his four-and-a-half years in charge, from the end of 1995 until the summer of 2000.

Happy homecoming

Apart from my match-winner at Old Trafford, two other Leicester goals that meant more than most to me came on my return to Upton Park for the final game of the 1997-98 campaign. I was only named as a sub and as I warmed up in front of the Doc Martens lower – where I used to stand as a kid in what was then known as the West Side – the home fans sang: *"Tony is a Hammer, Tony is a Hammer, la la la la..."* I indulged in a bit of a friendly banter with them and thought how nice it would be to get on at the ground where, 18 months earlier, I thought I'd never play again.

But within five minutes of coming on early in the second-half, I managed to score by putting one through French international keeper Bernard Lama's legs. As the ball hit the net, I raised my hands and looked towards the Bobby Moore Stand. I was momentarily shocked to see that no-one was celebrating with me. Then it dawned on me..."Oh shit, I'm playing for Leicester!" I turned away in embarrassment and walked quietly back to the halfway line.

I found the net again to equalise in the 83rd minute but Trevor Sinclair grabbed the Hammers' late winner to seal a 4-3 home win.

At the end of the game, I moved into the centre circle and clapped the Leicester fans at the Centenary Stand end (since renamed The Trevor Brooking Stand) before turning to each of the other three parts of the Boleyn Ground to salute the West Ham supporters who had given me such a warm reception. With my family watching from the stands, it made it another special Upton Park occasion for me and a great way to sign off my last ever appearance at my spiritual football home.

4

Wembley tears and trouble

AFTER 16 trophy-less years at West Ham and Everton, and with my 33nd birthday behind me, I'd almost given up hope of ever winning a championship or cup winners' medal. But such was the determination and collective spirit of Martin O'Neill's Leicester City that I had two chances in the space of a year to fulfil a lifetime's ambition.

My first appearance in the League Cup Final, against Tottenham Hotspur in 1999, ended in tears and trouble for me with the FA over our allocation of tickets for the Wembley showpiece.

A hamstring injury had ruled me out of the fourth round win against Leeds United and the quarter-final victory over Blackburn Rovers – both at home – but I returned for our first semi-final clash with Sunderland at their newly-built Stadium of Light. With Dad coming up to see the game, I was delighted to net both goals with my left foot (!) in our 2-1 victory to spark a night of celebrations.

Leicester were losing the second leg at home, 1-0, until I managed to get on the end of a cross to score the vital equaliser that saw us through to a 3-2 aggregate success and our meeting with Tottenham in the final.

I'd always had a good record against Spurs. By one of those strange quirks of fate, after scoring my debut goal as a 17-year-old for West Ham against our arch London rivals on New Year's Day 1983, I then netted my 100th league goal against Tottenham while playing for Everton and when I chalked up my 200th League strike I was wearing Leicester's colours against the same opposition. What I would have given to have scored against George Graham's Spurs again in the League Cup Final of '99 but the afternoon ended in bitter disappointment for us after Allan Neilsen's diving header in injury-time. Apart from that scrappy goal, the only major talking point from a dour game was Justin Edinburgh being sent off for tangling with Robbie Savage.

Tears of self-pity

I felt devastated. After 16 seasons without winning a trophy – the Malaysian League Cup didn't count – I assumed my last chance had gone. As the final whistle sounded, I just disappeared into my own little world of self-pity. No-one has a right to win any medal for sentimental reasons but I knew I'd put in 16 years of hard effort and still had nothing to show for it.

As the Spurs fans rejoiced, I walked around the Wembley turf in a daze, my

A hug from the gaffer at Wembley after defeat by Tottenham.

hands clamped behind my head in utter dismay. I didn't know where to turn and had wandered down to the penalty area where Spurs keeper Ian Walker was standing. I reflected fleetingly on the fact that, with just 10 minutes to go, he'd saved a half-chance I had squandered. Ian consoled me and it was as much as I could do to mutter "cheers" as he walked on towards the famous 39 steps to collect the winners' medal I thought should have been mine.

I just couldn't get it out of my head that this was it, my last chance to win something. Unable to control my emotions anymore, my eyes welled up and tears started rolling down my face. My next thought was, 'Oh no, now I'm crying at Wembley and I don't want anyone to see me doing that'. I remember Ian Marshall coming up to me and saying: "Don't worry, we'll be back next year."

I wanted to believe him but I didn't. "No mate, this is my last chance," I mumbled, still wallowing in self-pity.

As 'Marshie' moved away, I felt an arm around my shoulder and it was Martin O'Neill, who gave me a big hug. Martin knew that, of all the players at his disposal that season, I'd contributed most – in terms of goals – to get us to Wembley. As well as netting all three in the 3-2 aggregate semi-final victory against Sunderland, I'd also scored both goals in our 2-1 third round win over Alan Curbishley's Charlton Athletic at The Valley. Martin must have felt as dejected and deflated as the rest of us but he put aside his own personal anguish to show me the compassionate side of his nature.

Frank goes AWOL

Our preparations for the final hadn't gone too smoothly. If ever an occasion demonstrated Martin's strength as a manager, this was it. We'd travelled down to our Burnham Beeches hotel on the Thursday and went to the theatre that night to see a West End show. We trained on the Friday and Martin told us afterwards that we had a bit of free time in the afternoon before pointing out that we had to attend a team meeting at seven o'clock.

"Don't be late," were his last words as the players went their separate ways, trying to kill time.

As we were staying not far from London, Frank Sinclair decided to go into town to see a friend. God knows what happened to him – he must have lost track of time – but the bottom line was that he didn't show up for the 7.00pm meeting and wasn't back at our hotel until around eight o'clock.

Martin was absolutely raging.

The next morning, Steve Walford took us for our customary walk around the hotel grounds and he indicated that Frank would be left out of the final starting line-up for disciplinary reasons. As one of the senior pro's, he sought my opinion and I replied: "Frank is a mate and though it's not for me to say what the punishment should be, he should have been at that meeting like the rest of us."

Frank knew he was in the wrong and Martin decided to leave him out of

I had plenty to celebrate in my second season with the Foxes.

Another goal celebration, this time with Andy Impey, Muzzy Izzett and Neil Lennon.

the side. It was a blow to our chances because Frank was an important player – part of our usual back three – and it obviously caused a problem on the day.

My second season at Filbert Street started brilliantly for me, including a headed goal on the opening day at Old Trafford. Having gone 14 years without a goal there, I had now scored on consecutive visits – Emile Heskey having netted our first in the 2-2 draw. We led 2-0 before Teddy Sheringham got one back and, after the board went up to signal seven minutes of 'Fergie Time' to be added on, David Beckham grabbed United's late equaliser.

After scoring just five times during an in and out first season for Leicester, my second campaign with the Foxes proved very enjoyable and produced 16 goals. Some personal consolation for losing to that late Spurs winner at Wembley was being voted Leicester City's Player-of-the-Season for 1998-99 by the Foxes' supporters. The club doesn't have the same size fan base as either West Ham or Everton but from their very loyal supporters down to the tea lady, it was a very homely club full of good people. I was staggered by the fans' award, which meant a lot to me.

A fine mess

I became caught up in controversy five league games into my third season with Leicester when, on the morning of our match at Middlesbrough (where I scored in a 3-0 win), I picked up the paper and saw to my horror a back page headline that screamed 'PLAYERS IN TICKET SHAMBLES'. There had been a bit of crowd trouble at the Leicester-Spurs final months earlier, which led the FA's compliance officer Graham Bean and his colleagues to interview the Leicester players and ask us to explain how and where we'd distributed our Wembley tickets. I thought that would be the end of the affair and the FA would brush it under the carpet like they often do in these situations.

But the newspaper report suggested otherwise. It named Andy Impey, Graham Fenton, Scott Taylor, Neil Lennon and myself as the culprits and said I'd been fined something like £12,500 for breaching FA rules. It was news to me at the time but about two days after the Middlesbrough game a letter came through the post confirming the report.

We got the PFA involved and appealed against the decision at a hearing held at Heathrow. It just got worse for me, though, because not only was the FA's decision upheld, they increased my fine to £15,000 plus costs.

Basically, what happened was Leicester City had allowed all of its players to legitimately purchase 75 tickets each. A funny aside...Arnar Gunnlaugsson, our Icelandic player, sold off his 75 tickets but when the FA interviewed him about it, he gave them 75 made up and untraceable 'names' living in Iceland – and got away with it!

One of the lads at the training ground, who shall remain nameless, said he knew people who could "sort out our tickets" for everyone. Perhaps the club shouldn't have offered us quite as many tickets in the first place, but they had at least already satisfied the demand of all our fans who wanted tickets for Wembley and, back in 1999, we weren't earning the kind of money Premier League players get today. We viewed it as a little bonus for reaching the final.

We certainly didn't distribute our tickets with the intention of causing any crowd trouble. I needed a lot of my tickets for family and friends, some of whom went there to support me and Leicester, while others were there to cheer on Spurs. The tickets I didn't need, I gave to a friend of mine who said he could sell a few for me. As it happened, I ended up having to buy four more tickets I needed for friends from Garry Parker.

My allocated seats were at the side of the pitch, nowhere near the area where the fighting occurred, which is where Andy Impey's seats were. The reason I got into trouble was because one female Leicester fan wrote to the FA complaining that she had a Tottenham supporter sitting next to her. The Spurs fan didn't cause any trouble whatsoever but because she had drawn this to the FA's attention, I was held responsible and faced a tough grilling from them.

I might have avoided the 15 grand fine if only my mate had faxed the right ticket stubs to the FA when they requested them as part of their investigation. But instead of doing that, he faxed the stubs from the tickets I'd bought from Garry Parker, which simply opened another can of worms!

I know many of you reading this will argue that any footballer who is caught having dealings with ticket touts only gets what he deserves, and that's fair comment. I didn't make a financial killing – unlike some of the lads, one of whom turned up at the training ground with a suitcase full of cash – and I only made a small profit on about 15 of my 75 tickets. The rest were sold at face value.

While I'm not trying to excuse my actions or claim that what I did was right, making a few bob from reaching a cup final was simply the norm for the majority of players, and had been for many years. When Everton reached the 1989 FA Cup Final, we all made a little bonus from selling our ticket allocation – that's the way it was and I'm certain there are hundreds of players down the years who will have done the same as the Leicester players did in 1999 without getting into trouble with the authorities.

I can tell you this much. The 'little bonus' I received for my League Cup Final tickets was nowhere near the size of the fine I got from the FA.

5

Spanish inquisition

THE undoubted highlight of my time with Leicester City came on February 27, 2000, when we returned to Wembley and won the League Cup that had been snatched away from us the previous year. Injury had ruled me out of both semi-final matches against Aston Villa but with our new signing Stan Collymore cup-tied, I knew I only had to be fit to make the starting line-up in the final against Tranmere Rovers.

As part of our build up to the final, the club arranged for us to take a four-day relaxation break at the popular La Manga Club holiday and leisure resort. Steve Walford and John Robertson accompanied us on the trip, with the gaffer intending to fly out to south-east Spain and join us the next day. Martin O'Neill believed in the value of taking his players on mid-season 'bonding' breaks and we'd enjoyed previous trips to Tenerife and Ireland, which helped to further boost our all-for-one-and-one-for-all team spirit. There had been the usual high jinks on those overseas trips, with plenty of booze consumed, but no problems to speak of.

La Manga was a different story.

We arrived at the opulent Hyatt Regency Hotel in the early afternoon and a lot of the lads planned to play a round of golf on one of the complex's three 18-hole courses. I'd taken my clubs with me but felt so tired when we got there that I decided to stay behind in the clubhouse bar to chill-out with Tim Flowers and Ian Marshall. The others who weren't playing golf took the chance to get some sleep or relax in their hotel room. I just sat on the veranda sipping beer all afternoon and was well tanked-up by the time the lads came off the 18th green several hours later.

After dinner that evening most of us headed into the Piano Bar for more liquid refreshment but by about 10 o'clock I'd had enough and returned to the room I was sharing with Steve Walsh.

I slept soundly until around 1.00am, when I was awoken by the sound of our door almost coming off its hinges. It was Walshie accompanied by Stan Collymore. Our captain splattered my face with a glass of water and, just as I was coming to, Stan leapt on top of me – all 14 stone of him. He was clearly drunk and began to slobber all over me, pledging his undying love!

Steve and I eventually managed to chuck Stan out of the room and bolted the door tightly behind him to thwart any possibility of him returning. I asked Walshie if he'd had a good night but there was a vagueness in his response which suggested that perhaps all wasn't quite as it should have been.

"Yeah, we had a good night," he said, "but I can't remember exactly what happened near the end. There was all this white smoke floating around the Piano Bar..."

I didn't understand what he was going on about but everything would soon become very clear. There was no white smoke without fire.

I awoke at around 9.30am with a raging headache and feeling much the worse for wear but managed to put on my training gear in readiness for the scheduled morning session.

I went down for breakfast and bumped into John Robertson in the foyer. "Good morning, Robbo," I ventured.

"No it ain't a f****** good morning," he replied.

"What's the matter?"

"We're going home," he said.

"Home? We've only just got here!"

He explained: "F****** Collymore's let off a fire extinguisher in the Piano Bar and they're turfing us out of the hotel."

As each player in turn came down dressed in his training kit, he was sent back up to his room to change into clothing more suited to a return flight to England. By the time we were all ready to get on the bus for the drive to the airport, a few reporters and photographers had arrived. One or two of our lads were mucking about with them, making V-signs through the window, and it didn't help our defence later when a few pictures were published in the English press accompanied by sensationalised headlines that blew the incident out of all proportion.

When we landed back at Gatwick, our team bus came straight on to the runway to collect us as soon as we disembarked. Apparently, a herd of paparazzi had got wind of the rumpus in La Manga and were waiting for us in the arrivals lounge. In a way I was disappointed because I was looking forward to a bit of fun. Although I'd had a skin-full in the bar the night before, I knew I hadn't got up to any trouble and when you're in that position as a player it's sometimes funny to stand back and see everything unfold around you.

I also knew that the severe bollocking we were about to receive from Martin O'Neill would not compare to anything we'd had from him before.

We completely avoided the baying press pack and didn't even have to go through Passport Control – just straight back up to Leicester and the Hinckley Island Hotel, where the gaffer lay in wait.

The players were shown into a conference room amid a subdued atmosphere. Martin entered the room holding a copy of the Leicester Mercury – or 'The Freddie', as we all called the local paper. He threw it down in disgust and said: "What the f*** is all this about? You're a disgrace."

He immediately eyeballed Collymore. "What were you thinking?" he asked Stan, who immediately apologised but then somehow tried to justify his actions, saying he and the lads were 'just having a bit of fun'.

"A bit of fun!" said the manager with an air of exasperation. "There were other hotel guests present – little, old ladies – and you thought you were only having a bit of fun?"

A spokesman for La Manga claimed the Leicester players, who were reportedly rude and obnoxious to hotel guests, had been dancing on tables and were generally being a nuisance. He said their behaviour was "unacceptable". The report said that some 40 guests were covered in the contents of the fire extinguisher – the "white smoke" Steve Walsh vaguely remembered seeing the night before.

Martin went into one as Tim Flowers and I just sat there sniggering to ourselves like a couple of naughty schoolboys watching their class-mates getting the mother of all tongue-lashings from the headmaster.

And then Martin changed his point of attack. "Walshie," he barked. "What were *you* thinking?"

"What do you mean, boss?" replied the club captain with a genuine air of innocence.

"What possessed you to have your trousers around your ankles in the Piano Bar?" Martin added.

"I never had my trousers around my ankles," Steve protested.

But Martin had him banged to rights. "Walshie, it's in the local paper and I have it on good authority that you had your trousers down by you're ankles."

"No way," said an adamant Walshie, determined not to capitulate under pressure.

With that, Martin left the room for a few minutes and the players were able to enlighten the skipper on his late night antics in the Piano Bar. "Walshie, you did have your trousers down by your ankles," the lads told him.

Martin came back into the room five minutes later and repeated the question: "Walshie, what's all this about your trousers being around your ankles?"

"I can't remember having my trousers being around my ankles, boss," he repeated.

Ian Marshall was also in for it. During a moment of madness soon after we'd arrived at La Manga, John Robertson had given Marshie his phone and the big man proceeded to dial Martin O'Neill's number to ask when he would be joining us. The Gaffer didn't answer the call, so Marshie left a voicemail message.

Martin remembered this audacious act during his Spanish inquisition when he said: "Marshie, don't you ever f****** phone me again." Robbo also got a ticking off from the boss for having stupidly passed his handset to Marshie.

It was like a comedy sketch but the manager didn't see the funny side. He fined Stan Collymore two weeks' wages, while Walshie and Marshie were also hit in the pocket. The adverse publicity it brought the club was horrendous.

What I found unbelievable, though, is that some four years later, the club returned to La Manga and three City players found themselves embroiled in rape allegations. A Spanish court cleared Paul Dickov, Keith Gillespie and Frank Sinclair of sexual assault charges brought by three German women who were staying at the luxury complex but I was amazed that Leicester were even welcomed back to La Manga and, equally, that the club wanted to take its players back there again after what had happened on our trip.

The 1,400-acre La Manga complex is still a favourite destination for international football teams and leading clubs sides of Europe, including Chelsea, Real Madrid and Bayern Munich. Leicester City may not have achieved anything like as much as those clubs have in terms of silverware, but they somehow managed what no other football club has ever done...the dubious distinction of being thrown out of La Manga TWICE!

Stan the man

Of course, it was not the first, nor the last, time that Stan Collymore made headline news for what he got up to off the field, but I liked him and we got on really well. Sometimes it's just not possible to engage properly with other players but I could always have meaningful conversations with Stan. He was another one who most clubs didn't want to touch with a bargepole but Martin O'Neill decided to take a chance on a striker who hadn't fulfilled his obvious potential at Liverpool and Aston Villa and was allowed to leave Villa on a free transfer.

I was confined to the subs' bench soon after Stan signed for us in February 2000 and could only admire his brilliant hat-trick in a 5-2 home slaughter of Sunderland. He played up front with Emile Heskey that day and they were unplayable. Stan was really bought to replace Emile, who was destined to join Liverpool a few weeks later in a £11m deal. I was not only impressed by the way Martin dealt with the La Manga affair, but also how Stan put his hands up, admitted his guilt and accepted the consequences of his two-week

Martin O'Neill and Stan Collymore, who copped a fine for his antics in La Manga.

fine.

Stan certainly didn't upset the camp when he arrived – you weren't allowed to be a big-time Charlie at Leicester. He settled in quickly and proved a popular addition to all the other dressing room characters and 'misfits' we had.

He was a very good player on his day but it's been well documented that he had problems with depression that detracted from his football, which were known before he joined the Foxes. It was a real shame that he retired so early from the game, although I'm pleased he has re-emerged from his personal troubles to become a good broadcasting pundit.

Emile Heskey is considered by many to be an enigma, a much-maligned forward, and it frustrated me when people got on his case and criticised him for not scoring enough goals. What the critics always failed to appreciate was his overall contribution as an unselfish team player.

I always enjoyed playing alongside him because we had a great understanding. Basically, I knew that he would win most high balls down the middle and when he was smashing and crashing opposing defences around, I was often able to pick up the bits and pieces. When he ran down the wing, I knew he'd beat three players and then cross the ball – and it was my job to get in the box to meet his pass.

I'm sure Michael Owen, who had a similar tremendous understanding with Emile for both Liverpool and England, would echo my thoughts on the big man. Emile is not a natural goalscorer but he is a much underrated player and, as a team man, one of the best I played with.

Matt gloss

Martin O'Neill ended his rant over the La Manga fiasco by insisting: "You'd better win that cup final now" – and that's exactly we did.

Tranmere Rovers, with experienced forwards like John Aldridge and ex-Hammer David Kelly leading the line, were never going to be an easy pushover but we beat the underdogs 2-1 thanks to two goals by our centre-back and captain Matt Elliott.

I didn't play particularly well on the day and was disappointed to be replaced by Ian Marshall with about 10 minutes to go. But Marshie was

With Matt Elliott, who scored both of our goals in the League Cup Final victory.

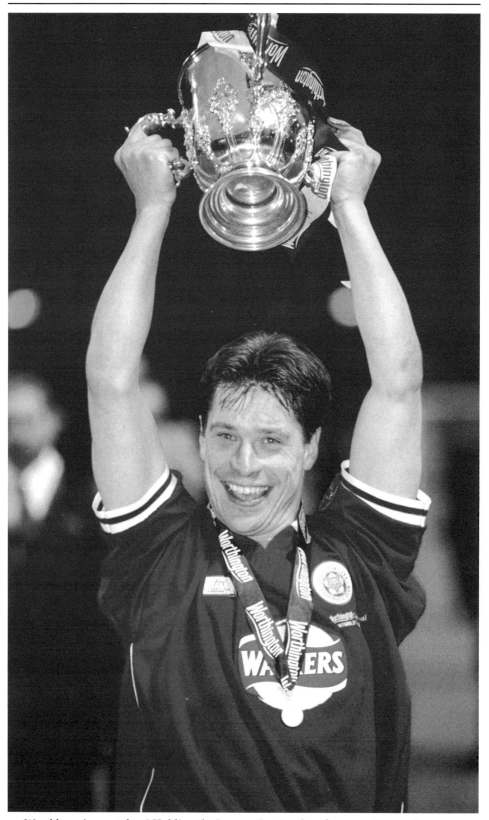

Wembley winner at last! Holding the League Cup trophy after our win over Tranmere.

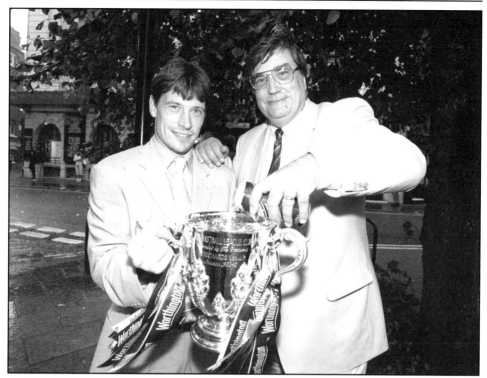

Showing off the League Cup with Leicester City chairman John Elsom.

going to be leaving the club soon, so in a way this was his farewell appearance.

At 34, I'd finally won my first winners' medal and it's difficult to describe the immense pleasure I felt as I stood on the hallowed Wembley turf – not far from the spot where I'd shed heartbroken tears of despair just a year before – clutching my cherished medal and The Football League Cup trophy.

Leicester had won it for the second time in four years. It meant we qualified for the UEFA Cup again and by the end of the 1999-2000 season Martin had completed his fourth consecutive top 10 Premier League finish – a remarkable achievement for a club of Leicester's size and limited budget.

We had some really good players, a wonderful team spirit but, more importantly, we had a truly great manager. When Martin O'Neill left Filbert Street that summer to accept an irresistible offer from Celtic, it signalled the end of my own fantastic adventure with Leicester City. It needn't have ended that way, though. I had hoped to remain at the club...in management.

Taylor-made for the job

Martin may have been a near impossible act to follow when he left Leicester to answer Celtic's call, but Steve Walsh and I were up for the task. It was obvious that Martin's two loyal assistants, Steve Walford and John Robertson, would go with him to Parkhead and before Leicester began considering their options, Walshie and I made our interest known to the people who mattered.

Walshie had been a loyal, long-serving player for the club and a real cult

Steve Walsh saw red again in La Manga, but we could have been a good combination in management at Leicester

hero among Foxes' fans, so I knew he'd be a popular replacement for Martin. He had great leadership qualities and with what I could bring to the table, between us we thought we had the makings of a good management partnership. Walshie would have been the main man and we had Garry Parker, another former team-mate of ours, in mind for the role of first team coach. With three ex-players at the helm, we would have maintained the famous Leicester team spirit that brought the club sustained success under Martin O'Neill, and I think we would have retained most of the important players too.

When I returned from holiday in Mauritius, Walshie, his agent and myself met Leicester City secretary Andy Neville and two board members at a hotel, where we stated our claims for the job. We did some research and identified a number of players we thought we could bring to Leicester, and how the proposed new management structure would work to build on what had been achieved under Martin over the previous four-and-a-half years.

The interview went well and, at a later date, Andy Neville admitted to me how we'd surprised the board with the professionalism of our presentation to them. Unfortunately, the bottom line is they had already made up their mind to appoint the former England Under-21 manager Peter Taylor. I don't think it really would have mattered how good or bad our presentation was – he already had the job in the bag anyway.

Taylor had a fairly impressive CV, so you could understand why the club viewed him as their best available option at the time. But I felt Leicester City needed continuity – not an outsider who would try to change things too much by dispensing with all the senior pros who were largely responsible for the team spirit and unity that existed under Martin O'Neill.

Despite Leicester's decision to appoint Peter Taylor, I still had my sights set on entering management. Ironically, Taylor's arrival at Filbert Street left a job vacancy at Gillingham – and I briefly had hopes of filling it. In the summer of 2000, I visited Priestfield for a chat with Gillingham's controversial chairman Paul Scully, who spoke of his ambitious plans to move the club into a new stadium. We discussed the possibility of me becoming the Gills' player-manager – they were a first division (now Championship) side at the time – and I thought our meeting went well.

We left it that Scully would phone me on my return from holiday but I never

did hear from him again and came home to the news that he had appointed Andy Hessenthaler instead. Andy was already an established key player at Gillingham, so if they were looking to appoint a player-manager then it obviously made sense for him to be given a chance. I was disappointed at the time and, it's fair to say, a bit apprehensive about continuing at Leicester City under their new manager.

I hadn't had much to do with Peter Taylor over the years but he always seemed a nice enough guy. As far as his training methods were concerned, though, us senior pros found it all quite basic, much like the stuff we did way back in our days as youth team players. I'd been there before at Everton, when Mike Walker arrived as manager and appointed coach Dave Williams who put on sessions – simple, monotonous passing drills – more suited to schoolboys than seasoned top flight professionals. Willliams called me in one day and asked what the problem was, so I told him that I didn't care much for doing the same things I'd done as a 15-year-old apprentice player at West Ham.

Feeling the strain

In truth, at 35, I'd reached the stage where I didn't want to train. My legs felt like lead after every game. I'd be very tired on Sundays and my knees would hurt so much that I would come down the stairs at home, crab-style, like an arthritic cripple. Even though I've got strong knees, I'd take extra care coming down the stairs for fear of pulling my hamstring. By Monday I could barely walk, although Martin O'Neill was good in this respect, too. He recognised my situation and would cut me some slack by allowing me to

spend Mondays doing simple stretches and having a massage. I'd do a little bit more on Tuesday, have Wednesday off, do shooting practice on Thursday, play in the five-a-side games on Friday and then play on Saturday. It was a routine that suited me and worked well at that advanced stage of my career.

When you're young it's not a problem playing two games in quick succession – at West Ham one season, we played on December 26 and then again the next day, which would be unthinkable now. But as I got older and the game became progressively quicker (though not necessarily better), it took increasingly longer for me to recover between matches and this became more apparent during my time with Leicester – a problem I exacerbated by continuing to commute from Essex. I'd get up at seven o'clock on Monday mornings, drop my daughter off at school before meeting up with the boys on the M1. By the time we reached Leicester's training ground at around 10am, my legs felt very stiff and my knees ached. It was ridiculous really.

By the end of my third season under Martin, I felt mentally and physically jaded. In fact, when he joined Celtic in June 2000, I more or less accepted that it was the end of my playing career.

Whether Taylor saw Steve Walsh and me as a threat to his position, I don't know, but I soon realised I wouldn't be figuring in his plans. He'd bought Ade Akinbiyi from Wolves for £5m and paid £1.3m to Cambridge United for Trevor Benjamin. They must have been getting two or three times the wages I was on but, nice lads though they were, they weren't better players than me – and certainly not better finishers.

I had the hump and with Walshie (eventually to join Norwich City), Marshie (Bolton Wanderers) and Stan Collymore (Bradford City) also heading out of the club, there was soon a distinct lack of senior figures in the dressing room. Maybe there were too many changes too quickly. Although Leicester enjoyed a good first season under Taylor – they led the table on October 1 and reached the quarter-final of the FA Cup but nine defeats in their last 10 games saw them slump to 13th in the final table – he was sacked after a poor start to the following 2001-02 campaign, which saw the Foxes finish rock bottom.

I did make one appearance in Leicester colours under Taylor at the start of 2000-01, coming on as a sub in a goalless draw at Bradford, but there were no more chances to add to my tally of 34 goals (27 in the Premier League) – not a bad contribution considering that many of my 100 first team appearances (84 in the league) were from the bench. I finished each of my two full seasons with the club as leading league and cup scorer, with 16 (twice as many as the next player, Emile Heskey) in 1998-99 and 13 in 1999-2000.

Hitting the buffers at Norwich

With the clock ticking on my playing career, Taylor accepted that I needed regular first team football and readily agreed to let me leave the club. In mid-September 2000, Norwich City manager Bryan Hamilton came in for me and I was further encouraged to sign for the Canaries when he indicated that I'd also be able to get involved on the coaching side at Carrow Road.

Travel wise, the two-hour drive from home to Norwich meant I more or less clocked up the same number of miles I'd been doing to Leicester and back. I'd signed a two-year deal – on the same basic money I'd been on at Leicester, who also paid up the 'signing-on' bonus at the start of the season, which was nice of them – but I knew within the first week of being there that I'd made a mistake. Instead of staying on in the afternoons to work with and coach the young players, I wanted to get back on the motorway and head home to my young family.

It became farcical one day. With petrol in short supply all over the country due to strike action and blockades at the pumps, I was forced to take the train up to Norwich. This involved taking a London Underground tube from Essex in to Liverpool Street, where I boarded an overground train heading north-east to Norwich. The fuel crisis was so bad, I had to stay in the city for a couple of days before I could get home.

At least I had a couple of familiar faces for company. Matt Jackson, my old Everton team-mate, joined us and then Bryan Hamilton took my advice and brought in Steve Walsh, who had played for him during his managerial spell at Filbert Street between 1986-87, and I was pleased to be reunited with them both.

I was at Norwich for just 10 games, playing up front alongside Welsh international Iwan Roberts. Although I scored a couple of goals at Carrow Road (in a 3-3 League Cup draw against Blackpool and a 4-2 league win over Sheffield United), I couldn't adapt to the frenetic pace of the first division. The Canaries were generally a fit, young side but that wasn't always good for me. During our pre-match warm-up the ball would usually fly everywhere – so much so, I'd come into the dressing room feeling knackered before we'd even kicked-off!

Technically, the Premier League is obviously far superior to the Championship but the second tier of English football is so much faster because the ball is pinged here, there and everywhere, which wasn't good news for an ageing 35-year-old. I don't know about a petrol shortage, it was me that was running on empty.

I was contemplating my future again when I happened to speak to Phil

Smith, from the reputable First Artist agency who had handled my transfer to Everton more than 12 years earlier. I hadn't spoken to Phil for some time but he mentioned that Barnet, who were usefully placed around seventh or eighth in Division Three (now League Two), were looking for a new manager to take the pressure off their existing boss, John Still, who was apparently looking for a less hands-on role at the North London club.

I immediately indicated my interest and asked Phil to approach Barnet on my behalf. My only stipulation to him was that I'd only consider joining them in a player-manager capacity. I wasn't interested in simply extending my playing days in the lower reaches of the Football League if there was no prospect of a management role.

It had always been one of my dreams to become a football manager. At Barnet, I realised again that dreams don't always come true.

6

Barnet: Wrong place, wrong time

IT had been my burning desire to become a manager but when the chance came my way at Barnet, I can honestly admit now that I simply wasn't ready for it.

After managing the Bees for the previous three seasons, John Still confirmed to me that he wanted to step back from being the manager. He said he fancied moving into a newly-created Director of Football role, where he could take an overview of what was going on, leaving me to manage the team on a day-to-day basis. It seemed an ideal arrangement. I only agreed to continue playing because, having finished sixth the previous season, John and the club's likeable Greek chairman Tony Kleanthous believed I would score the goals Barnet needed to push them further towards promotion.

At least that was the theory and the basis on which I accepted the terms – which amounted to just two-fifths of the money I'd been earning at Norwich – and a dual role as player-manager, but the reality was somewhat different.

Looking back, I'm sure that neither John nor Tony took my managerial ambitions very seriously. At my first meeting with them, when I'd again pointed out that I had absolutely nothing more to prove as a player and was much more intent on a future career in management, it didn't seem to fully register with them. Yes, they both nodded their heads at the right moments but what they were really saying to me was: 'OK, whatever you want to be or call yourself is fine by us, just as long as you do the business on the field'.

I should have twigged there and then. They really wanted me for what I could contribute as an experienced player, not as a rookie manager learning the ropes.

I was already questioning my decision to walk out on a secure two-year contract at Norwich – God knows what I must have been thinking at the time! – but money would soon be the least of my problems. The overriding factor in my decision to go to Barnet at the start of November 2000 is that I'd always wanted to be a manager but, as I said, I just wasn't properly equipped to deal with what came my way that season. I was nowhere near ready. I still had the mindset of a player.

I knew very little about Barnet as a club, other than that they were relatively new to The Football League having been promoted through the non-league ranks under the colourful management style of Barry Fry, one of the game's biggest characters. Ironically, my 146th, and last, goal for West Ham was a

There wasn't too much to smile about at Barnet.

late headed equaliser against Barnet in a 1-1 League Cup draw at the Bees' sloping Underhill ground in September 1996.

The chairman told me that the club had big plans, including a move to a new ground "in the near future", but, like Gillingham, they still haven't done so all these years later.

I didn't know John Still personally but I was aware that he'd had around 20 years' experience in management, most notably at non-league level with Dagenham & Redbridge, so I presumed I would only benefit from his knowledge. Sure, I was starting on the bottom rung of the league ladder but I hoped he would help to make my dreams come true. After all, John had led Barnet to two top seven finishes in the previous three seasons and knew what managing was all about at this level.

I arrived at Barnet without any coaching qualifications, because I never believed they were of any value. Brian Clough and Bill Shankly, two of the greatest managers the game has ever seen, never possessed any coaching badges either and there were numerous other examples of top bosses who learned their trade through their experience and knowledge of the game, not what could be taught in a classroom. Nowadays, you have to have them to get anywhere in pro football but coaching badges weren't mandatory when I joined Barnet and, rightly or wrongly, I viewed them as irrelevant and unnecessary. Looking back, I should have done the courses and got the FA badges before entering management. But I suppose I was more interested in becoming a manager than a coach – a Martin O'Neill as opposed to a Steve Walford.

The only two players I knew when I took over were left-winger Darren

Currie, who had been an apprentice in my first spell at West Ham, and midfielder John Doolan, a youngster at Everton in my time there. There was another West Ham connection, though, because we took striker Omer Riza on loan from the Hammers.

I had to quickly evaluate the squad and although I wanted to introduce my own ideas, I didn't expect to change things too quickly. At first I welcomed John Still's contribution to training, too, because I thought he'd have a lot to offer and, besides, he knew all the players and their capabilities very well.

My first game in charge was up at Rochdale, where it rained, causing the pitch to cut up badly and a half-decent performance, without ever playing too much football, earned us a 0-0 draw. I didn't name myself in the side for the game at Spotland to avoid disrupting the team so soon after taking over.

I found it difficult to get my head round the fact that the players were calling me 'gaffer'. Striker Scott McGleish was a good player, although a lively character and probably not the kind you would want to manage in your first job. He kept insisting on calling me gaffer and despite telling him that it was OK to call me by my first name, he wouldn't change the way he addressed me.

It was also hard finding the correct balance between being their team-mate and, at other times, trying to remain a little aloof when I had to put on my manager's hat. Successfully combining both aspects of the job is an art itself and the most difficult part of the player-manager role.

Not that there was anything testing about my first home game in charge, a 7-0 thrashing of high-flying Blackpool. I put us ahead after 18 minutes, the impressive Darren Currie grabbed a hat-trick, my strike partner Tony Richards scored twice and Mark Arber's header completed what is still Barnet's record league victory. Steve McMahon, the Blackpool boss, couldn't believe how we'd ripped his team apart. I didn't invite him into my office afterwards for a drink and a chat, as is the custom among opposing managers. I wasn't being inhospitable – I simply didn't have an office!

The battering of Blackpool on my dream debut at Underhill as

On the field for Barnet, which is where John Still and chairman Tony Kleanthous wanted me to stay.

player-manager raised the same question I'd asked myself after my sensational scoring debuts for both West Ham and Everton: where do I go from here? I achieved the pinnacle of my seven seasons at Everton in my first game, with a Goodison hat-trick against Newcastle United. I couldn't possibly top that in a blue shirt. It was the same with Barnet. From Underhill it was all...downhill.

Mentally draining

Initially, John Still was happy to let me get on with things but there was one particular home game – I can't recall the opposition – when I remember doing almost everything myself. I didn't have an assistant manager at that stage, so I arrived at Barnet's ground at midday, contemplated team selection and then had my usual pre-match chat with the chairman.

Players began to arrive and we had our team-talk at 1.30pm – I picked myself up front on this occasion. At 2.00pm-ish I organised the players' warm-up and when that was finished I went back into the dressing room and got myself ready for the game. Obviously, I had to give my team-talk before we went back out onto the field for the start of the match and then I spoke to all the other players as a group again at half-time.

At the end of the game, I had to try and analyse where we'd gone wrong in defeat before conveying my thoughts to the other players. Then we all trooped back out onto the pitch for the final warm-down.

After I'd showered and changed it was time to fulfil my obligations to the media by attending the post-match press conference. Before heading off home, I had another quick chat with the chairman, this time to try and explain why we'd lost.

I think I did just about everything that day except score a goal – oh, and I admit, I didn't actually make and serve the half-time tea! It was mentally draining and no way for any club to go about getting decent results.

I said to John Still before our next game that I needed an assistant, so we brought in Alex Armstrong to take the warm-up and warm-down sessions. As far as appointing my assistant was concerned, I ideally wanted my former Everton team-mate, Neil McDonald, who was coaching at Bolton under Sam Allardyce at the time and in 2011 became his No.2 at West Ham.

But with Barnet unable to pay much money, there was no way that Neil could even consider leaving Premier League Bolton to be reunited with me. We spoke about it but, understandably, 'Macca' just couldn't accept what amounted to a proposed 50% pay cut. I sounded out Garry Parker, a good friend from Leicester, who was still coaching there, but he said 'no' for the same reason Neil did. I also spoke to Steve Foley, the assistant coach at Norwich who I'd got on very well with in my seven weeks there, but just as we were about to agree a deal with him, Bryan Hamilton left Norwich and Steve stayed there after being promoted to a more senior role.

I then turned to Steve Wicks, who had been my manager in Malaysia. We'd got on well – not just on a player-manager basis, but also as mates. As well as a previous spell as assistant manager at Portsmouth, he'd also managed

*Trying to inject some skill and creativity into training made a
change from the usual basics.*

in the lower divisions at Lincoln City and Scarborough.

But I felt for Steve. He came in about halfway through my short spell there
and by then we'd gone from doing OK to hitting the buffers. He got caught
up in the crossfire a bit and the fact that he was commuting from Reading
also meant he couldn't spend perhaps as much time as possible with me at
the club, although I did appreciate his help.

I'd let John Still have a big input in training for the first three or four weeks
but his sessions were about as basic as could be – a case of get hold of the
ball and kick it forward as quickly as possible. He would always want
the full-backs to take quick throw-ins but, the trouble was, there was often
no-one in position for them to throw it to. It was typical Charles Hughes-
style POMO 'football' and totally alien to me. I found this rudimentary
approach strange because John is a West Ham fan and you would expect him
to encourage his teams to play neat, passing football but he didn't.

I could suffer the occasional dog turd on the training pitch and accepted
that we all had to take home our own training kit to be washed – it was all
part and parcel of operating at that level.

And I also appreciate that it's not always possible to play entertaining
football in the lower divisions and that you need to mix it up. I tried to retain
John's philosophy of getting the ball forward quickly while also introducing
a more passing game. One day I put on a keep-ball session and afterwards,
a young lad called Danny Brown said to me: "We've never done keep-ball
before." To me, keep-ball was one of the most fundamental practices you
could do, a way to improve passing, touch and technique, but this was

unchartered territory for the Barnet boys. I thought, 'Christ, what am I up against here?'

The players seemed to get caught between two stools, not knowing when to play the usual longer-ball game preached by Still or embrace the passing game I wanted us to play.

It was also obvious that several of the players felt a loyalty towards John. Even he admitted to me how they would go to him if they had a problem rather than approach me. I think it's also reasonable to assume that after stepping out of the manager's seat for three or four months, he'd started to miss it.

OK, so John Still wasn't Sir Alex Ferguson, but you have to respect what people have done in the game and I genuinely went to Barnet believing that I would learn quite a lot from him. Yet within four weeks of being there, I knew he could teach me very little.

During December, results deteriorated further. A 6-1 hammering at Hartlepool, when I rested myself a week after scoring a hat-trick in our 4-2 home win over Scunthorpe, representing the biggest low as Barnet continued on a downward spiral.

What didn't help was the chairman suffering an illness that restricted his involvement, which meant that instead of liaising with him, I had to take any issues to John, who effectively became a middle man. I didn't have a problem with that but the trouble was I never knew what John was then telling the chairman. Likewise, I couldn't possibly know if the chairman's true wishes were being accurately reflected in the messages John relayed from him to me.

John and I had talks about all manner of different issues – from the possibility of finding a new training ground, to wages, agents and funds for new players I hoped to bring in. The two I did bring to Underhill were Lee Flynn, a decent left-back who cost £35,000 from non-league Hayes, and my biggest legacy, then 22-year-old midfielder Mark Gower, who was signed from Spurs for £32,500.

Gower made nearly 100 appearances for Barnet, including two seasons spent in the Conference after I left, before five seasons with Southend United and then joining Swansea City in 2008. I can take satisfaction from the fact that one of the two players I paid money for went on to play three seasons for the Swans in the Championship before appearing for the Welsh club in the 2011-12 Premier League.

It's not until you become a manager that you fully appreciate how much more there is to managing a football club, especially one as small as Barnet, than simply picking the team and playing matches.

My handling of the players was also being compromised. I fell out with a couple that I didn't think were putting in the required effort and there was a time when I felt it was necessary to bollock the players. But after expressing my thoughts to John, he would talk me out of it. "No, don't do that, they're only youngsters," he'd say. I took his advice but then I'd find myself driving home from the ground and regretting not going through with my initial instinct to let the players know, in no uncertain terms, that they weren't all giving their very best efforts. This led to indecision on my part and I could see that some players sensed this. You couldn't blame them for asking themselves: 'who's in charge here?'

Within a week of joining Barnet, I made a phone call to my old West Ham boss John Lyall, hoping to pick his brains. I had so much respect for John and if anybody could point me in the right direction it was him. But, to be honest, he didn't really say much. Whether he was still feeling bitter about the way he had been dismissed at West Ham in 1989, I don't know, but he seemed a bit detached and he kept the conversation brief. One bit of advice he did give me, though, was: 'Be your own man'.

I wish I'd taken his advice.

Another example of indecision on my part came after I introduced the 'yellow jersey award'. This would be handed to the worst trainer – as voted by the players – each Friday and whoever received it would have to wear the top in training throughout the following week. It was something we did at Leicester, where Stevie Walford would invariably hand out the yellow bib to poor Steve Guppy after the Friday morning five-a-side session.

It was a bit of harmless fun and I decided to bring in it at Barnet. My only stipulation was that the players couldn't vote for me – I didn't think it was right for their manager to become the butt of their jokes.

Anyway, after about three weeks, John Still told me that a few of the players had approached him and said that they didn't feel it was right that they weren't allowed to vote for me. At first, I rejected John's request to change the rule on the yellow jersey award in line with the players' wishes, pointing out that I knew they would simply all vote for me rather than nominate a team-mate.

When I relented, you can guess what happened. Yep, they all voted for me, so I swiftly abandoned the idea!

Whether they did it to try and undermine me in front of John, I don't know. What I do know is that I'd ignored John Lyall's advice by once again not acting on my own instincts and allowing myself to be swayed by John Still's opinion. I was gullible and maybe too respectful of John, lacking the self-confidence to act on my own initiative more than I did.

My contribution as a player began to suffer as the winter struggle dragged on. Although I remained Bees' top scorer right up until I left the club, I started to miss games through fatigue. So, like the other players, I also found myself falling between two stools – I wasn't managing well and then I began letting my standards as a player dip, too.

One incident that particularly bothered me came in our FA Cup second round defeat at Walsall, where I missed a sitter. We'd gone 2-0 down but I scored a cracker to bring us back into it. Then, in the last minute, our keeper moved up into attack for a corner and won a header. The ball bounced in front me and I had what can only be described as a fresh air swing at it. My finishing let me down and had I made any sort of contact with the ball, I would have scored past Jimmy Walker and taken Walsall back to Underhill for a replay. I rank it right up there as one of the five worst misses of my career.

I was so gutted afterwards – my embarrassment enhanced by the fact that the Sky cameras were present to record my miss for a live audience – that I booted the skip in the dressing room afterwards and hurt my foot in the process!

To compound my misery, when the FA Cup third round draw was made the following Monday, Walsall were paired with West Ham. Walsall were a league above us and we may not have beaten them in the replay, but you can imagine how I felt at just missing out on the possibility of a plum third round tie against my former club. Looking at the bigger picture, an attractive third round money-spinner would have given everybody associated with Barnet a big lift, but it wasn't to be.

The uncertainty at Barnet couldn't have been easy for John Still and Steve Wicks either. They must also have been affected by it, so it was an unsatisfactory situation for all concerned.

Visit from John Still

Things came to a head early in March 2001, when I received a phone call from John asking if he could come to my place for a chat. In the four months that I'd been at Barnet this was the first time he'd asked to see me at home, so it was obvious something was up.

I welcomed him inside and the first thing he did was comment on my seven England caps that were framed on the wall. "They're nice," he said, sounding as pleasant as he could be before I asked him to quickly get to the point of his surprise visit.

"Obviously we've got some problems at the club. We're hurtling down the table and need to stop the rot," he said. "I've spoken to the chairman and we both feel that the only way out of this situation is for you to go back to being a player, scoring the goals we need to get us out of trouble, and I'll return to managing again."

I immediately made it very clear to him that I wouldn't be happy with those arrangements, reminding him that I hadn't joined Barnet to be just a player. I added that it's in times of adversity that young, inexperienced managers like myself need all the advice and support they can get to be able to handle problems and resolve them.

"I'm only passing on what the chairman has said," John replied.

I demanded to see Tony Kleanthous, who asked if we could meet on neutral territory. We chose the Wembley offices of First Artist, directly opposite the national stadium, where Tony explained that he felt he had to be guided by his Director of Football. He reiterated what John Still had said at my house – the only way they believed the club could climb up the table was for me to concentrate solely on playing.

I repeatedly expressed the view that I'd joined the club on a player-manager basis. If I relinquished the management part of my job and the team still got relegated at the end of the season, then everyone would blame me. I was prepared to accept that responsibility if I could retain my dual role, but not if John was being brought back in to manage, which would have given me no control over my own destiny.

I put it to the chairman that he had a decision to make. Either he followed John's advice and wishes, or he honoured the agreement we made when he appointed me as player-manager.

Tony said he needed five minutes to think about and disappeared out of the room, presumably to phone John Still. In the meantime I had a quick word with my former agent Phil Smith, who advised me not to resign in a huff. He pointed out how difficult it would be for me to get

On the touchline with John Still during difficult times.

another job in management if I walked away from Barnet. While I understood what he was saying, it was a matter of principle as far as I was concerned.

Tony came back into the room and said he felt obliged to back his Director of Football. "There is no point in me having a Director of Football if I'm not going to take his advice," he reasoned.

"That's fine," I replied, "but as manager, I'm not going to be dictated to by a Director of Football and I won't have him picking the team if, at least in theory, I'm still the manager in name."

The relatively new Director of Football role is a contentious one and I'd advise any manager not to work alongside one. I don't believe the relationship between the DoF and the manager can work effectively. It certainly didn't for me. I liked John Still as a bloke but in footballing terms, we were many miles apart.

Table football with the Chairman

Tony and I quickly reached a mutual agreement to terminate my contract and we had a very harmonious parting of the ways on March 16, 2001. In fact, there was a somewhat surreal end to my four-and-a-half months with Barnet, when the chairman challenged me to a game of Table Football, which was stood upstairs in the office.

"Do you fancy a game of table football before I leave?" the chairman asked.

I never really got to know Tony as well as I'd hoped to due to the fact that he was missing from the club through ill health. His absence came in the middle of our bad run and this breakdown in communication was certainly a factor in the club's problems that season. A likeable guy in his 40s, his father used to help out in the kitchen at the club and also cooked the food on our away trips.

Barnet chairman Tony Kleanthous – a nice guy but not too good at table football.

"Yeah, no problem," I said, looking down at the players of the opposing Table Football teams. They were coloured blue and red and, knowing Tony was an Arsenal fan at heart, I suggested: "You be Arsenal and I'll be Everton."

I told myself that there was no way in the world that I was I going to allow the Barnet chairman to beat me and I was so pleased that he didn't. With the fabled Twin Towers hovering in the background (well, OK, just across the road!) to add a sense of romance and drama, for the record, Everton beat Arsenal 10-8.

Tony Kleanthous and I shook hands for the last time and that was the end of me at Barnet.

Doomed to fail

I felt hugely disappointed that it hadn't work out. Whether I liked it or not, my arrival created turmoil at the club and, although I was top scorer with 10 goals, my 18-match spell there was probably doomed to fail from the start. I'm not saying it was all the fault of John Still or Tony Kleanthous. Of course I made mistakes, I'm very aware of that. I made a lot of mistakes but I can only recognise that now when I look back on my short time there.

When John got his wish to resume control of team affairs in mid-March, I've no doubt that he saw it as a chance to prove himself as the Bees' saviour following my departure. He was quoted as saying: "Tony Cottee's ideas didn't work." Which was another way of saying that we had directly opposed views on how we believe the game should be played.

It annoys me when I hear people say I was sacked and that I took Barnet down, because neither was true. I scored nine league and one cup goal for them and although they were in the bottom half of the third division table when I left, there were still 10 games to play.

But if I ever apply for another job in management, I've no doubt that my Barnet experience would be thrown back at me. The same stigma is attached to many young managers who fail at the first hurdle with clubs where it's very difficult to have a big impact and many factors conspire against you. They become tainted by the experience and, in many cases, this is totally unjust.

Just as I did at Barnet, my former West Ham team-mate Alvin Martin had a tough time managing at Southend United in the late 90s and has never been given another chance to show what he can do, despite winning 17 England caps and spending 19 years with West Ham.

As it happened, Barnet continued to slide down the division under John Still and were relegated from the Football League at the end of that season. Yet had the club retained me as player-manager and kept me happy, I have no doubt I would have scored the goals that would have kept them up.

These are the bare facts from that season:

Managed by John Still (August-November 2000)
P-17 W-6 D-6 L-5 Pts-24

Managed by Tony Cottee (November 1-March 16)
P-19 W-4 D-2 L-13 Pts-14

Managed by John Still (March 17-May)
P-10 W-2 D-1 L-7 Pts-7

Before another training session at Barnet. Despite everything, I'm glad
I at least had a brief shot at management.

The two most influential people at the club may have felt that they could replace me as a manager but what ultimately decided Barnet's fate in 2000-01 is that they couldn't replace my contribution as leading scorer. Surely it would have been better for the club and everyone concerned if the question of my future as player-manager, and whether Still should have resumed the role of manager, had been left until the end of that season, once we'd hopefully avoided relegation to the Conference. After all, the Bees finished just two points adrift of Halifax Town at the bottom and only four points separated the bottom five clubs. What difference would a few more goals from me have made in the crucial final 10 games?

The Director of Football and chairman had to live with the fact that they made what turned out to be the wrong decision and I have to accept that I blew my chance in football management by accepting the first offer that came along.

It was a case of wrong place, wrong time.

I'm glad I had my time at Barnet, though. Up until the last three weeks, I mostly enjoyed the experience. I left there hoping I might be given another crack at management but, as events were to prove, my life was about to change direction again.

7

End game

ONE of the first chants younger West Ham fans learn is the one that begins: 'We 'ate Millwall and we 'ate Millwall...' They are the sworn enemy according to many Hammers supporters and the aggro that has tarnished a number of matches between these London rivals over the years speaks for itself. The hatred between large sections of the respective clubs' support dates back years, to the rivalry in the London dockyards, and there has been little sign of a ceasefire in hostilities.

So you can understand my reservations as I considered my options before the transfer window closed in March 2001...and reached the dubious decision to enter the Lions' den.

It seemed a million miles from sunny Florida, my preferred destination.

Ignoring offers from a number of lower league clubs in England, I flew out to the USA, where Major League Soccer were holding a series of trials ahead of their upcoming season. I was only there for a couple of days and it was nice to bump into a few familiar faces from my Everton days in Robert Warzycha, Mo Johnston and the Serb Predrag Radosavljević, or 'Preki' as we knew him.

MLS, who effectively own the players, allocated me to a team in Florida, where I played up front in a trial match alongside an unknown Brazilian. I can't recall his name but he reminded me of the former Newcastle United striker Mirandinha – he'd get his head down, try and beat a thousand players and never once considered passing to me.

I thought I did all right by scoring a goal but the club hadn't offered me a deal by the time I boarded the return trans-Atlantic flight and I soon heard that they had opted for the Brazilian solo artist instead. A pity because, as a family, we would have fancied a move to America's 'Sunshine State'.

I managed to convince myself that I had to consider the prospect of joining Millwall from a professional's point of view, not through the eyes of a diehard Hammers supporter. Apart from offering me the best financial deal, more money than I'd been earning at Barnet, they were the nearest club to my Chigwell home and chasing promotion in the equivalent of League One at the time. Managed by Mark McGee, they also possessed some really good players, including Lucas Neill and Tim Cahill, who both went on to establish themselves as Premier League and Australian international stars.

Although it was only a very minor consideration, it hadn't escaped my

The look says it all about my last days as a footballer with Millwall.

notice that joining Millwall in the third tier would give me the chance for me to put my name to a quirky achievement of having played in all four divisions of the English league in the same season. With the transfer windows now in place, it's a unique record impossible to achieve today. I have to admit, having previously played for Leicester City (Premier League), Norwich City (Division One) and Barnet (Division Three) earlier in the 2000-01, the 'anorak' in me quite fancied the idea of joining a second division team.

As it turned out, my sum contribution in seven weeks with Millwall amounted to just 19 minutes of first team football. My two appearances for the Lions were both as a sub. The first time I came on for quarter-of-an-hour and the next outing was for a mere four minutes.

A strained stomach muscle, a problem that arose during the American trials, prevented me from making the impact I'd hoped to. I felt pain whenever I tried to kick a ball and had to sit out the last three weeks of the season.

It was a good time for the club, who won promotion to what is now the Championship, but I just didn't feel able to join in the celebrations. There were many nice people among the staff at Millwall and they did everything possible to make me feel welcome. Even their fans, the rougher elements of which are not exactly known for their warmth and humanity, especially towards those in claret and blue (and vice-versa, it should be said), gave me encouragement. Naturally, some of them were quick to remind me where my allegiance lies. 'Wot you doing 'ere, West Ham boy?' one of them demanded to know. But, all things considered, they were generally good towards me.

It's fair to say, though, I never felt a part of Millwall. I didn't even attend their final game and, despite an invite from Mark McGee, I also shunned the celebration party that followed. I felt uncomfortable there because I hadn't contributed anything towards their success.

Millwall was the only one of my eight clubs (including loan spells) that I didn't score for – I don't even think I even touched the ball! – and there is no denying it was a rather unglamorous end to my playing days.

People still say to me that it was quite an achievement to have played in all four divisions in one season and maybe it would have been had I worked my way up through the leagues. But it was plainly ridiculous to think that I'd started the 2000-01 campaign in the Premier League and ended up two rungs further down the league ladder in the equivalent of today's League One.

Scrambled mind

My career had reached another crossroads. During my time at Barnet, I reluctantly agreed to enrol on an FA coaching course. Not that I particularly wanted to, but because it was felt that, as player-manager, it seemed the right thing to do. The course was scheduled for May, immediately following the end of that season, and my enthusiasm for it hadn't improved when we arrived for the first day's tuition. Not having fully recovered from the rejection and disappointment I'd felt at Barnet, I couldn't have been in a worse frame of mind when I turned up to find that the course in Hertfordshire was being run by my former West Ham team-mate Geoff Pike.

It was Geoff's job, on behalf of the FA, to coach the would-be coaches and for all my cynicism where the accumulation of coaching qualifications is concerned, it has to be said that 'Pikey' put on a good course. Gus Poyet, the former Chelsea and Spurs midfielder and now manager at Brighton, was among those of us trying to gain the UEFA B Licence. Ex-Arsenal defender Steve Bould, who became Arsene Wenger's No.2 at the start of the 2012-13 season, was another former pro who joined us.

Although Pikey was in overall charge of what went on, the way it works is that the coaches take it in turns to coach each other while attempting to demonstrate different drills and practical skills. I say 'attempting' because it was laughable watching the one and only school teacher on the course trying to explain to Poyet, a Uruguayan with 23 international caps and an outstanding goalscoring record for club and country, how to make penetrating midfield runs. The poor lad was totally out of his depth. It was a complete nonsense.

Another farcical situation developed when one of the other coaches tried to show Bould, once a key member of the famously resolute Arsenal back four, how to play the offside trap! Under George Graham, 'Bouldy, Tony Adams, Lee Dixon and Nigel Winterburn were the ultimate masters at it.

We all had to muck in and help each other to try and attain the coaching badge but after witnessing the first session on day one of what should have been a two-week course, I could only describe my brain as totally and utterly scrambled. I just couldn't get my head around it all.

Geoff Pike, who did his best to encourage me to become a coach, with his FA Cup winners' medal and shirt from 1980.

Each of us were given a specific topic and it says everything about my indifferent attitude to the course that I can't even remember exactly what I was supposed to try and teach the others. It may have been the art of midfield runs or something similar. Anyway, after I'd given out the bibs, we started an eight-a-side game and the idea was that I should stop the match at various intervals to highlight mistakes in play and make other relevant observations.

I blew the whistle once after a minute or two and had a few words with the lads, but then I proceeded to let the game flow for several more minutes without taking another pause in play to make any further points. As I say, my mind was scrambled and after standing by and simply watching the match go on for several minutes, Pikey eventually blew the whistle himself and shouted 'stop!' He asked me why I hadn't stopped play before he had but I just apologised and told him that my mind had been miles away.

I got home that night and decided I couldn't continue with the course. I'd been so anti-FA coaching courses throughout my playing career that I didn't see the point of them and had convinced myself that it was something I didn't need to bother with. I did actually complete the first week of the course but on the Friday at the end of that first week, I told Pikey I probably wouldn't be back on Monday morning.

I found the experience a painful one and totally against everything I've ever believed in. I didn't even want to become a coach – I was only interested in being a manager. Geoff remained very positive about things and did his best to talk me into continuing but I phoned him again that Sunday to confirm I'd had enough of coaching.

Calling it a day

There were still a number of clubs interested in signing me as a player the following season, especially Cheltenham and Stevenage, who were then still a rising force at non-league level. I had a massive decision to make but the option to play on didn't appeal when I took account of the fact that I felt both mentally and physically drained.

Barring a miracle, I wasn't going to be offered a manager's job at the start of the 2001-02 season, so, during my summer break, I did some sums and wondered if I could possibly earn enough from media work to cover all our family overheads. I quickly worked out that we had enough money left in the bank to go another nine months before I needed to find new work to cover all our outgoings. Chloe was attending private school and my boys were four-years-old and also about to enter private education, which doesn't come cheap.

Believe it or not, I hadn't paid off our mortgage – albeit a relatively small one – and had made the mistake of paying my surplus earnings into a pension fund rather than invest it in property.

Trudging off the pitch at Millwall wasn't the way I wanted to bow out as a player, so I asked West Ham if they would grant me use of their facilities so that I could invite a number of people – family, friends and associates from my time in the game – to gather together at my spiritual football home for an official retirement party. My old club were very happy to oblige and on July 11, 2001 – my 36th birthday – I called a press conference to announce that, after 19 years as a pro footballer, it was time to hang up my size eight boots.

Any hopes that my immediate availability as a media pundit might draw attention in the following morning's papers were somewhat dashed, however, when the news that Tottenham had sacked George Graham broke that day. Bloody Spurs!

Seriously, I hadn't called the conference expecting it to make big news – it barely got a mention on the sports pages – but it seemed an appropriate place to bow out. West Ham, especially their press officer Peter Stewart, were very good about it. Ironically, given the extent of how our relationship would deteriorate a few years later, Terry Brown was also on good form. The chairman presented me with an inscribed silver salver on what was only the second occasion I'd met him – the first being when I'd returned to the club as a player in the mid-90s.

To paraphrase Kenneth Wolstenholme, playing wise, now it really was all over for me.

Highlights and disappointments

Scoring at least 200 league goals had been one of my biggest career targets when I first set out on the long path to becoming a pro. I respect any striker who scores 200 league goals, especially if most of them come at the highest level, so that was very satisfying. If you play for 20 seasons, then it's the equivalent of netting 10 goals per season. It sounds easy but it isn't when you consider how injuries can disrupt things and there will inevitably be spells when you are simply out of form.

My 714 first-team appearances produced 306 goals – conveniently, I've included the 14 I scored in Malaysia to take me beyond the magical 300 mark!

There wasn't a lot else let for me to achieve as a player and I look back with a lot of pride and personal satisfaction. To be paid to do what you love doing

Check out the dodgy strides and shoes! One of my career highlights was being named PFA Young Player of the Year in 1986. I also won the Fiat Uno Young Player of the Year award that year and among those at the award ceremony along with representatives of sponsors Fiat were Ian St. John, Joe Mercer, Ron Greenwood and Bill Nicholson.

– and earn good money in the process – is a privilege I have very much appreciated and still do to this day.

I was fortunate to meet so many nice people from all walks of life and different countries and cultures. When I met David Essex, a big West Ham fan, for the first time after a home game, he knelt at my feet. "What are you doing, you're an international pop superstar," I told him. I could never get my head around the fame thing in football. Apart from being a musical legend from the 70s, David is a very lovely man and the way I saw it, I should have been bowing to *him*.

In terms of my top three career highlights, scoring on my Hammers' debut against Tottenham in 1983 is still the pinnacle. It's crazy really that my first senior appearance should still hold the most cherished memories. My hat-trick debut for Everton against Newcastle United and my England debut, against Sweden in September 1986 (even though we lost), are right up there. Winning the PFA Young Player-of-the-Year award in 1986 and moving for a British record fee in 1988 were also gratifying landmarks.

It's much easier to pinpoint my disappointments. The biggest regret is that I never scored for England, even though the time I actually spent on the pitch for my country added up to only 171 minutes (my thanks to Trevor at Sky's Soccer Saturday for that ridiculous stat!). I'd love to have experienced the thrill of scoring with the three lions on my chest.

In one of my last appearances for the Hammers. I only wish
I'd ended my career at Upton Park.

I wish I'd stayed at West Ham throughout my career, as Sir Trevor Brooking did, and I'm not just saying it for the benefit of Hammers' fans. While I experienced a lot of great times at Everton and Leicester, I can't turn back the clock and I accept now that joining Everton in 1988 was the right move for me at that time. When I left West Ham the second time to go to Malaysia, I didn't want to leave and maybe, looking back, I should have dug my heels in and stayed to fight for my place. Some time after I returned from Selangor and joined Leicester, Harry Redknapp admitted to me that he'd given serious thought to bringing me back to West Ham for a third spell with my club. I only wish he had.

But if I'd stayed at Upton Park instead of leaving for Everton, who can say whether the Hammers would have subsequently reached a Cup final or managed to avoid relegation, as happened a year after I left? While I don't lose sleep over the fact that my last professional appearance was in a Millwall shirt, if I could have planned it to perfection I would much preferred to have finished in claret and blue.

The regrets, though, are very few and far between. There were many more highs than lows and there isn't much I'd change from a career that gave me so much to be proud of.

8

After the thrill has gone

ACCORDING to official Professional Footballers' Association (PFA) figures, around 70% of players get divorced within five years of retiring. It's a stunning statistic that makes a mockery of the old cliché of giving up the game to spend more time with family.

For many, the problems begin straight away, from the first day you are at home. On retirement, you are in the house much more and your income is greatly reduced or even non-existent. This leads to questions like 'can't you go out and get a job?' because your wife isn't used to having you around and also her spending allowance usually gets cut.

As a divorcee I can speak from personal experience. The cracks in my marriage to ex-wife Lorraine started to appear soon after I retired from the game in July 2001. I was never worried about my wife wanting me for my money because we met at school when she was 13 and I was 15. We were married for 20 years. But after I retired there was too much time at home, less money and the arguments started.

The careers of Premier League players usually come to a close in their early to mid-30s. From the women's perspective, their husbands often lack the maturity and life experience of so many other men of a similar age.

My generation of players were probably the last to earn decent money – if not really big sums – before Sky TV came in, changed the face of football and players' wages went spiralling through the stratosphere.

I've been lucky in that I quickly found regular work as a pundit and reporter for Sky but if I hadn't done so, I would have found it very hard to cope in retirement.

Along with the absence of the big monthly pay cheque, the thrill and adrenalin rush of playing before packed stadiums has suddenly disappeared. Having focused on only one thing for more than two decades, players are then faced with a very difficult question: 'What's next?'

As a footballer, your life is disciplined and you pretty much know what you are doing, day in and day out. Getting used to a new way of life for both husband and wife is the hardest thing.

What disappoints me is that the PFA don't bother to make a quick phone call to recently-retired players to check if they are OK. The PFA do so much good work in many other areas but it would have been nice if they had picked the phone up and asked if I was OK. They tend to be reactive rather than proactive.

I believe the PFA should look at introducing a programme that helps prepare players for the off-field challenges in their lives that come once the roar of the crowd has died down.

You very quickly become forgotten and all the hangers-on, the so-called advisors and 'friends', disappear when you can no longer get them tickets and they're looking to jump on the next bandwagon. I found this very hard to come to terms with myself.

For many, retirement must feel like being pushed through an open door and once you're on the other side, you try to push your way back in but there is no handle on the door. There's that sudden and painful realisation: Shit, now I'm in the real world!

Some players don't even know how to change a light bulb or pay an electricity bill. I wasn't one of them but there are plenty who must struggle with everyday issues that normal people never give a second thought to.

Some of today's generation of elite players have an entire entourage to pamper and protect them from the grind of everyday life. So in the same way that financial rewards have increased, the future challenges may also be greater. Modern players are in a celebrity bubble and when that bubble bursts the money they earn will become irrelevant for many of them.

Problems looming

I see problems looming for today's multi-million pound earners of today when they leave the game. The vast riches they receive now will not necessarily make retirement any easier – on the contrary, it is more likely to fuel their problems – when their playing days are over.

The more famous and recognisable a player is, the harder it may be for them to settle into everyday life when their last ball has been kicked and they walk the street with no-one stopping them for an autograph or a photo. They have more to lose than the far less recognisable faces who have earned a living from playing in the lower divisions.

The Premier League players of today might have 10 million quid in the bank when they drive their Bentleys into the training ground for the last time but having all the money in the world won't replace that special buzz they got from playing the game at the highest level.

People often ask if I miss playing and I can honestly say that I don't. The reason is because it was bloody hard work, mentally and physically demanding. I spent most of the first 35 years of my life where everything totally and utterly revolved around football. I know we were not as aware of the need for good diet in the way modern players are but we still had to dedicate ourselves to the game and remain disciplined.

I recall a chat I had with my dad when I was about 13. He asked: "Do you want to be a footballer?" to which I naturally replied "yes."

"Right," he said, "if you want to be a footballer, you can't drink, smoke and must keep girlfriends to a minimum and concentrate fully on your football." And he was right. While some of my friends were doing drugs, going nightclubbing and getting into all sorts of things, I kept clear of all that. My life was simply football.

Physically, it was very demanding. Our pre-season routine at West Ham meant 10-mile runs through Epping or Hainault Forest slogging our guts out, whereas now they probably don't run more than 400 metres at a time but we didn't know any different back then. By the time I came to the end of my career I was physically and mentally shattered.

In my latter playing days, I could barely walk down the stairs at home. I came down like a crab, going sideways, because my joints were knackered and I couldn't put any weight on my knees. Yes, pitches got better but they also became harder and that did me no favours either. I found it hard going in my last season at Leicester and even harder when I moved around the divisions in my final year.

By the time I actually called it a day, I had very sore knees and both my groins were hurting. Luckily, I just rested and didn't actually need a hernia operation but I was a physical wreck.

What I miss most

I don't really miss the dressing room banter much either, as a lot of ex-players do. The Boys of 86 at West Ham have met up regularly to appear in shows and attend social functions in the past decade or so, so we've all kept in touch with each other. Then I'm fortunate to enjoy the 'banter' with the other ex-pros I work with at Sky, which is fantastic.

The one and only thing I still miss is the thrill of scoring a goal. Where do I go in life to recapture that unique sensation? Netting the winner for Leicester

Emile Heskey tries to catch me as I celebrate scoring for Leicester at Old Trafford. How can you possibly recreate the sheer buzz those special moments bring?

at Old Trafford in front of 55,000-plus...how can I possibly repeat the buzz I got from doing that? Sex? No, nothing compares with scoring a goal in front of tens of thousands of people, especially when your team wins.

The best buzz I ever got from scoring a goal was my first against Spurs on my debut at West Ham when I was 17. But I can honestly say that I got as much buzz scoring for Barnet, in front of just 1500 fans, as I did when hitting the target for any of my previous clubs.

I can't replicate the thrill of scoring a goal but I guess I'll keep searching, even though I know I'll never find it.

That's where former players who have recently left the game usually struggle. The highs are so high and the lows so low. If you visualise a graph with a straight line in the middle, in most people's lives they tend to go a little bit above the line and also at times a tad below it. But for most footballers, it's extremes – miles above the line and miles below it.

Dealing with depression

We will probably never know the circumstances that drove him to his death, but the Gary Speed hanging tragedy in November 2011 brought the issue of how retired players often have to battle to stave off depression sharply into focus. The fact that Gary earned good money from football as a top player, appeared to have a settled family life with a wife and two sons and was doing very well as Wales' national manager when he ended his life, only added to everyone's anguish and bewilderment.

The tragic Gary Speed left football shocked and bewildered.

My former West Ham team-mate and strike-partner, Jeroen Boere, was another who took his own life. The big Dutchman had drug and gambling problems and obviously couldn't face life anymore.

Several of the lads within our own tight-knit Boys of 86 group, Mark Ward, Frank McAvennie and George Parris, have found themselves in trouble concerning drugs or gambling in the years since they stopped playing. When you can no longer find the unique buzz that sporting competition provides, or you fall on hard times and you have no close friends to turn to...or all of those things and more, life can

Jeroen 'Yosser' Boere is another who sadly took his own life.

Frank McAvennie and Mark Ward before our Boys of 86 tournament at West Ham in 2009, shortly after 'Wardy' was released at the end of his four-year prison sentence.

feel desperate and the PFA have to realise that there are a lot of old pros out there who need help and guidance.

This life of extremes must apply to all sportsmen and women. We've heard of a number of rugby players and cricketers also committing suicide because they are unable to adapt to everyday life once their playing days are over. Injuries that leave once fit competitors partially disabled or plagued by painful arthritis are other contributory factors to mental stress.

After Gary Speed's death, I read somewhere that the PFA sent out 50,000 leaflets to retired ex-players asking them if they needed any assistance. I never received one.

The PFA need to address the question of depression and the problems retirement can often bring for the more vulnerable ex-pros. Perhaps it's time for them to appoint a footballers' counsellor...

9

Reach for the Sky

IF I couldn't make it as a manager, then it was my aim to stay in football as part of the media. Happily, the 2001-02 season was just weeks old when my chance first came to work for Sky, who have revolutionised the game in England since the FA Premier League was formed in 1992.

I first worked for Sky on a freelance basis following an approach to producer Jonty Whitehead, who I'd got to know on previous visits to their studios for shows such as *Soccer AM*. The Copa America tournament was about to be staged in Colombia that summer and I jumped at the chance to ease my way into the world of football punditry by expressing my views on a tournament that, although packed with skilful South American players, was not exactly compulsive viewing for most fans of English clubs who prefer the cut and thrust of our game.

"Come along and we'll see how it goes. The first match kicks off at 12.30," said Jonty.

"Great," I replied, eager to take my chance.

"That's 12.30 in the morning," Jonty emphasised.

"Oh."

"...And the second game kicks off at 2.30am!" he added.

On the upside, at least if I made a few mistakes on air there wouldn't be too many people around at those unsociable hours to witness them.

I enjoyed the experience and must have done OK because Jonty invited me back for the games scheduled for the following two nights. He then introduced me to Ian Condron, producer of their *Soccer Saturday* show, who was on the look out for possible new guests. Although I'd heard of the show's increasing popularity as the best way to access live scores and news updates from games all over Britain, I'd not seen much of it myself because I'd obviously been playing most Saturdays. 'Condo' invited me onto the show soon after hosts Colombia won the 2001 Copa America and the English domestic season had begun.

I think the first panel of *Soccer Saturday* experts I worked alongside were Rodney Marsh, Frank McLintock and Alan Mullery – I was a real rookie among a trio of experienced, fully established media pundits. To say I was nervous is a massive understatement. I sat sheepishly at one end of the panel and let the others do most of the talking in response to promptings from Sky Sports' acclaimed anchor man, Jeff Stelling.

For those who aren't familiar with the show's format, it runs from midday until 6.00pm and the panel spend the first three hours previewing the Premier League games of the day. After the matches have finished, we provide a reflective round-up of what happened. Six hours might be less than the average working man and woman has to put in each day but it's quite an endurance test when the cameras are fixed on you.

We tend to arrive at the studios at around 11.00am and begin work by scanning the Saturday papers for any news items surrounding the matches we'll be focusing on that day. Sky supply us with a stats pack, so we're fully informed of every team's recent results, scorers and just about all the other relevant info you could wish to have at your fingertips. Whether we fully digest it all depends on the individual characters!

At around 11.30am we go down to the make-up department, where they apply powder to our faces to ensure that none of us appear to have shiny foreheads. Just before midday, the four panelists take their seats in the studio, where Jeff will already be fine-tuning his preparations, and await the countdown from the floor manager before the live show begins.

I was sat next to Frank McLintock on my first appearance and the former Arsenal double-winning skipper was a massive help to me. He showed me how the buttons worked and gave me lots of simple, but sensible, bits of advice, such as writing down all the players' names and numbers for easy identification when they appeared on the screen immediately in front of me. Both Frank and 'Mullers' were invaluable to me in those early weeks on the show.

At the end of my first appearance, after removing my headphones and moving out of the glare of the powerful studio lights, I came away feeling mentally exhausted and nursing the biggest headache I'd had in a long time.

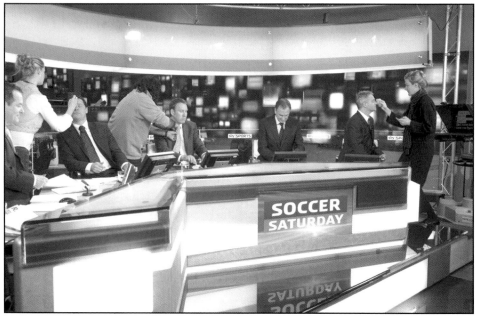

The make-up ladies get to work in the Sky Soccer Saturday studio before I go on air with Jeff Stelling, Paul Merson, Phil Thompson and Charlie Nicholas.

I'd concentrated so hard and felt more pressure in 'performing' on *Soccer Saturday* than I'd ever done playing or managing.

Throughout that first show I kept telling myself: 'Don't make a gaffe, don't swear, don't do anything stupid'. This is live TV, a bit like playing a football match. You can't take back what you've said on air, just as you can't smack the ball over the crossbar and ask the crowd to throw it back again to let you have another shot.

Rodney Marsh usually sat nearest to Jeff. He prided himself on trying to be more controversial, outspoken and wittier than his colleagues. He was wonderful entertainment value but also a powerful presence on the show. With Jeff also being a strong character, they would often enjoy a lot of banter. Rodney also liked to wind up Frank as often as possible.

Although Rodney was all right with me on my first few appearances, as I became more confident he relished putting me to the test. One week I made the mistake of saying what a "great team" West Ham had. Rodney jumped on the comment immediately and barked back at me: "What do you mean, West Ham have a great team? What have they done in the past couple of years?"

He was very abrupt and straight to the point. He threw the question straight back at me and I immediately sensed all eyes were on me, eagerly anticipating a response. I quickly tried to explain that what I meant to say was that they had a great squad in terms of strength in depth.

What Rodney did was good, though, because he'd put me on the spot and I had to give a rapid response. You can't just throw out a comment on television and not be able to back it up, or else you'll be found out very quickly.

Unfortunately for Rodney, he was sacked by Sky in January 2005 after making a tasteless joke about the Asia tsunami disaster on a phone-in show. The former England, QPR and Manchester City star made what the station called "offensive and inexcusable" remarks on *You're On Sky Sports.*

It worked out well for me at Sky in those early days, though, because Clive Allen had just left to join the ill-fated ITV Digital while George Best was going through one of his difficult periods, so they never quite knew when the Manchester United legend would be available. I basically just slotted into the vacant gap and when West Ham were playing away, they invited me on the show. To make it even more interesting for me, I'd invariably be allocated a game featuring one of my three former Premier League clubs.

It's fantastic to be able to watch football, express some opinions, enjoy plenty of banter with your mates and get paid for it. To me, it's the next best thing to playing.

Whoever came up with the concept of *Soccer Saturday* and convinced the top men at Sky, Vic Wakeling and Andy Melvin, that it would be the success it very quickly became, deserves much credit. It would have been easy to have dismissed this bright idea as a non-runner. Basically, they were asking the viewers at home to watch four ex-players watching football matches that (due to Premier League rules which prevent live coverage of games kicking-off at 3.00pm on Saturdays) the TV viewers themselves weren't able to see.

Jeff Stelling keeping the lads in check and the show ticking over nicely.

But with the brilliant Jeff Stelling at the helm, it has established itself as compulsive viewing for millions every Saturday and also in midweek.

I can't emphasise enough just how accomplished an anchor man Jeff is. He remains totally unflappable on screen, plucking the most unlikely nuggets of information from seemingly nowhere as he relays each goal and goalscorer, linking with each member on the panel...while at the same time having to absorb and react to incessant instructions from producer 'Condo' in his earpiece. But it's a measure of Jeff's skill in the presenter role that he takes it all in his stride.

It's also nice that he supports Hartlepool United, rather than one of the glamour clubs. It means he takes a genuine interest in what is going on in the lower divisions, which only serves to emphasise that *Soccer Saturday* is not a show aimed solely at supporters of the elite clubs.

Of course, the Premier League matches remain the focal point of the show and these are the games we enjoy covering most. We're looking at a 12-inch TV monitor in the studio and if it's a Premier League or Champions League game, it means we are provided with full live commentary and action replays of goals and all major incidents. So even if you're not totally sure which player has scored, the chances are that within a few seconds you will see confirmation on the screen in front of you before finishing your bulletin, so you're able to convey this important piece of information to the viewers.

The challenge comes when you're working in the studio in midweek and you've been allocated, say, Huddersfield Town v Bristol Rovers on a dark night. There is no live commentary to assist you in identifying players or confirming scorers, you are barely able to recognise any of the players (especially as their numbers appear so small on screen and, worse still, are covered in mud) and there are no replays available. A few of us have been caught out once or twice when covering a game from the lower divisions, especially if you've been distracted by a Champions League glamour tie on the screen in front of the colleague sat immediately next to you.

Gaffes and goals

After a few seasons working for Sky, I became increasingly involved in what we call In-Vision – providing brief, live updates from the ground while the match is in progress. Another name for it is 'Kamara Cam', on account of Chris Kamara's uniquely frenetic match-reporting style. Chris pioneered this technique, no-one does it with more gusto and now they have eight or nine ex-players reporting from grounds all over the country every Saturday afternoon.

In-Vision work presents different a challenge to the studio aspect of Sky. At Brighton's Withdean Stadium one night, years before moving to their excellent Amex Stadium, we had no shelter from the rain, so there I was holding an umbrella while water got into the wiring and caused my monitor to break ...just as a penalty was awarded! When you are talking on air, you are always told to look straight into the camera, not over your shoulder at what's going on down at pitch level. If I did that you'd only see the back of my head on the telly and I'd have the producer screaming in my ear telling me to turn around.

But on this occasion, with no picture on my monitor, I had little choice but to abandon protocol and watch the penalty being taken. The TV monitor is positioned just below the camera, which explains why you'll notice the commentator's eyes flicking up and down as he talks into his mic. If a goal happens to go in while you're talking and staring into the camera, it's not easy to keep your eyes on the monitor at the same time.

Working outdoors presents other problems that are beyond your control. I was once describing a goal at Southend when a group of excited Blues' fans started jumping on my back. And we've all seen how the pundits at Blackpool have to contend with the noisy beat from the local drummer.

Inevitably, we all drop the occasional clanger. One of my biggest bloomers

Among legends on the Sky Soccer Saturday panel, with Alan Mullery,
George Best and Rodney Marsh.

came about two years into my work for Sky. As a player, you know whether you've played well or not and it's the same as a pundit or commentator. On this particular occasion I thought I'd had a good show and, having completed my final analysis of the game I'd been watching and with Jeff winding down studio proceedings, I foolishly allowed myself to switch off mentally. I was thinking about what I'd be having for dinner at home later that evening when, quite unexpectedly, Jeff suddenly fired another question at me. It was relevant to a short clip they had just shown, possibly to do with West Ham's opponents the following week, but I hadn't even seen it and was in the dark about what he expected me to comment on.

I was completely lost for words, other than to say: "I'm sorry, Jeff, I don't understand the question, so why don't you ask Rodney..."

I didn't deal with that unexpected situation at all well and perhaps should have mocked myself on air for not paying attention. I'd 'played well' for five-and-three-quarter hours but let myself down with a lapse of concentration in the last few moments of the show. It was an important lesson and I've since prided myself on getting things right and staying focussed until we're off air.

It's also very important to learn that your microphone is always 'live' even when you think it might not be – as Ron Atkinson infamously discovered to his cost while working for ITV.

My sons, Matt and Billy, on the day they joined me in the Sky studios at Isleworth in 2011.

I learned from experience that it always pays to get to a ground early and get organised but on the day Leeds United visited Gillingham for a League One fixture in April 2010, I was caught up in traffic on my way to Kent and didn't arrive at Priestfield until about quarter-past two for a 3.00pm kick-off. I struggled to find a car park space and by the time I picked up the team sheet from the press room, made my way up to the TV gantry and clocked in with Carly Bassett at Sky, who is the link between me and the producer, I had to very quickly scribble down the line-ups on my notepad, as I routinely do.

As I hadn't seen either team play before that season, the last thing I needed was an early goal. In the eighth minute Gillingham launched a long throw into the box, which was flicked on at the near-post and then headed in by their number 14. "Goal!" I shouted into my microphone and Carly said they would be back to me within a few seconds, when I would describe the goal to Jeff Stelling for the benefit of our viewers. I looked into the camera and described how Gillingham had a throw-in on the left-hand side, which was flicked on and Jonathan Howson, the number 14, scored with a header to put the Gills one-up.

I thought that was that, until I heard Jeff's witty follow up

On the gantry at Fulham. Judging by my expression, it looks like West Ham have just conceded again.

comment through my headphones: "Well, that's quite an amazing goal... Gillingham have taken the lead...the goalscorer's Jonathan Howson...and he plays for Leeds!"

Because I'd arrived late and been all over the place, and didn't really know many of the players in either side, I'd unfortunately looked down at my notes and read out the number 14 of Leeds in error, instead of the correct Gillingham number 14 who was Adam Miller.

Jeff quite rightly slaughtered me for my blunder – a stark lesson that a commentator should always arrive at a ground well before kick-off and prepare properly.

My other memorable cock-up made it onto one of Sky's end-of-season funny clips. I was reporting from Colchester and got totally tongue-tied when trying to pronounce the surnames of home players Chris Iwelumo and Karl Duguid, who, to my embarrassment, came out sounding something like 'Iwuliamuuu' and 'Digwid'.

Thankfully, those type of clangers have been few and far between and, after six years with Sky as a freelancer, I was delighted to gain my first contract with them from the start of the 2007-08 season.

Down the pub with McAvennie

Although Sky now occupies most of my working week during the football season, I have kept busy and remained in close contact with football through various other opportunities that have come my way.

Soon after announcing my retirement I went along to West Ham's pre-season friendly at Rushden & Diamonds, who at that time shared the same sponsors as the Hammers in Dr Martens. The Doc Martens bosses, Max and Stephen Griggs, had invited me to the hospitality suite, where I

Working together with Frank McAvennie was always going to be good fun.

happened to bump into Sue Page, West Ham's commercial director. Sue asked to speak to me after the game, when she explained the club wer looking for an ex-player to host the two main hospitality lounges within the newly-built Dr Martens Stand. Naturally, I was immediately interested and about a week later she suggested that it might be a good idea if I worked alongside my old strike partner Frank McAvennie.

I'd seen Frank earlier that year while he was filming a documentary on his colourful life. He asked if I'd play a small part in the film and invited me to join him in the Boleyn pub, just a couple of hundred yards from West Ham's ground, on the corner of Green Street and the Barking Road. The fans mobbed us and afterwards we watched the game together. It was great to see Frank again for what must have been the first time in 14 years. We'd always got on fabulously well and when we met up again in 2001, it was just like old times.

Anyway, following up on Sue Page's suggestion, I phoned Frank at his home at Gateshead, on the outskirts of Newcastle, to ask if he fancied making regular trips down to Upton Park to renew our double act and he jumped at the chance. We usually went down well with the corporate guests, except when it came to reading out the quiz questions and they had trouble understanding Frank's broad Glaswegian accent.

There was a funny moment before one game when Frank turned up clearly feeling the effects of a cold. Purely for medicinal purposes, he'd downed a few vodka and cokes to lift his spirits...but forgot he'd already been taking prescribed medicine. By the time he got up on stage to join me in conducting the traditional pre-match quiz, he was already half-cut and slurring his words.

The club decided that I should host the Castle and Premier Lounges on my own in the second year, although they asked me to invite along a different ex-Hammer or celebrity to join me at each home game, which I continued to do until March 2005.

Another small sideline I enjoyed was promoting my dad's insurance company, Chase Insurance, which basically meant meeting his top clients and talking football with them over lunch or on golf days. This PR work helped to gain new customers and in 2005 we sold out to Towergate, who employed me on the same basis for the next three years.

The Boys of 86

One of the most pleasing aspects of recent years has been the way West Ham's record-breaking team of 1985-86 has reunited on numerous occasions for social events under the Boys of 86 banner. I had the idea to form the limited company after attending the dinner to celebrate the 15th-year anniversary of our best-ever league season, held at the Prince Regent Hotel in Chigwell back in May 2001. It was Tony McDonald, a good friend of mine who worked closely with me on both my first book and this one, who had the original idea to bring all the players from that season back together again for what was a memorable night attended by some 300 supporters.

Later that year, Tony and his mate Danny Francis wrote the successful book, The Boys of 86, containing interviews with all the players that made it happen. I had no problem whatsoever with Tony Mac's Football World company earning a small profit for their endeavours – good luck to them for having the original idea – but I thought us former players should get in on the act, too.

What the success of that dinner and the book demonstrated was the warmth and affection West Ham fans who had watched us in that unforgettable season still had for the players who pushed Liverpool and Everton all the way to the wire in that epic championship race. We finished third in the final table but the enthusiasm shown by Hammers fans in reliving their memories of that famous season was all too evident. I first spoke about the commercial

The Boys of 86 at the first dinner held in our honour at Chigwell in 2001.
Back row, left to right. Neil Orr, Alan Devonshire, Greg Campbell, Tony Gale,
Alvin Martin, Paul Hilton, George Parris, Rob Jenkins (physio).
Front: Alan Dickens, Ray Stewart, Frank McAvennie, Mark Ward and me.
Obviously, co-hosts Galey and Alvin gave me stick for the bright suit.

opportunities to Tony Gale and then, along with our fellow former team-mates Phil Parkes, Alvin Martin and Ray Stewart, we formed 'Boys of 86 Ltd' in 2002.

We have since put on numerous gala dinners of our own, enjoyed fabulous days out at the races, organised other corporate events and, of course, played charity football matches in the name of Boys of 86, where we were able to test the elasticity of claret and blue replica West Ham shirts and shorts at various non-league grounds in the south-east. Our corporate football day on the main pitch at Upton Park, where fans got the chance to play against the ex-players they used to cheer from the terraces, evolved into a hugely successful annual event.

Apart from having a lot of fun, the Boys of 86 company was also able to generate a small amount of revenue that has gone directly back to the ex-players themselves. In several cases, for those who have endured tough times since giving up the game, it has been a welcome boost. There's not one player from that squad who is financially secure. We all need to work for a living, so it was always our intention to raise as much money as we could, while at the same time give our loyal followers from that era some entertainment in return.

The highlight of all the events we've been involved in was the lavish dinner staged at the Britannia Hotel on London's Isle of Dogs in September 2005. It was organised to jointly celebrate the 25th anniversary of the club's last FA Cup victory and the 30th year since the previous Wembley triumph, in 1975. Billy Bonds, who captained both cup-winning teams, got the standing ovation we all expected. But the reaction our guests reserved for our manager John Lyall was something else.

Before the Boys of 86 football tournament at Upton Park in 2003.
Back row, left to right: Alan Dickens, Jimmy Quinn, Tony Gale, Greg Campbell, Kevin Hitchcock, Mickey Phillips, Allen McKnight, Alan Devonshire, Paul Hilton, Neil Orr, Alvin Martin. Front: Nick Berry, Bradley Walsh, Steve Potts, Perry Fenwick, Frank McAvennie, George Parris, Mark Ward, me, Geoff Pike, Paul Allen and Bobby Barnes.

Another Boys of 86 reunion, this time before our tournament in May 2009 when Alan Dev and Galey were our non-playing joint managers.

Sadly, one dinner I wished we'd never had to consider putting on was the tribute evening in honour of John, soon after he died of a heart attack in 2006. His widow Yvonne and son Murray attended what was for all of us a very emotional evening at Upton Park, where John had masterminded so many great victories we'd shared together.

The team spirit that existed between the players in 1985-86 is as strong now as it was back then. And no matter what any West Ham team achieves in the future, I very much doubt that those players will experience the same enduring camaraderie still enjoyed by the Boys of 86. We closed the company following a private dinner involving the ex-players and our friends in London in 2011 and when I look back I'm proud to have been part of it.

It's not as if the Boys of 86 still don't meet up from time to time, especially those of us – the likes of Alvin, Galey and myself – who have progressed onto the after-dinner circuit. Len Herbert, a long-time West Ham fan who helped out behind the scenes for the Boys of 86, first got me involved when he asked Frankie Mac and I to speak at his local football club's annual dinner held at Dagenham & Redbridge FC. Soon afterwards my comedian friend Russ Williams got me along to a golf club function, where most of those present happened to be cricket fans who didn't have a clue who I was talking about when I mentioned Bobby Robson.

It's never easy going on stage after a comedian who has had the place in stitches, and it became even harder when a couple of pissheads at the front of the audience started talking over me. What should have been a 40-minute speech was cut by half – I just kept talking as quickly as possible to get it over with – and it was the most excruciating 20 minutes of my life.

I sought advice from my friend, Florida-based Michael Hockton, who is one of the funniest blokes I know, and he was very helpful with tips on how to fine-tune my stage act. Now I feel comfortable with a structured routine based on my football experiences. I'm not proactive on the after-dinner

On stage with Galey at the Queens Theatre, Hornchurch in December 2011, where we were appearing in the 'Galey and Friends' show organised by Jeff Garner and Tony Hoskins of Football For Fans.

circuit but at least I now have a proper 40-minute script to adhere to when making occasional guest appearances.

As well as being a punditry colleague at Sky, Tony Gale and I have also shared a stage in theatres and clubs on many occasions in recent years. It's really football's *Little and Large* show, with me predictably on the wrong end of Galey's relentless piss-taking about my short legs, not to mention my abortive attempt to take over at West Ham. I've learned how to handle him, though.

10

Time to act

IT was on the heartbreaking return journey from Cardiff, where West Ham had just suffered a dismal 1-0 defeat by Crystal Palace in the 2004 Championship Play-off Final, when the idea that I should try to change things at the club first entered my head.

It hadn't been a good season, football-wise, but after all the problems manager Alan Pardew had to contend with following his delayed arrival from Reading a couple of months into the season, most of us felt grateful to have snatched fourth place in the final table to reach the end-of-season play-offs.

The semi-final victory over Ipswich Town, when Mattie Etherington scored a great goal to send us on our way to the Millennium Stadium, was one to savour. The atmosphere at Upton Park that night, with 35,000 fans jumping for joy and singing *Twist and Shout*, took me back to my teenage days spent on the terraces.

I felt so excited as I set out at the start of a day that I hoped would end with victory over Crystal Palace and my beloved Hammers back in the Premier League. As a match day host in the hospitality lounges at Upton Park, I flew from Stansted to Cardiff on a charter flight organised by West Ham's commercial department. I knew most of the fans on board from seeing them in the Premier Lounge or Castle Suite at each home game.

On the flight to South Wales, I got talking to the guy next to me. I didn't know him at the time but it was Lee Horton, sports editor of the *Sunday People*. We chatted away and, like all other West Ham fans on the trip, I felt buoyant and fully expected us to beat Palace.

On landing in Cardiff, our bus took us from the airport to Jury's Hotel in the city centre, where I got up on stage and did what I usually did prior to home matches – a bit of chat about the game, a quiz, that sort of thing – as the fans enjoyed their pre-match meal. And drank...and drank...and drank. None more so than my younger brother Paul and his mate Shaun Parmenter, who had travelled to Cardiff by train. While I was doing my best to entertain the fans, those two got steadily pissed. Never mind, I thought we'd all be knocking back celebratory drinks later on. At about 2.30pm, I remember belting out a rousing 'let's get back to the Premier League' rallying cry as I stepped down from the stage and we all prepared for the short walk to the stadium.

We had three great seats in an executive section of the Millennium Stadium and I couldn't wait for the action to begin. The first half was interrupted by Paul and Shaun disappearing to the toilet, their earlier thirst-quenching efforts having taken its toll. They returned to their seats about 10 minutes later, followed swiftly by a steward who asked: "Are these two with you?"

When I confirmed who they were, the steward told me they had been wandering along the concourse and upsetting some of the bar staff. They were clearly a bit drunk and the steward pointed out that as their antics had been captured on CCTV, he had every right to throw them out of the stadium. Thankfully, I managed to placate the steward by apologising for Paul and Shaun's behaviour and reassuring him that I'd settle them both down and keep them quiet for the rest of the game. The problem was half-solved anyway when Shaun fell asleep. He had the right idea, as it turned out.

Neither of them missed much as a pretty average first-half degenerated into a shambles after the break, when Pardew bizarrely took off all of his forwards – Bobby Zamora, Marlon Harewood and David Connolly – at one-nil down and still contrived to lose the final thanks to Neil Shipperley's tap-in just past the hour mark. Apart from Zamora's first-half shot that was parried by the Palace keeper, West Ham created very little else, except a half-hearted penalty appeal in the second-half that was turned down after Michael Carrick fell on the edge of the box.

I couldn't believe what I'd seen. The inexplicable removal of all three forwards aside, the standard of football was dire, much as it had been for

Alan Pardew wearing the t-shirt bearing the slogan referring to Bobby Moore.

most of the season. Lacking any class or guile, it wasn't the West Ham I wanted to see.

To add insult to injury, the management and players had taken to wearing motivational T-shirts, introduced by 'Pards', bearing the slogan 'Moore Than Just a Football Team'. I suppose it was meant to be some kind of acknowledgement of Bobby Moore and all that he stood for at the club but, instead, the dross served up by Pardew's team was an insult to the great man's name. No-one needs reminding who Bobby Moore was or his contribution to club and country. This totally unacceptable PR stunt just wound me up and the feeble manner of the defeat by Palace only compounded a miserable afternoon.

At the final whistle, I was in no mood to hang around. I left my brother and his mate in the stadium to drown their sorrows while I made my way to the pick-up point outside the ground where our coach was meant to be waiting for us. As if this miserable day couldn't get any worse, we had a two-hour wait because the coach driver had fallen asleep in the car park!

While enduring this agonising wait, I spoke to other West Ham supporters who were all as dejected as me. We questioned the performance of the team, the manager, his selections, his substitutions and his tactics. And, above all, we questioned where the club was going from here.

When we finally boarded the bus for the journey back to Cardiff airport, I made a point of sitting next to Lee Horton again. I told him the club was going nowhere and that, like so many other despondent fans, I'd just about had enough of it. I was fed up with West Ham being widely regarded as a yo-yo club, where there had long since been a lack of investment in players. On the contrary – most of our best players had already left and a few more would soon join them through the Upton Park exit gates.

Lee listened to my gripes and, in his senior role at the *Sunday People,* offered to help in any way he could. I didn't know at that moment if he could be of any help at all, because my head was in a spin, but I knew that something drastic had to be done to turn it all around at West Ham...

Brink of disaster

The Upton Park malaise had set in from the start of the 2002-03 season that ended in relegation from the Premier League under Glenn Roeder's management. It was Roeder's second season in charge and my second back at the club as a host in the corporate hospitality lounges. I could readily identify with the fans' frustration as this disastrous campaign unravelled.

The die was cast in the first home game, a 2-2 draw with double winners Arsenal who should have suffered their first defeat in 23 matches. Joe Cole and Frederic Kanouté gave the Hammers a two-goal lead before Thierry Henry pulled one back for the Gooners midway through the second half. But with one of the worst penalty misses you are ever likely to see, Kanouté blew a golden chance to make it 3-1 and seal the game in the 75th minute...only for Silvain Wiltord to snatch an 88th minute equaliser. Who knows what victory over Arsene Wenger's high-fliers would have done for West Ham's confidence. Instead, they had to wait another five months before winning another home league game.

As December dawned, it was obvious to most of us who followed West Ham that a change of direction was required, starting with the manager. This isn't hindsight – West Ham were staring relegation in the face some six months before the inevitable conclusion.

Roeder had done well to claim a seventh-place finish in his first season after succeeding Harry Redknapp but, despite boasting a talented squad brimming with quality – including the likes of Cole, Michael Carrick, Paolo Di Canio, Trevor Sinclair, Kanouté, David James and young Jermain Defoe – he just couldn't get them to perform. It took until the last day of January to record their first home league victory, 2-1 against Blackburn Rovers.

Chairman Terry Brown and his fellow directors should have terminated Roeder's reign in December 2002, or certainly by early January, to give his replacement enough time to turn things around. There was talk of George Graham, who was sacked by Spurs the previous March, coming in and although I would have preferred a 'West Ham man' at the helm, at least Graham – renowned for organising the most water-tight defences in the land at Arsenal – would probably have kept Hammers' in the top flight.

The board's failure to act decisively proved financially catastrophic in terms of how relegation decimated a team brimming with quality prospects. It is arguably the best team ever to have been relegated from the top flight, certainly the most talented since Brian Clough's Nottingham Forest side of Nigel Clough, Roy Keane and co. went down 10 years earlier.

In the course of working at Upton Park, I often bumped into Paul Aldridge, Brown's No.2 and managing director, but they were never going to take any notice of what I said. West Ham had a tradition for keeping faith with their managers – only nine full-time appointments in 100 or so years said it all – but they dithered too long in Roeder's case. Since he became executive chairman in 1996, Brown was being paid a substantial wage to run West Ham but he didn't stand up to be counted in the 2002-03 season.

Neither did some of the highly-paid players who also let their club down. Paolo Di Canio was a big fans' favourite at Upton Park but the volatile Italian didn't travel north of Watford too often when the pressure was on and Roeder needed everyone pulling in the same direction. French-born Mali international striker Fredi Kanouté was out for long spells through injury and illness and there were others who just didn't perform. Glenn probably gave the senior players too much leeway at times.

Down and out...Fredi Kanoute and Trevor Sinclair after relegation was confirmed at Birmingham in May 2003.

Two fans at St. Andrew's trying to come to terms with the unthinkable.

OK, I accept that they went down in exceptional circumstances. To be relegated with 42 points was very unfortunate, although even victory on the last day at Birmingham, which would have taken them to 44 points, wouldn't have saved them. It was a travesty but one that could, and should, have been avoided.

Counting the cost

On the day relegation was confirmed with the 2-2 draw at St. Andrew's, I was working as a pundit in the Sky studios and literally had tears in my eyes as the club's fate was finally sealed. The consequences for everyone, especially the long-suffering fans, were absolutely horrendous. Working at the club on a part-time basis meant I had close contact with the commercial department, in particular, so I knew the devastating effect of relegation and the drastic cut-backs that would have to be enforced in the weeks to follow.

While several of the players quickly put the season behind them and left the club to enjoy new signing-on deals and lucrative

Sub keeper Raimond Van Der Gouw consoles Paolo Di Canio at Birmingham.

contracts elsewhere, those left behind had to count the cost. Members of staff, many of them earning a pittance anyway, either had to take a pay cut (as I did) or, in some cases, face redundancy.

The players didn't suffer and neither, in personal terms, did Terry Brown. There were reports of him and Paul Aldridge taking a significant pay reduction but, as far as I know, they ended up being wage deferrals. When West Ham gained promotion back to the Premier League in May 2005, I understand they both recouped the earnings they would normally have received over the course of the club's two years in the Championship. It was just another insult to the fans.

I've criticised Glenn Roeder for taking the team down, as he had to accept ultimate responsibility, but Brown should also have considered his position once relegation was confirmed in May 2003. But given the ridiculously high salary he was on at the time, he was never going to jack it in and managed to retain the support of the shareholders.

When the shit hit the fan in 2003, Brown did a good job of keeping his head down and out of the firing line. It was always Roeder who copped the flak. Brown was sometimes described by the press as a 'faceless chairman' but the fans don't want a figurehead who is virtually invisible, especially during the most difficult times.

The board compounded their mistake in not sacking Roeder earlier by then bizarrely dismissing him just four games into the following season, which then forced them to ask Trevor Brooking to help out again in a caretaker capacity. If they were going to change managers, then it should have been done in the summer, which would have given Roeder's successor time to bring in new players and formulate his own ideas – not, as Alan Pardew did, inherit a club in turmoil and have to try and pick up the pieces in October.

Fire sale

By the summer of 2004, with their play-off hopes shattered and their financial state becoming bleaker by the day, if not quite having reached meltdown, West Ham were left with little alternative but to sell off all that remained of their crown jewels. That summer Joe Cole (£6.6m) and Glen Johnson (£6m) were sold to Chelsea and Trevor Sinclair (£2.5m) left for Manchester City. Within six months Jermain Defoe (£7m to Tottenham, with Bobby Zamora in part-exchange) and David James (£1.5m to Manchester City) had also departed, while Michael Carrick (£3.5m) and Fredi Kanouté (£4m) were released to our arch rivals Tottenham.

Remembering how Rio Ferdinand had been sold to Leeds United for a British record £18m in November 2000, followed by Frank Lampard's £11m transfer to Chelsea in the summer of 2001, West Ham supporters dare not dwell on the fact that they had seen their club sell eight full England internationals – past, present and future – in the space of less than four years for a combined haul of £60.1m.

Just look at this team of stars West Ham could have put out if the club had been managed differently. Look and weep, because all bar the Czech

Joe Cole posing with his new Chelsea shirt in the summer of 2003, along with Blues' manager Claudio Ranieri and Juan Sebastian Veron.

Republic defender Tomas Repka were sold for financial reasons, although I accept that Frank Lampard's departure was more or less a given after the club sacked his uncle and his father's position as assistant coach became untenable...

David James

Trevor Sinclair   **Rio Ferdinand**   **Tomas Repka**   **Glen Johnson**

Michael Carrick   **Frank Lampard**   **Joe Cole**

Paolo Di Canio   **Fredi Kanouté**

Jermain Defoe

The fact is, though, if the club hadn't sold off its best players as a direct result of relegation in 2003, it would surely have gone into administration.

The debacle of relegation was the biggest problem, but not the only one. Puzzled fans demanded answers to other pertinent questions like: Why did the club spend as much as £40m on a new stand? Even after the opening of the Dr Martens (old West Stand), the stadium redevelopment was still incomplete, because the club – heavily in debt – was unable to finance a rebuild of the East Stand that has stood since 1968.

The bitter frustration we all felt wouldn't go away and losing the 2004 Play-off Final only deepened the gloom that had engulfed our club. Instead of looking forward to a bright future with an entertaining team packed with some of the most talented, sought-after youngsters in English football, the club was staring into the face of oblivion. What if we didn't gain promotion at the second attempt under Pardew in 2005, after which the parachute payment from Sky TV would have ended? What if we 'did a Leeds United' or a Nottingham Forest and ended up dropping into the third tier? Would there ever be a way back for us?

West Ham badly needed solid, progressive leadership. It was crying out for a saviour to give it new direction.

As I brooded some more on the flight back from Cardiff to London, churning over in my mind what could have been and fearing what possible further disasters lie ahead for the club, it was then that I vowed to myself to try and do something to put things right...

Jermain Defoe and Michael Carrick were both sold to arch rivals Tottenham.

Trevor Sinclair and David James were offloaded to Manchester City.

11

Chasing the dream

IT was one thing wanting to change things for the better at West Ham, but actually doing it was something completely different. Let me say from the outset that I had nothing to offer personally other than honest commitment and a burning desire to bring about the changes at the top that I, and many thousands of others, knew were necessary if the club was ever to go forward again. I had no spare cash to invest in any takeover bid – everything I earned from my part-time work with Sky and West Ham, along with one or two other small sidelines, was needed to feed my young family and cover all my overheads.

I knew that if my initial thoughts, first sown on that depressing flight back from Cardiff, were ever to reach fruition, the millions required to buy-out Terry Brown and his fellow major shareholders would have to come from elsewhere, so my mission was to find a consortium of wealthy businessmen, ideally long-term Hammers supporters, who shared my passion for the club and a strong belief that changes had to be made and a new hierarchy installed at Upton Park. West Ham had become a second tier club with massive debt and a bleak future, which for many fans was unacceptable.

In the course of helping Dad at his insurance company, I met quite a number of people from the business world who were as concerned as I was about West Ham's plight. It wasn't just me expressing heartfelt fears – plenty of others told me that they, along with many of their friends, were fed up with how the club was being run and wondered where it would all end.

I didn't start out with a specific plan. All I knew is that I felt compelled to do *something*. I couldn't just sit back and do nothing. Who would come up with the money, how any new shareholding would be divided if, and when, the takeover happened, which directors would fill executive roles at the club ...these were things I hoped would only become relevant further down the line.

It wasn't my intention to set out to find any financial backers who simply had lots of money to throw at the club. At first, it was very important to me that anyone who I managed to gain significant investment from fully understood the history of the club and what it stood for in the eyes of its fans. This may be an unrealistic ideal in today's world, where Premier League clubs, as well as others lower down the scale, have become a magnet for overseas investors looking to cash in on the Sky TV boom, but that's how

I wanted it to be.

As well as seeking investors who had a close affinity to the club, I wanted to keep the group as small as possible. Six was the maximum limit I had in mind.

Brainwashed since birth

We estimated that West Ham probably has a massive worldwide fan base in the region of one million people. If the team was very successful, a 60,000 capacity stadium wouldn't be big enough, because it would be full every game.

Few people fully appreciate just what great potential West Ham United has. Wherever you go in the world, from Africa to Australia, Belgium to Bolivia, you'll always see somebody wearing our distinctive claret and blue shirt and the mere sight of it makes you feel a little closer to home.

I always say that football mirrors life itself. West Ham fans have come to expect their fair share of ups and downs...Just like my dreams, they fade and die and all that. I'd characterise a typical Hammers fan as follows: We tend to duck and dive a little bit but we don't mind working hard. We graft for our living and we enjoy the rewards but we know full well that, just around the corner, there's going to be a little hiccup and you might lose some of what you've earned. But then what do you do – sit around moping about it, or get on with life? West Ham fans just get on with it.

For loyalty, our fans are unique. It's passed down through generations of families – just like mine – and it's in our DNA. When my two boys were born, I didn't *ask* them which team they fancied supporting. I *told* them they were now West Ham supporters. They were helplessly born into it, just as I was and thousands more who have followed our club through thick and thin.

One thing's for sure, when you commit to supporting West Ham for life, you know you're in for one hell of a rollercoaster ride and it will rarely be dull.

I took my then six-year-old twin sons, Billy and Matt, to the opening Saturday home game of the 2004-05 season against Wigan Athletic. I'd brainwashed them from birth that they would be West Ham fans and there was no alternative. Their big moment had arrived – they put on their claret and blue kits for their first-ever live match, which is a proud moment for any father who wants his kids to follow the family tradition of

I brainwashed the boys from birth that they were born to support the Hammers.

supporting their local team.

Every new season tends to herald fresh optimism and a feeling that 'this could be our year'. These false hopes can be seen etched on the faces of excited fans in the stands at most grounds on the first day of every season but, in most cases, they quickly disappear once reality dawns and you accept that your team doesn't justify your initial optimism.

My boys must have decided West Ham were in for another season of struggle, because within 20 minutes of the kick-off, with the Hammers already a goal down in five minutes, they asked if they could play with

The twins on their first day at their new school in 2005.

the GameBoy consoles they had thoughtfully brought with them. As any father in my position will tell you, it feels important for your team to win on the day your kids see them play for the first time – not only because you love to see their happy, smiling faces at the final whistle, but also to help justify all the pre-match hype and years of indoctrination which precedes their first visit to the ground.

Wigan rolled us over, 3-1.

Afterwards, I think it was Billy who asked: "Dad, do West Ham always lose?"

Although I tried my best to explain that setbacks and rollercoaster rides were all part of the inherent suffering West Ham fans of all ages have learned to endure, it was a habit we'd had to get used to more often in recent years.

It's not easy for youngsters in these situations. I've got a mate, Dave Walsh, whose son James defected from West Ham to Arsenal during our two years spent in the Championship following relegation in '03. Dave and his two other sons, William and Sam, remain staunch Hammers but with so many of his school friends electing to follow Arsenal, Chelsea and Manchester United, young James decided to take up supporting the Gooners.

I'd hate to have been in Dave's position but his son simply couldn't accept that his team was floundering in the Championship while his mates were always boasting about their teams' pursuit of the major trophies with big-name players – in some cases, ex-West Ham stars who were sold from under our noses.

But even supporting one of the so-called 'big' clubs can have its drawbacks. The reason James, now 14, started supporting Arsenal was the brilliance of their 'Invincibles' – the team that went through the entire 2003-04 Premier League season unbeaten. They won the FA Cup in 2005 but I still take great pleasure in reminding him that they haven't won another trophy since then!

It was a difficult time for everyone at West Ham. I could see the dejection

on the faces of the corporate lounge brigade when they trudged back to their tables at half-time or at the final whistle. Even after we'd won, they were still often far from impressed by what they had seen. There was a real hangover from the previous season when, even before the play-off misery, there had been too many dire performances.

Watching the 2009 Boys of 86 tournament on the pitch at Upton Park.

Remember that shocking goalless draw with Stoke City on December 9, 2003? There were 24,000 hardy souls there on a midweek night to see Alan Pardew's team plumb the depths. As we came back into my lounge at the end of that wretched game, I had to go back on stage to read out the results of our quiz, which became a bit of a ritual. Now I always try to be positive no matter how woeful things might appear on the field, but on this occasion I stood up and could do nothing other than admit that it was one of the worst games I'd seen in 32 years as a West Ham supporter.

At which point some wise guy stood up and said: "That's the worst I've seen in 45 years."

It was quickly followed by a cry from an older gent, seated just behind him, who blurted out: "No, that's the worst I've seen in 55 years."

Then, believe it or not, an old boy at the back of the room, who must have been around 80 if he was a day, topped the lot when he shouted: "That's the worst I've seen here in SEVENTY TWO YEARS!"

It was like a Cockney version of Monty Python's famous 'Four Yorkshiremen' sketch. These were desperate times at Upton Park and, according to my sons, the following season wasn't shaping up too well either.

Yes, something definitely had to be done.

Short list

I drew up a short list of people who I thought might be interested in coming on board. One of the first I spoke to after resolving to put together a group of West Ham-supporting businessmen was Mick Villiers, who I'd chatted to at one of Dad's corporate golf days. Mick, who lives at Emerson Park in Essex but spends almost half the year based in Antigua, runs a successful finance company and after sharing our concerns about the state of things at West Ham, he gave me his phone number and said he'd like to hear from me again if I did manage to make any progress with my plans.

An obvious one to sound out was Clinton Lewin, whose father Don named his Clinton Cards business chain after him. Although I met Clinton in the

Cottee hoping card family join his pack

BY RAOUL SIMONS

A TAKEOVER battle could be on the cards at West Ham after Tony Cottee today ·stepped up his attempts to get serious financial backing for his consortium hoping to buy the club.

The former Hammers striker is understood to have approached Don Lewin, multi-millionaire founder of Clinton Cards, in a bid to attract investment.

Cottee is close friends with Don's son, Clinton, managing director of the greetings card chain, and is hoping to persuade his father, the company chairman, to get on board. Together the two Lewins, who are both West Ham supporters, are estimated to be worth around £40million.

Cottee this week admitted he had held talks with potential investors who he described as "lifelong fans who want to put the club back where it belongs".

As local boys made good, the Lewins would appear obvious candidates. The son of a chimney sweep, Don was born in the East End, where he worked on market stalls from the age of 10.

He started selling greetings cards from the boot of his car at 26 before opening a shop in Essex in 1968 which he named after his infant son.

The business has since ballooned into a Stock Exchange-listed company — with a market capitalisation of £200m — which now sells one in four of the two billion cards bought in Britain each year.

In a recent interview, Don, 71, said: "I have been poor and I have been rich, and rich is better — there's no question about that. I enjoy my money. I can have anything I want now, and it's a great feeling."

Despite his immense wealth, Don has stayed loyal to his roots in West Ham's heartland. Clinton's headquarters is in Loughton, Essex, and he has also passed on his support for the club to Clinton through regular visits to Upton Park.

Standard Sport understands that Don is giving careful consideration to a proposal sent to him yesterday by Cottee's consortium, though he has so far made no decision as to whether or not he is willing to invest.

It is, however, unlikely that any takeover attempt would rely on a single backer, and Cottee would also require the support of other interested parties.

West Ham are estimated to have debts of £25m and could face more financial problems if they fail to win promotion back to the Premiership this season.

Nevertheless, any move to buy the club is complicated by West Ham's ownership structure. Chairman Terry Brown has 38 per cent of the shares, while the majority of the others are held by the Warner and Cearns families. One of these block shareholders would need to be persuaded to sell for a bid to succeed.

Brown, who has been personally blamed for the club's decline by a section of West Ham supporters, had previously said he was willing to listen to offers from interested parties.

Racehorse owner Michael Tabor, Birmingham City director David Sullivan and another unnamed consortium have all been linked, but no deal has been forthcoming.

The club claim to have a net asset value of £40m and it is understood that outside investors would need to find £25m to be taken seriously.

Cottee said: "I want what is best for the football club and I'd like to think we will be able to get the necessary funds together. That will only be possible if the chairman is in agreement."

My approach to Clinton Lewin made headline news.

Premier Lounge at Upton Park from time to time, he'd previously done some insurance business through Dad, who had also met Clinton socially. Although Don Lewin wasn't a big football fan, Clinton was very much a West Ham man. We spoke just before Christmas 2004 and although he indicated some possible future interest in what I was trying to achieve, it was a very brief and vague conversation and didn't go any further than that.

Another I knew I should approach was Robbie Cowling whose thriving internet recruitment company, JobServe, was Hammers' main shirt sponsor at the time. The other person who quickly sprang to mind was David Sullivan. Although previously well known in football circles as the co-owner of Birmingham City, he and fellow directors David and Ralph Gold had been linked with a possible takeover of West Ham in the past.

But I didn't attempt to contact either Robbie or David at that stage. At first they were no more than a couple of names on a piece of paper. They were in my head and no more than that as 2004 fizzled out and West Ham struggled to stay among the top six promotion contenders.

On January 13, 2005, Dad and I were visited at his Chase Insurance company by Gary White, a chartered accountant who I'd met for the first time in September 2003 while playing for the Boys of 86 team in our first-ever match at Heybridge Swifts FC. The event had been a huge success, with over 1,000 fans turning out to see a load of old codgers trundling around the pitch. Afterwards Gary approached me in the marquee for a chat. We never discussed anything about West Ham that night but we hit it off immediately and I have since discovered that Gary, who played against us in the Heybridge side, is a compulsive networker. He had his family with him that day and our respective teenage daughters – Gary's Katie and my Chloe – quickly got chatting and soon became friends, so we all agreed to keep in touch.

Gary visited Dad's office at Brentwood in his capacity as a partner and sales director in an Essex-based firm. Following my first meeting with Gary at Heybridge the previous year, we had arranged to meet up with the intention of discussing how his company and Chase Insurance could forge further business links. A huge Hammers fan, the first thing he said when he came through the door was: "I'm so disappointed with what's going on at West Ham. Have you ever thought about getting together a consortium to take over the club?"

As soon as those words left his lips, I confided to him that his idea was something I'd been working on – albeit mostly in my head at that point – for the past three or four months. Anyway, we spent an hour-and-a-half discussing West Ham and only the last half-an-hour talking insurance.

Gary immediately pledged his support for my initial idea and suggested that he had one or two clients it might be worth us approaching. He also pointed out that he knew West Ham's main sponsor, Robbie Cowling, which was music to my ears.

Having been a fan since his first visit to Upton Park in 1969, it was immediately obvious to me that Gary not only shared my passion for all things claret and blue, but he also understood the club's traditions and could readily relate to supporters' expectations. That meeting, where our shared commitment to try and shake things up at West Ham was reinforced, marked the start of a genuine friendship and business relationship between Gary and I that continues to this day.

His enthusiasm in joining forces with me gave my dream some much-needed direction and purpose that had been lacking before, but it's fair to say that we were both going into the unknown as co-founders of what we called 'Project TC'. Although I knew Gary would be excellent with figures, neither of us had any real knowledge at that stage of exactly how to go about buying a football club.

Apart from a bit of part-time work for Dad's company, I'd had no experience whatsoever of the business world. I was a total novice and didn't really know how to go about doing what was required if my dream – at that early stage it was still only the basic shell of an idea – was ever going to go anywhere.

Just how naïve we were in those early days became very clear when Gary and I visited Kevin Stevens, a West Ham fan and Upton Park box-holder and the owner of Woodlands International, a large freight company based at Coggleshall. We met in Brentwood on February 3, 2005, when I began by explaining how unhappy we were about West Ham and why we were beginning the process of trying to meet wealthy businessmen with a view to forming a consortium capable of buying the club.

The first thing Kevin asked was: "Where's your business plan?"

He said that although he had money and might be willing to get involved, we needed a proper structure in place to present to him before he would even consider it. He politely told us to go away with the recommendation that we returned three weeks later with three key documents in our possession:

a) A Business Proposal

b) A Background Report

c) An Investors' Report

Quite rightly, he pointed out that if he, or anybody else, was going to invest serious money with us, then there were very important questions that needed answering, such as: how would his money be used and for what purpose?; what sort of return could he expect on his investment?; and what was the exit strategy?

By drawing these important points to our attention, he also offered sound practical advice and nothing was said in a patronising way. As he made clear, the three documents he urged us to produce before we went any further were simply the ones every serious businessman would expect to see, and so we had to have our answers prepared in a well presented, structured way. Being an accountant, Gary knew he would have to produce relevant figures to back up our plans but there was much more to it than that.

To be honest, when I started the ball rolling I probably imagined it would more or less be a case of finding the right guys to come up with the money needed to buy the club. Then I'd plonk the cash on Terry Brown's desk and wait for him to say 'thanks very much.'

As I quickly realised, it was never going to be like that.

12

Chairman of the board

I MAKE no bones about it, I wanted to be the next West Ham United chairman. The way I saw it, this was my baby. I'd instigated the takeover bid and was the driving force behind it. After my family, I love West Ham more than anything in the world. I saw myself as the club's ideal new figurehead – a vital link between the supporters and the boardroom.

Apart from having a good understanding of West Ham fans, I'd also built up a strong relationship within the football media – by then I was part of it – over many years and I saw this as another big plus for a club that had made too many PR gaffes in the years following the ill-fated bond scheme fiasco of 1991-92.

I'd briefly considered calling myself Director of Football or Chief Executive Officer but felt the title of chairman would be most appropriate. I wanted to work full-time from the Boleyn Ground in an executive, hands-on role.

I decided from the start, though, that I would have had no intention of interfering in the manager's role or telling him which team to pick. I would probably have gone to the training ground no more than once a week, to ensure that all was well with the manager and to give him the chance to discuss any problems with me. I'd always have been there to lean on for advice and would have advised my board colleagues on football matters, of course, but there is no point in appointing a manager if you don't let him get on with his job without meddling in tactics and team selection.

Likewise, it wouldn't have been right for me to have taken major financial decisions alone, which is principally the responsibility of the Finance Director following consultation with the rest of the board. With his accountancy skills, Gary was the obvious choice as our future FD even though, like myself, he had none of his own money to invest in West Ham. His fellow senior partners were fully aware of his involvement with me in the takeover project and, although understandably worried at the thought of losing a partner from their business, they accepted that his future may possibly lie in a new hierarchy at Upton Park, if acceptable to the investors concerned.

Despite my lack of personal financial resources, I would certainly have worked hard to help bring much-needed revenue into the club by working alongside the commercial department – going out to meet potential sponsors and advertisers, which is what I did in a part-time consultancy role years later. West Ham needed to be much more proactive in this respect and I hoped that my past connections with the club as a player would have opened a lot of new doors commercially.

I saw myself as an ambassador. I wouldn't have tried to hog the limelight as some high profile chairmen and CEOs in football like to do, but there is a balance to be struck between those on an ego trip who crave publicity and the so-called faceless men in grey suits who remain permanently out of sight and become almost unaccountable.

Meeting various supporters groups and attending a regular series of fans' forums – and then, in turn, communicating their opinions back to my boardroom colleagues – would have been another important part of my responsibilities.

I also saw it as my job to give media interviews and promote West Ham in a PR capacity – and not just when things were going well on the field either. One of the problems Glenn Roeder had to contend with while his team was struggling badly was constant pressure from the media as well as supporters. He could have done with someone shielding him from the spotlight at times, and that's what I would have done had our manager suddenly found himself under intense pressure. With the advent of social networking sites such as Facebook and Twitter in recent years, as well as the internet forums that have been with us since the late 90s, managers cop it from all directions these days. It obviously helps if they have very thick skins but I also believe that senior club executives also have a part to play in protecting them from much of the flak.

At the time we embarked upon Project TC, the West Ham United board comprised of the following seven directors: Terry Brown (Chairman), Martin Cearns (Vice-Chairman), Paul Aldridge (Managing Director), Nick Igoe (Finance Director), plus Charles Warner, Scott Duxbury and Chris Manhire. The Cearns and Warner families founded the club in 1895 but the one we were most keen to retain as part of our board was legal expert Scott Duxbury, probably in the role of company secretary.

I toyed with the idea of including two former Hammers team-mates on the new board and tentatively pencilled in Tony Gale for the role of Vice-Chairman and Bobby Barnes as MD. As a regular contributor to West Ham's match day programme and its website, 'Galey' – one of my best friends in football, if not the best – understands the club better than anyone. He later became an ambassador for West Ham while at the same time developing his successful career as a very respected commentator at Sky. At the time we were trying to move things forward behind the scenes, he also had his own weekly column in The Sun and, like myself, had established extensive media contacts.

But Galey wasn't the right man for us at the time. I think he found it a little difficult once I became publicly linked with a takeover bid, because he understandably felt a loyalty towards Terry Brown, especially, and Paul Aldridge. Brown had sponsored Galey through his Sussex Beach Holiday Village business and they had been good friends for many years, right back

Bobby Barnes would have been well suited to an executive role in a revamped management set-up.

to the days when Terry was one of the first corporate 'Academy Club' members at West Ham, before being invited onto the board in 1990. But it would have been great if we could have got Galey involved with us because he has so much to offer the football world beyond his media roles.

A lightning-fast winger at Upton Park in the early 80s, Bobby Barnes has made his mark in football administration with his excellent work for the Professional Footballers' Association, so he too was an obvious consideration.

Pardew's replacement

In the spring of 2005, with the Hammers far from assured of a play-off place by May, it's fair to say that we would certainly have sacked Alan Pardew and replaced him with a 'West Ham man'– a former player who understood the club's heritage and what it stood for in the hearts and minds of most Hammers supporters.

Pardew had been given a brief to gain promotion within his first two seasons and if he hadn't achieved it by the end of May 2005, then he would have failed and had to go – regardless of who was running West Ham.

I drew up a short-list of five possible candidates, four of them former Hammers players in (in no particular order) Iain Dowie, Alan Devonshire, Alan Curbishley and Martin Allen.

Dowie might not have been a very popular player in claret and blue – a wholehearted performer who grafted for team-mates who appreciated his contribution more than the fans – but he had quickly established his reputation as a young English manager with a bright future. After excellent work on a shoestring at cash-strapped Oldham Athletic – his Latics team knocked Glenn Roeder's Hammers out of the League Cup in 2002 – he then

Iain Dowie celebrates leading Oldham to a League Cup victory at West Ham in 2002.

performed heroics in his first season at Crystal Palace.

The Eagles were strong candidates for relegation before Dowie arrived and transformed them completely. They soared up the Championship table, snatched sixth place and then beat West Ham in the 2004 Play-off Final to gain promotion to the Premier League. OK, so they came straight back down again the following season, but that was widely expected given the limited resources available to Dowie at Selhurst Park.

This is perhaps an opportune part of the book to make the point that you have to put much of what you read within these pages, especially where managers and players are concerned, into retrospective context. As I write this in the summer of 2012, Alan Pardew has just enjoyed a fine first season as manager of Newcastle United, elevating the Magpies to fifth place in the Premier League, only five points short of third spot and an automatic Champions League berth.

On the other hand, Iain Dowie – another established member of the Sky punditry team – has been out of work as a manager for two years since failing in a nigh impossible shot-term bid to keep Hull City in the top flight failed in May 2010. But when we began planning a takeover bid at West Ham, Dowie's stock among young English managers (he was 40 at the time) was high, while doubts had surfaced about Pardew's ability to make further progress following the good work he had achieved with Reading followed by a dismal first season at Upton Park.

As a West Ham fan in his youth and having played for Hammers in two spells, I identified Dowie as someone who knew what the club was all about.

Martin 'Mad Dog' Allen would have brought more bite to the dug-out.

And after leading Palace to promotion in May '04, I knew he had what it took to do the same at Upton Park. At that time, my former West Ham strike partner was probably my No.1 personal choice to succeed Pardew, although it would obviously have gone to a vote by all of our new board members.

Martin Allen, a big character who became a cult

fans' favourite in his playing days as a forceful midfielder who always played with plenty of passion at Upton Park, was another young manager making rapid progress in the game. He might have been a bit unconventional, but 'Mad Dog' demonstrated in his first season of management at Brentford in 2004-05 that he was likely to attract the attention of clubs at a higher level. He has since had nine different clubs in 10 seasons but...as I say, apply a little context!

Alan Dev has made his mark at non-league level.

It's a travesty that Alan Devonshire has still to be given the chance to manage in the Football League, especially when you consider his sustained success in the higher echelons of the non-league sphere, with Maidenhead United, Hampton & Richmond and, most recently, Braintree Town, who he comfortably guided to a mid-table finish in the club's first season of Conference Premier football in 2011-12 – on a shoestring budget a fraction of what a number of his rival managers in that division are given to spend each year.

A huge favourite with the fans, 'Dev' is old school and had to be a serious consideration for us because he's very knowledgeable and his football philosophy has West Ham stamped all over it. He doesn't have as many coaching qualifications as others higher up the league ladder but, by God, does he understand the game and know how to manage players. He grew up as a footballer under John Lyall and how good it would have been to have given him his big chance back at the club where he is a living legend.

Alan Curbishley earned himself a deserved reputation as one of the most successful English managers at Premier League level, having kept Charlton Athletic in the top flight for so long on relatively small resources. He was interviewed for the England job and, indeed, West Ham sought his services after sacking Harry Redknapp in 2001. He didn't come to Upton Park then and, had West Ham remained in the Championship in 2005-06, it's very unlikely that our consortium would have been able to tempt him away from The Valley either. When he finally did return to

Alan Curbishley turned down West Ham years before he took the job.

Upton Park in December 2006, so much had changed on and off the field.

If we'd been unable to appoint a former West Ham player, then Martin O'Neill would have been my perfect choice. As covered earlier, I knew from having played under the Northern Irishman at Leicester City for three years just what a brilliant man-manager he was, and still is, although it would have been virtually impossible to have lured him away from Celtic at that time.

Our new manager would obviously have nominated his first team coaches, so I can't speculate here on who they would have been. I did, though, intend to retain Tony Carr as the head of youth development, with two more ex-Hammers, Geoff Pike and Paul Brush, pencilled in as possible new members of the coaching set-up. Pikey made a good impression on me despite my indifference to the whole process when I saw him coaching at close quarters after my short spell with Barnet a few years earlier.

Geoff knows coaching inside-out, while 'Brushy' coached and managed at Leyton Orient before going on to coach successfully at Southend United. Two more former team-mates of mine, Alan Dickens and George Parris, who has worked for Liam Brady in the Arsenal youth academy, also came into my thinking. Essentially, I wanted as many West Ham people as possible involved in a restructured academy. I wanted them to come in, coach the kids, work their way through the system and hopefully become genuine future candidates to take the top job at the club. That's how it should be.

I'd hoped to retain the services of important backroom staff John Green (Physiotherapist), Ges Steinbergs (Medical Officer) and Eddie Gillam (Kit Manager), while I considered it a good idea to bring Ronnie Gale back to the club as Chief Scout at academy level. There has been none better at spotting good, young talent for West Ham than Ronnie, who 'discovered' the likes of Stuart Slater, Paul Ince, Steve Potts and myself before he unfortunately left the club under a cloud during the Redknapp years.

On a separate hand-written sheet of paper, I mapped out a provisional commercial set-up. I'm obviously unsure if the people concerned would even have accepted the jobs I'd earmarked them for but, for what it's worth, this is the structure I had in mind. We would probably have brought in a newcomer, Sue Crowley, who has worked in the hotel business and is currently at Woburn Golf Club, to head up the commercial and hospitality section, with Sue Page hopefully retained as commercial manager. John Ball (stadium manager and safety officer) and Steve Kitcher (ticket office) were also in our initial plans, with retro *EX* magazine writer and keen West Ham historian Tim Crane (memorabilia and museum) also earmarked for a role.

Scout Ronnie Gale with two of his discoveries,
Steve Potts and myself.

13

Making plans

IT was my task to put together the Business Proposal. As well as explaining my football background, West Ham's history and why the club had got itself into such a mess, I outlined my proposed role as chairman and set out our key objectives within a 10-year plan. (To the pedants out there, I know the top flight was in fact titled the 'Premiership' in 2005 but it will be known throughout this book by its current name of the Premier League.)

Between us, Gary and I wrote the Background Report, outlining our reasons for launching a takeover bid and why it was a good investment opportunity. Apart from what we regarded as the general under-performance at the club, we also highlighted other areas where West Ham had fallen down badly. We quoted a number of examples where the club committed PR gaffes or missed out on major commercial opportunities:

*The CEO of a substantial windscreen company, on visiting the commercial manger to discuss a shirt sponsorship deal, was kept waiting for up to an hour. He was so disgusted he chose to sponsor Chelsea instead, despite being a life-long Hammers fan. West Ham was then the only club in the entire Premier League not to have a shirt sponsorship deal that season, which seems unthinkable when considering the exposure this provides to the advertiser and the revenue to the club.

*A potential investor in the club contacted one of the directors to ask how he could inject £2m in the club and the level of percentage shareholding this would achieve. West Ham did not even return his call, even though he was very well known to the club and its directors.

*The poor timing of the chairman's statement published in the match day programme for the visit of Southampton in November 2002. The statement was prepared before the start of the season, soon after the club had finished seventh. However, by the time of the Southampton match, the club was bottom of the Premier League and police had to disperse angry fans outside the stadium after the 1-0 defeat.

Our Background Report went on to say:

I passionately believe that the future of West Ham United involves giving the club back to its fans, for it to be customer-focused by building strong relationships with those that love the club, are prepared to put their money where their mouth is and who are not scared of taking tough financial and football decisions. Modern-day business is very different from the days of the 60s and 70s, when the Cearns family ran and owned the club.

These days, successful clubs are too big to be funded by a board that favours a closed shop mentality, because professional expertise is required. This is sadly lacking at West Ham from both a football and corporate viewpoint.

Among a number of pertinent questions we posed were:

*Why was Glenn Roeder appointed as manager in the summer of 2001, when much more experienced candidates were available? Why did such candidates not want the job? Could it be that they felt the board of directors were not ambitious enough? When it became clear that Roeder was not capable of keeping the team in the Premier League – the team had not won a single home league match before the end of January 2003 – why did the club not opt for a change of management? I never met one West Ham fan who wanted Roeder to stay and despite being a good man and doing his best, possibly to the extent that it caused him very serious illness, he was clearly not good enough for Premier League management.

*How can a club trade at such a huge loss each year? Whilst the present board may wish to blame Harry Redknapp for signing players on excessively lucrative contracts, surely it was the board who ratified these decisions and who authorised the transactions. Whilst accepting that there are some highly dubious transfers that take place in football, this was surely no excuse for such operating losses which needed to be covered by £57m of player disposals over three years.

The Investors' Report naturally became Gary's responsibility. He put together a comprehensive 7,000-word dossier that ran to 16 A4 pages. Here is a brief extract from it:

*Our first aim was for our consortium to raise an initial £25m, which we projected

Terry Brown, the chairman and largest shareholder who I wanted to replace in the boardroom.

Disgruntled fans made their feelings known after the home defeat by Southampton in early December 2002. Glenn Roeder should have been relieved of his duties that night.

would be sufficient to gain ownership of the club and provide an injection of new funds to strengthen the squad.

We budgeted on the probability that it would take another two seasons – until May 2007 – to win promotion and regain Premier League status (although we would obviously have adjusted all our projections had promotion been secured earlier).

During this two-year period £10m of the projected £25m capital investment would be used to buy new players.

We budgeted for a further injection of £15m to redevelop the East Stand from before the start of the 2008-09 season to bring the Boleyn Ground capacity up to 42,000 within a fully-enclosed arena. However, we didn't rule out the possibility of moving to a new, bigger stadium in Essex.

Before you scoff at the originally projected buy out price of £25m, remember that these reports were compiled in March 2005, by which time the team had slipped out of the top six in the Championship. Automatic promotion was virtually impossible by then and even one of the four coveted play-off positions was far from assured. In fact, by March 18 and following a run of five league matches without a win, Pardew's lack-lustre team had slumped to eighth place and the outlook appeared bleak.

To underline the fact that we weren't just looking to go in and implement a short-term fix, we mapped out a plan for the next five seasons and included an appendix that covered all of our detailed financial projections, including:

Profit & loss business plan (5 years)

Cash flow business plan (5 years)

Balance sheet business plan (5 years)

Funds flow business plan (5 years)

The introduction to our Investors' Report set out the structure of the club's hierarchy and the share value as it existed at the time, as follows:

West Ham United PLC currently have an issued share capital of 20,202,352 ordinary 25p shares, having a nominal value of £5,050,588 on the balance sheet, as at its last published accounts to May 31, 2004. Although the company currently has over 2,000 entries on its shareholder register, 67% of the shares are owned or controlled by three individuals who are all current board members as follows:

T.W. Brown (Chairman) 7,392,000

C.J. Warner 4,252,000

M. Cearns (Vice-Chairman) 1,844,000

Full steam ahead

Gary and I spent all day and night compiling these reports at his Essex village home near Witham. Once they were completed it was then a case of full steam ahead, getting out and about and trying to meet as many potential investors as possible. Paul Miller, the former Tottenham centre-half who has strong connections with corporate clients in the City, was a starting point. I bumped into Paul at a function where he confirmed that he knew of a number of disgruntled, though wealthy, West Ham fans who he thought might be interested in becoming investors.

On February 9, 2005, Gary and I met him in London along with Paul's solicitor friend, Michael Segen. It was suggested by Michael and Paul that we should write to West Ham expressing our interest in acquiring the club. It was only a tentative initial enquiry and was made simply to test the lay of the land. The letter, signed by Michael and typed on Michael Segen & Co. headed notepaper, was dated February 16 and addressed to Terry Brown. It read as follows:

I have been instructed by a consortium of potential investors who would be most interested in purchasing your shareholding in West Ham United FC. At this stage, I am not at liberty to reveal the identity of my clients but confirm that I have acted for a number of them for some years and am firmly of the opinion that they could raise the necessary finance.

If you are considering divesting yourself of your shareholding in principle at least, perhaps you (or your professional advisors) would kindly contact me to indicate the price at which you would be prepared to sell.

Perhaps it might assist if I say that my clients comprise supporters of the club who would wish to keep all matters strictly confidential and then, at the appropriate time, make joint releases to the press in a form to be agreed by you which advise the fans that all matters have been arranged on a most amicable basis. My clients are also planning strategic investment to allow substantial purchase of players in order to assist the club in regaining its rightful position in the Premier League.

I trust that this will be of interest to you and look forward to hearing from you in the near future.

Kind regards.

Yours sincerely,

MICHAEL SEGEN

About a week later, Terry Brown responded with a letter that highlighted the naivety of our initial approach to him. I admit it, I hadn't realised the implications of trying to buy a Public Limited Company. Although we knew from the outset that West Ham United was a plc, we didn't appreciate the full implications from a legal perspective. More surprisingly, neither did solicitor Michael Segen! As the club wasn't quoted on the stock exchange, we hadn't realised that they were still subject to Takeover Panel rules.

When Terry Brown responded with his letter dated March 24, he might have guessed, but couldn't have known for certain, that Michael Segen had written to him on behalf of Gary and myself.

Buy by then the shit had well and truly hit the fan at West Ham and he certainly knew that I was orchestrating a takeover bid that would hopefully lead to his departure.

Our Ref: TWB/ajl

24th March 2005

Michael Segan Esq
Michael Segan & Co.
7th Floor, Bath House
52 Holborn Viaduct
London
EC1A 2FD

Dear Mr Segan

Thank you for your letter dated 16th February.

You will know that, as West Ham United plc is a public company, the provisions of the City Code on Takeovers and Mergers will apply to it. Under Rule 9 of that Code, if a person acquires 30% or more of the shares of West Ham United, he must make an offer for all of the shares, at the same price. As I hold over 36% of the West Ham United shares, an acquisition of that shareholding by your clients would trigger a requirement to make a cash offer for all the West Ham United shares, not just mine.

You will therefore appreciate that in deciding whether to entertain offers for my shareholding, one of my primary concerns would be the ability of any purchaser not only to fulfil his obligations in respect of my shareholding but also in respect of the other shareholders. Moreover, I would also be concerned to know that thereafter the best interests of the Club would be safeguarded.

I would remind you that under Rule 1(b) of the City Code, the identity of your client must be disclosed at the outset of any approach with a view to an offer being made.

It is impossible for me to proceed and address all of the concerns referred to above without knowing who your clients are, how they propose to finance the acquisition of the shares and seeing evidence of the level of commitment from the banks or others which are to provide that finance. I would also suggest that if your clients are serious they will be able to assess the value of my shareholding and produce a sensible offer for me to consider in the context of the other information requested.

Yours sincerely

Terence Brown
Chairman

WEST HAM UNITED PLC

REGISTERED OFFICE: BOLEYN GROUND, GREEN STREET, UPTON PARK, LONDON E13 9AZ
Telephone: 020 8548 2751 Facsimile: 020 8472 0328 www.whufc.com Registration No.3407691

Terry Brown's reply to our initial, though naïve, approach.

14

Sacked by West Ham

FROM the moment I first set about trying to assemble a consortium to buy West Ham, it was never my intention to de-stabilise the club or jeopardise the Hammers' bid for promotion in any way.

It would have been very easy for me to have utilised my many good media contacts and leaked information to them about our plans – and maybe I should have done so. Perhaps I would have moved things forward much more quickly had I come out and declared my intentions very publicly in the weeks immediately following the 2004 Play-off Final defeat. But I never did. Our initial letter to Terry Brown didn't reveal the names of our consortium members and I hoped to keep my involvement confidential for as long as possible.

West Ham were playing at home to another of my former clubs, Leicester City, on Friday, March 18, 2005 – a game televised live by Sky. At about one o'clock that afternoon my mobile rang and it was Rob Shepherd, an old mate, a big Hammers fan and a well known journalist who was with the *News of the World* at the time.

He told me that on Sunday his paper would be running a story revealing that I was trying to put together a consortium to buy West Ham. I'd known Rob for years and tried to appeal to him to sit on the story for a while, or even spike it completely. I explained that if the story broke now, it would be of no benefit to me or the club, because I wasn't ready for the news to come out.

Although sympathetic and sorry that he'd put me in a very difficult position, Rob pointed out that an ex-Premier League player trying to buy his old club was a big story and that the *NOTW* would be running it. He further justified the paper's stance by adding he'd rather give me the chance to put my side of the story than print it without a response. I suppose it was better than someone at the tabloid hacking into my mobile phone. Then again, had they done that, I might be due a few bob in compensation from the nation's now defunct best-selling Sunday tabloid!

I had to think on my feet. I was due to be hosting the hospitality lounges at Upton Park that night and, as a part-time employee of the club, I felt obliged to forewarn them of what would be published in the *NOTW* two days later.

I felt as if I'd been caught between the devil and the deep blue see. On one hand the club were paying me to do a job on match days and on the other, I

I had to break the news of my takeover bid to West Ham MD Paul Aldridge.

was working on a plan to oust the chairman for what we considered to be the long-term good of West Ham. Even so, it's true to say that I did feel a bit guilty about it, so I decided to put the club's MD Paul Aldridge in the picture.

I'd always had a good working relationship with Paul. Although unhappy about the way the club was being run, I put that largely down to Terry Brown, not Paul. I'd never had a relationship or any dealings with Terry and, at that point, I think I'd only spoken to him about twice in 10 years. When I arrived at the ground on match days, before starting work I'd sometimes sit down with Paul and have a chat over coffee but this was obviously going to be a difficult meeting with him.

I phoned Paul that afternoon and made an appointment to see him a couple of hours before the game. I came straight to the point: "I'm very sorry but I'm going to be honest with you. I've had a phone call from a journalist at the *News of the World*, who tells me his paper is going to print a story on Sunday saying that I'm trying to put together a consortium to buy West Ham.

"The story is true. I have been talking to some friends and businessmen but our plans are still very much in the early stages. We are not at the stage where we're going to be making an offer tomorrow."

Paul seemed shocked and a bit taken aback by what I told him. He didn't seem to know how to react as I went on to say that even if I ignored the *NOTW,* they would go ahead and print their story anyway.

Paul didn't bother to ask me who I'd been speaking to or the identities of my fellow consortium members. He just ended our brief meeting by saying that he would let Terry Brown know what we'd discussed.

I worked the lounges as usual that night – another two home points dropped as Marlon Harewood missed a poorly struck penalty and Leicester claimed a 2-2 draw – but my position at the club quickly became untenable. We didn't even have to wait until Sunday for the news to get out, because it broke the afternoon after the West Ham-Leicester match, while I was at Blackburn covering Rovers' home game for Sky's *Prem Plus.*

It was a 12.45pm kick-off at Ewood Park but I was there nice and early, at around 10 o'clock, and having a cuppa on the Sky bus where they serve food and refreshments to their staff before the game. I was sitting there chatting about West Ham with commentator Alan Parry and Geoff Shreeves, their pitchside presenter, when I made a casual comment about having received a call from the *NOTW* the previous day. Geoff latched onto it immediately and when I elaborated on the content of the paper's story, he pointed out to me that if anyone was going to break an exclusive on my proposed takeover at Upton Park, then it should be Sky, my main employers. He added that if the story was going to break the next day anyway, then it would make sense to release it on my terms.

He was right, so Geoff phoned Andy Melvin, his boss at Sky, and I hastily agreed to be interviewed on air by Jeff Stelling after the Blackburn game. Jeff asked me if the story about to break was true and although I confirmed that this was the case, I deliberately tried to remain as vague as possible. The producer took the decision to show the clip – it was no more than a minute or two long – and as well as airing it on Sky, they passed the feed on to TalkSPORT who broadcast it on the radio later that day.

That's when the football world first learned of my takeover plans.

I'd managed to keep Rob Shepherd at bay until Saturday evening and when I called him back, ironically, it was to apologise for having to break the story on Sky. As an experienced national newspaper journalist, Rob knew very well how the media worked and he didn't express any anger towards me about leaking his original story to Sky. Although he was a mate, I didn't owe him anything and I certainly didn't owe the *NOTW* either. I didn't provide him with any printable quotes but he had his job to do – I had no problem with that – and I accepted that his tabloid would print their story, as planned, the next day. I don't usually buy the paper but I don't mind admitting that I bolted round to my local newsagent's first thing the next morning. And there it was, on the back page, a picture of me sitting in the main stand at Upton Park alongside the story about how I hoped to take over the club.

I sat at home that Sunday evening feeling down and surveying the fallout wreckage. My hopes of keeping everything under wraps until we were at least in a position to make the club a solid offer had been blown out of the water.

I naturally wondered how my name had been leaked to the *NOTW* – I never did ask Rob Shepherd on the basis that journalists should never reveal their sources – and can only guess that I must have been spotted by one of the guys on the trading floor at the Royal Bank of Scotland, where I'd recently visited a director called Steve Ashley, who had been recommended to me by a friend. Steve is a big Hammers fan whom Gary White and I met on a few occasions at the RBS office in Liverpool Street. Any football fan working on the RBS trading floor who had seen me walking through the building carrying my briefcase and looking very businesslike would have guessed that I hadn't just popped in for a casual chat with a mate.

Indeed, soon after news of my plans broke in the media, I was surprised to receive a call from my friend, Michael Hockton, in America who said: "Oh yeah, I heard about you and your West Ham consortium two weeks ago! My mate works on the trading floor in London and he saw you there meeting one of the directors."

If it hadn't been somebody at RBS putting two and two together and getting four, then there were plenty of other people who could have leaked it. You know how it is...you tell a mate, he tells his mate and, before you know it, Chinese whispers spread like wildfire.

With good friends Michael Hockton and Richard Wilson in the USA in 2012. Michael heard about my visit to the RBS trading floor.

I'd like to make it very clear, though, I never deliberately tried to rock the boat at West Ham at such a delicate stage of the season when the team was still chasing a play-off position. I wasn't seeking publicity or on an ego trip and I insisted to everyone I spoke to before the news broke that our discussions were to remain confidential. I wanted to remain in the background for as long as possible and was bitterly disappointed that the news came out when it did.

But probably not half as angry as Terry Brown was.

He saw me as a traitor who was plotting against West Ham. Instead of working for the club on a match day, he assumed that I was spending most of my time in the lounges going round tapping up prospective investors, like a wild west cowboy rounding up a bunch of outlaws.

Without knowing the facts or the circumstances, he also no doubt assumed that I had deliberately broken the story, using my position at Sky to broadcast it to a television audience of millions in the hope it would lure investors.

I could understand Brown's anger and how it must have looked from his perspective – after all, he was paying me to entertain the supporters. But the truth of the matter was not how he viewed it. I did the job I was paid to do and yes, one or two of those I spoke to did frequent the lounges at Upton Park, so it was inevitable that I'd come across them in the course of my role there.

But the fact is, I'd already built up plenty of contacts of my own during and since my playing days at West Ham through meeting most of these businessmen at numerous corporate golf days and other functions.

Terry Brown had made up his mind about me, though, and I very swiftly became *persona non-grata* at Upton Park. On the Monday afternoon, I received a phone call from Paul Aldridge saying that the chairman "feels it would be inappropriate for you to carry on with your lounge work at West Ham."

There was no malice in Paul's voice but neither was there a 'thank you' for my efforts at the club over the previous three-and-a-half years. It was basically a short, sharp conversation to inform me that I'd been sacked.

A few hours earlier, I'd received a call from a woman at The Takeover Panel. I thought it was a wind-up, until she informed me that she had read of 'weekend speculation in the media' and was interested to know more about my plans. I tried to placate her by saying it was mere speculation, that I'd only spoken about it to a few friends, but she pointed out that I was not permitted, under rule 1(b) of the City Code, to talk about buying a public company such as West Ham.

She went on to demand to know the identity of my investors as well as the name of my accountants and legal representatives, so I put her on to Gary and slammed the phone down in exasperation.

It was obvious that West Ham had prompted that call from The Takeover Panel.

A couple of days later I received word from Tony McDonald of *Hammers News Magazine*, telling me the club had also instructed the magazine's publisher to terminate my regular monthly column, which I'd always enjoyed writing. I'm not sure that Alan Pardew always appreciated my view of events on the field at Upton Park, though,

Alan Pardew wasn't happy with my comments in Hammers News Magazine.

after he let it be known immediately after joining the club that he was unhappy to read that I'd rather the club had appointed a manager with previous Hammers connections.

Although I had expected to lose my match day host role, it still came as a blow to be axed from the club magazine's editorial team. I took pride in always typing my own columns before emailing them to the office in Romford. I never had a ghost-writer do it for me, although when I think how slowly I typed the words onto my home computer, perhaps I could have done with a secretary to save me an hour or two!

What really annoyed me, though, were the comments that appeared in the papers in the week of my sacking. On March 24, the *Daily Telegraph* ran a story, under the heading 'Phantom Offers Failing To Spook West Ham Board', who reported talk of "four consortia being ready to buy the club" and said "the board claim they are not in the financial straits that many imagine."

Nevertheless, the *Telegraph* speculated that Alan Pardew's position was under serious threat and went on to say: "These have been worrying times for the board. There has been vitriolic press comment and phantom takeover bids, and the board have forced newspapers to print apologies for untrue stories."

It was the next paragraph of their report that really got me. It said: "The so-called offer from Cottee added to the general unease. Cottee works for West Ham as a matchday host, talking to fans in the corporate lounges, for which he is paid about £420 per match."

Where would the *Daily Telegraph* have got details of my earnings from if not a senior source at West Ham? 'About' £420? That was, in fact, the EXACT AMOUNT I was being paid by the club. I could understand the hierarchy at

West Ham being upset with me, but to provide details of my earnings to a national newspaper was below the belt. The fact is, my money had been cut from £500 per game (in the Premier League) to £420 in the Championship anyway, so I don't consider I was overpaid for six hours' work.

Another cause for annoyance, which came out about two weeks later, was an *Evening Standard* report that I still hadn't paid the FA since being fined £15,000 over the 1999 League Cup Final ticket fiasco (full story chapter 4). The new spin on this very ancient story was that if I ever did manage to take over at West Ham, I wouldn't be allowed to run the club because of an outstanding FA fine.

I didn't agree with the fine – and that's another story – but the point was, if ever I took another job in football, either as manager, coach or director, then obviously I would have fully paid up my fine with the English game's rulers at Soho Square. As it happened, I did eventually settle the fine in 2010 but, at the time this story appeared in the *Standard*, it was still academic.

Again, it seems someone at West Ham had conveniently taken great delight in drawing this to the attention of the *Standard*, who ran it as a pro-West Ham story that reflected negatively on my part. I'd never discussed the FA fine with anybody at West Ham but someone at the club had used it to try and besmirch my character. The leaked reports that contained exact details of my earnings at West Ham and the (then) unpaid FA fine hurt me more than actually being sacked by the club.

Sue Page, West Ham's then commercial manager, valued the work I did in

After the shit hit the fan.

the lounges and she had nothing to do with my sacking. She was caught in a very awkward position and was embarrassed when, a few days after my phone conversation with Paul Aldridge, I popped into her office to hand back the club's all-areas swipecard pass that had afforded me privileged access to all parts of the Boleyn Ground. It meant I could no longer enter the stadium for free, or buy tickets from the club for friends, and my stadium car park place was also withdrawn.

To me, news of my takeover plan coming out the way it did in mid-March 2005 seemed to be the worst possible thing that could have happened and I truly feared it would spell the end of my hopes of ever buying out Terry Brown. I'd been outed and ousted and could see only negativity emerging from that weekend's press coverage and subsequent piece about my outstanding FA fine.

As it turned out, it was the best thing that could have happened in our efforts to raise awareness of what we were trying to do. And the 'dirty tricks' campaign I suspected one or two people at West Ham of perpetrating only reinforced my resolve to bring about big changes in the Upton Park boardroom.

I spoke of my sadness at being sacked by West Ham in an interview with the retro EX magazine.

15

That's Zamora!

IN the days immediately following my sacking by West Ham, I received numerous phone calls from people who either expressed their interest in joining our consortium, or were looking to put me in touch with others who might be.

The press were also on my case, hoping for a follow up piece to the news that I was fronting a takeover bid. But having already said as much as I'd wanted to publicly, I rejected their offers to recruit would-be investors via the media. It wasn't necessary anyway. Pretty soon, wealthy West Ham supporters were approaching us direct.

Someone employed by the club, who shall remain nameless, phoned me to say that they had been contacted by a corporate box-holder at Upton Park who was interested in talking to me. He turned out to be Russell Bartlett, the owner of a Shenfield-based commercial property company called R3 Investment Group Ltd, who also had a number of joint-venture interests.

Gary and I met him for the first time at his office on April 6, 2005. Russell was immediately very positive and professional, as he was in all his dealings with us. A pleasure to deal with, he became an integral part of our consortium over the next 18 months.

I had a phone call from South African-born lawyer Jonathan Klein, the Seattle-based CEO of the world famous photographic agency Getty Images Inc. A highly respected entrepreneur and innovator, Jonathan co-founded the company with its chairman Mark Getty and he also owned a venture capital company. He was intrigued by my plans and after exchanging emails and meeting his London representative called Zac on three occasions, he pledged to invest up to £5m.

Another potential investor to emerge from the States pledging £1m was Mike Winstone, a director of a Texas oil company who claimed he had a Russian friend who might also be interested in what we had to say.

Via a friend, I received an email from a West End-based Hammers fan named Chris Ward, a PR man, who indicated that he and a fellow supporter called Richard Davis, who was in the music industry, could have £1m to invest. Gary attended the premiere of the film *Green Street* with Chris, who had founded two PR marketing companies and worked on behalf of the Friends Reunited website owners.

There was some interest from a Norwegian, John Fredriksen, who I met at the Berkeley Hotel in Knightsbridge. John owned a forestry business but nothing came of it.

I received a phone call from Ben Mansford, who worked for the Leeds-based solicitors Walker Morris. Although a Yorkshireman himself, Ben told me his father happened to support West Ham and he had read about my link to a takeover bid in the papers.

He introduced Gary and myself to his colleague. David Hinchliffe, who explained that Walker Morris were a leading law firm who also had a wealth of experience in relation to football transactions. They had acted for the Yorkshire-based consortium that purchased and then sold Leeds United. They had acted for clients in buying Hull City and Huddersfield Town and were involved in the flotation of Newcastle United. They were also involved in administration matters at Bradford City, York City, Ipswich Town and Leicester City, so they clearly knew their stuff and, after meeting them for the first time on April 15, we were more than happy to instruct them as our solicitors. After our *faux pas* regarding plc implications, we were clearly in need of good legal advice.

My mobile phone number had remained unchanged for about 10 years but it still amazed me how complete strangers, including two men I'd never even heard of in America, managed to get hold of me, although I was obviously delighted to hear from them all in the circumstances. From being the disaster I feared, the initial adverse publicity surrounding my dismissal by West Ham turned out to be a blessing in disguise. I couldn't have hoped for a better reaction from the business world if we'd placed a full-page advertisement in the *Financial Times*.

One of the more amusing episodes followed a tip off I received from Ray Graves, a West Ham fan based in Gidea Park, Romford who was a friend of Gary's brother, Steve. Ray pointed us in the direction of an Irish contact of his called Charlie Shirling. Although Charlie, who must have been in his 60s, wasn't a football man, he suggested that he might well be willing to invest £5m into our project.

This sounded very interesting, so Gary and I arranged to meet Charlie and Ray at Langan's Brasserie in Mayfair on April 11. The meeting was going well until Kenny Sansom, the former Arsenal defender, approached our table. Alone and looking for company, England's then most capped full-back had clearly had a few too many by the time he bowled over to our table that afternoon. But as soon as he recognised me he insisted on sitting down with us, oblivious to the fact that we were in the middle of a very important private meeting.

A somewhat secretive character, Charlie clearly planned to keep a low profile. You really had to concentrate hard to follow his broad Irish accent and at one stage he whispered: "Come closer...walls have ears."

It took us about an hour to get rid of Kenny Sansom and although we did meet up with Charlie Shirling again a while later, nothing came of it.

Mick Woodward is a big East End character who I'd previously met through Alvin Martin, while making a guest appearance at a five-a-side event they were both involved in. Mick paid me for turning up and, as the then wealthy owner and chairman of Grays Athletic FC, Essex's premier non-league club, he naturally came onto our radar and we arranged to meet him on April 25.

Now while I wouldn't quite have put him down as a pentathlon contender for the 2012 London Olympics, he was definitely an able bodied guy. Yet when Gary and I pulled in to the Brentwood Moat House Hotel car park, we saw what turned out to be Mick's Bentley Continental GT cheekily parked in a disabled bay!

Mick, who also ran Westview Rail, a railway maintenance company, was wearing a Chelsea replica shirt – for a wind-up – and talking on his mobile phone. It turned out that he was organising tickets for Grays' FA Trophy final against Hucknall Town at Villa Park, which turned out to be one of the greatest day's in the Thurrock club's history following their penalty shootout victory. I think we spoke to him about our plans for West Ham for about 10 minutes and the other 25 minutes he spent taking orders for tickets.

A very well connected guy, Mick's involvement with West Ham was conditional on the club leaving the Boleyn Ground and moving to a newly-built stadium near Lakeside shopping centre, where he apparently had an option on some land. In fact I went to view the area in question but one of the problems would have been public transport access to the site. Mick was very keen to become involved and said he could bring other investors to the table. We had a second meeting with him but, for whatever reason, the land deal never materialised, so that ruled Mick out of the reckoning.

If Mick tried to wind us up by wearing a Chelsea shirt, there was no doubting Robbie Cowling's allegiance when we met him at the head office of his JobServe company in Tiptree, Essex. He was wearing his West Ham home shirt with his company's name emblazoned across the chest. He didn't just put it on to try and impress us – he often wore it to work.

I'd chatted to Robbie on a number of occasions during the course of his sponsorship of West Ham, which began when JobServe became the main kit sponsor following relegation in the summer of 2003. Typical West Ham...we go down, backroom staff lose their jobs, star players are shipped out to new employers and we sign a new shirt deal with an employment recruitment company.

A likeable, laid-back man, Robbie has always been a big Hammers fan. One of nine children, he was born and brought up very close to the Boleyn Ground before his family moved out to Jaywick, near Clacton-on-Sea in Essex, when he was seven-years-old. It must have been a dream come true for him when he became the club's biggest commercial backer 10 years after launching the world's first online recruitment business, which is now worth millions.

Former IT contractor Robbie was said to be worth at least £200m when we spoke to him and he could have been a serious player for us. Although he was clearly interested in our plans, he said that it was "three or four years too soon" for him to consider. This more or less proved to be the case, because in September 2006 he bought Colchester United, the club JobServe used to sponsor.

Robbie helped West Ham at a time when they were at a very low ebb, struggling hard to find a main sponsor to replace Dr Martens. They snatched his hand off for the sponsorship money when they were in desperate need of it but they didn't treat him as well as they should have done or as well as any major benefactor has a right to expect. For example, prior to the FA Cup semi-final against Middlesbrough at Villa Park in April 2006, he had to organise his own car park pass, which is a bit much to ask of a guy who was giving the club almost half-a-million quid a year.

It did, though, prove to be a bargain deal for Robbie. Although the club had just plummeted to the Championship when JobServe first appeared on their shirt, they were FA Cup finalists and doing well in the Premier League in the final year of his contract with the club. When the time came to renew the sponsorship, he did it on the understanding that it would cost him £250,000 if West Ham remained in the Championship, as they very much looked like doing at the time, or £450,000 if they were promoted. As it turned out, Robbie possibly negotiated the cheapest shirt sponsorship deal in Premier League history and, considering the takeover that happened halfway through his final season as the club's main backer, he couldn't have asked for two more high profile years to be associated with the Hammers.

I had a link to then Birmingham City co-owner David Sullivan because one of his two sons attended the same school as Chloe. I bumped into David in the school car park one day and asked if we could meet in more businesslike surroundings. I thought he might be interested in hearing what I had to say because he'd been linked with possible takeover bids at West Ham before. On the day the *News of the World* reported the news of my having formed a consortium, I was working for Sky at Birmingham. I happened to speak to

David Sullivan at his Essex mansion, where he told me in 2005 that West Ham was over-valued.

Blues' manager Steve Bruce and club chairman David Gold, who both suggested I have a chat with Sullivan, whose estimated £600m empire was built on the success of Sport Newspapers, publishers of the *Daily Sport* and *Sunday Sport,* but mainly due to his property portfolio reportedly worth around £500m.

As David said he wasn't keen on meeting accountants, Gary was disappointed to miss out on this meeting and I went alone to Birch Hall, Sullivan's palatial mansion set in 12 acres in the Essex village of Theydon Bois, on the fringe of Epping Forest. It's a quite amazing place, not unlike a huge roman temple. Apparently, at a cost of £7.5m in 1992, it was said to be the most expensive home built in Essex at the time.

Prior to winning promotion in 2005, we had valued West Ham United's total share value at around £15m but David said he thought that was too much money for a club that was £25m in debt and needed another £20m spent on new players, as per our projections. The fact that he was already a director of Birmingham City precluded him from having a simultaneous role at Upton Park but he didn't completely rule out any future involvement at our initial meeting.

Chatting away in his office, David was friendly and welcoming and said he admired what I was trying to do, although he warned me that making West Ham an attractive investment opportunity to any serious businessman would prove a very difficult task. Presumably, he felt a bit differently by the time he and David Gold bought the club in January 2010!

There was a curious sequel to my meeting with Sullivan. Soon after visiting his home to discuss my takeover attempt in 2005, I bumped into Peter Storrie, the former West Ham MD who had since taken up the position of chief executive at Portsmouth. I was working at Fratton Park for Sky when I met Peter, who pointed out that he still held a 2% shareholding in West Ham and would give us first option on them if we ever did get to the stage where we were ready to make an offer for the club.

When I contacted Peter again a year later to discuss the possibility of taking up his offer, by which time we were considering strategic share purchasing, he revealed that he'd already sold his shares...to David Sullivan.

After Storrie reluctantly confirmed how he'd disposed of them, I phoned David at home and said: "I didn't think you were interested in West Ham."

"I'm not," he replied.

Peter Storrie with Harry Redknapp during their time together at Portsmouth.

"So why have you just bought shares in the club?" I countered.

"I already own some shares in West Ham and just bought another couple of per-centage because there has been a lot of speculation about a possible future takeover. I got them pretty cheaply. Peter needed the money and so I bought them for a rainy day."

I learned that Sullivan bought them from Storrie at a cost of £1 per share. At that time there were 20,202,352 West Ham shares in issue, so Storrie's 2% holding was worth £368,000 when he sold them. Just over a year later, when the club changed hands, Sullivan sold them on to the new Icelandic owners for £1.54m – a 300% profit that netted him a tidy £969,000 bonus. This, on top of the West Ham shares he already owned, which increased his total shareholding to 4.9% by the time he sold them.

The constant round of meetings Gary and I undertook brought us into contact with businessmen and entrepreneurs of all shapes and sizes. We spent a whole afternoon with Daniel Harris, a box-holder at Upton Park and chief executive of Alba plc, the consumer electrical goods group that distributed brands such as Bush, Goodmans and Grundig. Although our lengthy chat with Daniel had been very positive, within about two weeks of the meeting Alba's share price dipped, they were hit by a profits warning and he said that the time was clearly not right for them to become involved with us.

One who did initially pledge £1m to our plan was James Light, a West End-based residential property developer who we met at the Landmark Hotel in Marylebone.

The most interesting call I had came from a friend who knew someone called Steve Smith, who in turn had a wealthy businessman friend based near Marbella. The contact in Spain was in fact a wealthy Iranian oil man named Sasha Shojai, who had no links to football or much knowledge of the game but was very interested in looking at Project TC from a purely business perspective. It started out as one of those 'friend of a friend' type scenarios but we had to pursue it and it turned out to be a very significant development.

I met Sasha for the first time at a top West End hotel. An immaculately dressed man in his 50s with a floral tie, he was an articulate gent who made a big first impression on me. It quickly became clear that he appeared to have enough financial clout to become our biggest single investor, with the ability to bring in other backers too. Sasha would prove a very strong ally throughout much of the process.

Guilty thoughts

I remember vividly the first game I attended at Upton Park following my sacking by West Ham. It was the vital clash with fellow promotion rivals and Championship leaders Sunderland on the evening of Friday, April 29 – the last home match scheduled for that season. A friend of mine invited me along as a guest in his box in the Bobby Moore Stand.

As I walked into main reception, there was a look of shock on the faces of the security staff and other club employees who I'd got to know well over the previous three years. It felt liked I'd grown two heads, as if they were anticipating an explosive situation. I'd heard on the grapevine that I'd been banned from attending the ground – I think there was a snippet to that effect in one of the papers – but that was never made official to me, so I saw no reason to stay away.

I'd kept in touch with Rob Shepherd and told him that I planned to attend the Sunderland game, although there was a slight doubt whether I'd be allowed in. Sensing another sensational scoop, Rob sent along a *NOTW* photographer in the hope of capturing the moment I was turned away from the ground but it proved a waste of the photographer's time. As an invited guest, I had a ticket for the game, so there was no way I could be refused admission and, thankfully, it never came to that.

On the contrary, the security guys waved me through into the main foyer, where I said 'hello' to a number of friends and other familiar faces who seemed very surprised to see me back. Before making my way upstairs and through the narrow corridors that led to the Bobby Moore Stand behind the goal at the southern end of the stadium, I bumped into Paul Aldridge, who happened to be standing in reception. We shook hands and exchanged formal pleasantries before I continued on my way to the corporate box for a night of high tension.

It was a surreal experience, the most horrible feeling Gary and I have ever experienced as West Ham fans. The vast majority of the 33,482 packed inside the Boleyn (Gary watched from his seat in the East Stand), plus many of those watching the game live on Sky, were praying for a home victory to inch sixth-placed Hammers a step nearer the play-offs with just one more game to play, away at Watford. There was good travelling support from Sunderland, who turned out in force in the hope of seeing their team not only clinch promotion, but the Championship title itself.

And there were two very nervous Hammers supporters chewing their fingernails and hoping for the unthinkable...a defeat for West Ham that could have brought matters at boardroom level to a head sooner rather than later.

I want this book to be a totally honest account of what really happened so, yes, it's now time to confess my sins. For the first time in my life, I hate to say it, but I didn't mind my team being beaten. I wouldn't say that we went to the game actually *hoping* the Hammers would fail to win, but a draw or a defeat would have helped our takeover cause.

There was so much riding on this final home league game of the normal season. If West Ham won it, they would virtually have been assured of a place in the play-offs and therefore a big step nearer their ultimate goal of returning to the Premier League. If that happened, our hopes of taking over the club would not have been completely shattered, but they would be dealt a very serious blow.

Gary and I went to Upton Park that night knowing that victory in the 2005 Play-off Final would change everything. Alan Pardew's position would be strengthened and he would be handed a big transfer budget to try and keep West Ham in the top flight the following year...the lucrative Sky money would come flooding back in and greatly ease Hammers' perilous financial position...and, most crucially, the club itself would immediately increase in value. It would obviously cost us millions more to purchase West Ham as a newly-promoted Premier League club than it would if the team missed out on the gravy train and had to endure another season in the second tier on rapidly decreasing revenues.

Marlon Harewood put Hammers ahead with a scuffed effort that went in off the post just before half-time but the evening turned sour for Pardew's men when Arca equalised for Sunderland soon after the break and then Elliott netted their winner three minutes from time. While part of us was gutted that our team had lost this crucial match, Gary and I knew the visitors' title-clinching victory was a much better outcome for our long-term ambitions.

The way I justified our private thoughts was that, although most fans didn't realise it at the time, this defeat could well have helped to hasten the change of ownership at Upton Park. It was a case of short-term pain for long-term gain but as I looked at all the dejected people trudging away from the ground that night, they were thinking only of the short-term effect – the dreaded prospect of another season outside the elite. I tried to console some of those downbeat West Ham fans in our hospitality box at the final whistle by telling them that the 2-1 defeat by Sunderland was not the end of the world, but they looked at me as if I was mad. How could failure to gain promotion be perceived as anything but bad news?

I felt guilty for not feeling as gutted as most West Ham supporters were at the end of that torturous night – it was horrible and Gary and I would never wish to go through it again.

But joy returned to the supporters' faces nine days later, on the last weekend of the normal season, when the Hammers came from outside the top six to snatch a priceless win at Watford on May 8. At the start of the day, Sunderland were already confirmed as champions, with Wigan Athletic and Ipswich Town chasing the other automatic promotion spot. Preston North End, Derby County, Reading and West Ham were competing for the four play-off positions.

Reading's promotion hopes had suffered a major blow when they were beaten at home the previous weekend by Wolves, despite having taken the lead, which left the Royals level with the team led by their former manager, Alan Pardew, on both points and goal difference. The Berkshire club faced by far the more difficult last day task, though, and went down 3-1 at promoted Wigan...while West Ham snatched a priceless 2-1 victory at Watford which clinched their place in the play-offs.

If Gary and I had been nervous before the Sunderland game, we were now expecting the worst outcome as far as our business plans were concerned. And so it proved. If Pardew and his team had been fortunate to scrape into the play-offs after another largely dismal season, there was nothing lucky about their aggregate 4-2 victory over Ipswich in the semi-final. I was one of Sky's studio guests at Portman Road for the second leg which they covered live. The tie was settled by two Bobby Zamora goals and the mixed feelings

Killer goal: Bobby Zamora slots home the winner in the 2005 Play-off Final that proved costly to our consortium.

I'd had around the Sunderland home game a few weeks earlier resurfaced. Everyone I work with at Sky knows I'm a West Ham man so, if anything, I try to play down my natural allegiance whenever I'm covering one of their games. I think I did a professional job in front of the cameras again that night, agreeing with Sky's presenter that it was a great result for the club.

Inside, though, I knew very well that if they went on to win the final at Cardiff against Preston on May 30, it was going to make our takeover bid that much more difficult to execute than it was already proving to be. We'd been beavering away in the background for months, getting all our ducks in a row, but the late push for the play-offs left our consortium in limbo.

Bobby Zamora couldn't

Match-winner Bobby Zamora is mobbed by sub Mark Noble.

have known the full significance of his 57th minute Play-off Final winner at the time. The media labelled it the '30 Million Pound Game', with West Ham's annual income from the Sky TV revenue alone said to rocket from £1.1m to £17.75m. Demand for tickets and club merchandise would also increase following a traumatic season that unexpectedly turned into an End End celebration party.

I couldn't be at the Millennium Stadium to see the game and didn't even watch it on TV. At the end of each season I usually attended kids' prize-giving evenings, where I'd give out medals to the players, and I'd agreed way back in January '05 to do one in Great Yarmouth on May 30 – the date of the Play-off Final. How poorly West Ham had performed for much of the first half of the season and even well into the New Year could be measured by the fact that I hadn't even bothered to check the Play-off Final date before accepting the football club booking.

To be honest, when it was known that West Ham would meet Preston in the final, I remember feeling inner-turmoil and couldn't face going to the game. I thought, 'if I can't go there and cheer West Ham to victory alongside many thousands of other fans who would go ballistic if we won...if I can't share in their total ecstasy at winning promotion, then I don't want to be there'. Supporters reading this might consider my thoughts to be an act of treason, especially given the success that followed in the 2005-06 season and all the happiness another Cardiff cup final brought, but there was so much at stake for us at the time.

Jubilant young fans after Bobby Zamora scored THAT goal at Cardiff that meant so much for different reasons.

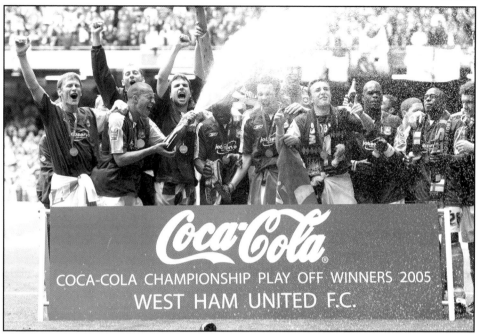

The West Ham team at Cardiff after victory over Preston in the 2005 Play-off Final, but we were unable to share their delight at the time.

So I honoured my commitment to do the children's football club presentation at a holiday camp in Norfolk. The big game in Cardiff actually kicked off during the presentation ceremony and I remember a lad coming up to me, his face full of joy, and saying: 'West Ham have scored...Bobby Zamora!' I smiled back at him and, trying to look as delighted as he was, said something like: 'Oh, that's good'.

When the final whistle went in Cardiff, a different bloke came up to me and said: 'West Ham have won, they're promoted!' I didn't know whether to laugh or cry.

Our original proposal was only ever going to be a rescue package. If the club was going to be condemned to a third consecutive season in the second tier, then our hand would have been considerably strengthened. The fans would undoubtedly have turned on Terry Brown again, Alan Pardew's position would have become untenable and the groundswell of support we would have engendered on the back of that scenario, both financially and in terms of goodwill from disgruntled fans, was obvious.

But after the 2005 Play-off Final, I thought 'that's it, game over'. My immediate reaction was almost one of heartbreak, as if a year's work had gone down the pan through no fault of ours and due to a major slice of good fortune Pardew and his team had in scraping in to the play-offs. I didn't think at that moment that we would have any chance of buying the club.

I walked disconsolately out into the car park at the holiday camp and phoned Sasha, the Iranian businessmen who we expected to become our biggest backer, to let him know the result and to get his thoughts. I was immediately heartened by his response. 'Yes, we might have to pay a bit more money for the club', he said, 'but, as far as I'm concerned, nothing has changed'.

It didn't strike me as such at the time, but that conversation effectively changed the course of the club's history. If Sasha had said at that point that he couldn't go any further with us, then I would have thrown in the towel there and then too, and the Icelandics would never have moved in on West Ham.

I phoned Gary to tell him what Sasha had said and by the time I left Yarmouth and drove home at the end of a day that had brought a rollercoaster of emotions, I felt positive again. We weren't kidding ourselves, though. The goalposts had moved completely. Instead of me and my band of musketeers hoping to buy the club for a few bob, we were now in need of serious investment and had no option but to switch to Plan B.

16

Browned off

IN June 2005 I phoned Paul Aldridge to say I would like to meet him and Terry Brown informally to discuss my consortium's intention of making an imminent offer to buy the club. He suggested we met at the Tower Hotel by Tower Bridge, so Gary, myself and our two legal lads, Ben Mansford and David Hinchliffe from Walker Morris, went there on June 21. Brown didn't show but Aldridge and the club's new finance director Nick Igoe were present to hear what we had to offer. I felt pretty nervous about leading the meeting but read out our plans from handwritten notes that ran to three A4 pages.

Our actual purchase offer, subject to due diligence, was for £40m to be used as follows:

*£15m (or 75p per share) to buy out the main shareholders, Terry Brown, Charles Warner and Martin Cearns.

*£25m to service the club's bank debt.

*We were also pledging £20m to invest in new players and the youth academy, so the total cost of purchasing the club would have been £60m.

We knew that further down the line we would also need to negotiate a buy-out of Brown's employment contract with the club – effectively a redundancy payment. Partly for that reason, we included in our offer to him a presidential and consultancy role, plus boardroom facilities, a seat in the directors' box and car park pass. We also pledged the normal football perks of

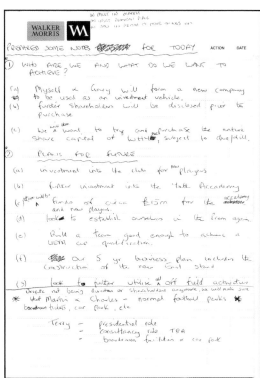

The first page of my scribbled notes I read from at our secret meeting with two West Ham directors.

boardroom access, directors' box tickets and car park passes to the two other major shareholders, Martin Cearns and Charles Warner.

In light of the fact that Brown and his colleagues eventually sold out to the Icelandics for £4.21p per share in November 2006, the initial offer we made some 18 months earlier seems relatively paltry now. But, again, we come back to that word context. The club was in a mess and our offer was the first concrete offer anyone had made to Brown and co. since Michael Tabor's £8m takeover bid was rejected by the West Ham board in 1996. OK, so I was hardly Don Corleone making an offer they couldn't refuse! But if you go to buy a house, you very rarely, if ever, offer the full asking price on first viewing.

The way we saw it, despite returning to the top flight, West Ham still had a very average squad of players who had crept into the play-offs via the back door on the final day of the normal league season. Without decent investment in new signings, many people agreed that they looked every inch relegation candidates and likely to go straight back down.

Promotion meant the club would receive a fresh injection of TV money but all that would have done was alleviate their debt. They still needed to spend money on new players for the top flight, which in turn would hike their wage bill.

The important thing to remember is that we intended investing £20m on new players of Premier League quality while at the same time eliminating most of the debt that had suffocated the club for the previous couple of years, and which almost brought it to the brink of disaster following relegation in 2003.

Neither Paul Aldridge nor Nick Igoe uttered a word as they listened to my three-page spiel but afterwards it came as no surprise that the only figures they were interested in was our valuation of the directors' shares. They were at the meeting to represent the major shareholders, not necessarily the best future interests of West Ham as a whole and certainly not those of the fans. It didn't matter one iota to the two West Ham board members present that we were promising to wipe out the debt and spend unprecedented millions on probably half a dozen new players.

"Thank you for the offer," said Paul, "but we believe the club is worth three-to-four times what you are actually offering."

He said they valued West Ham at somewhere between £45m and £60m, which meant we were miles apart. Within half an hour the meeting was over and we were left with plenty to ponder. The most obvious thought that struck me again was the cost to us of Bobby Zamora's strike at the Millennium Stadium, because promotion had clearly moved the goalposts as far as our bid was concerned.

If only that Preston defender hadn't slipped on the turf as the cross arrived at Bobby Zamora's feet.

If only Zamora had sliced his shot wide.

Life is full of if onlys...

After a brief period of feeling sorry for ourselves, we had to be realistic. It's fair to say that had the club missed out on promotion again in '05, there would probably have been other vultures circling the Boleyn Ground to compete with our bid. One mooted interested party was the Hyperion Group, fronted by Brendan Harris, a Coca-Cola executive, but that soon fizzled out.

West Ham would have become a sleeping giant – many would argue it still is – although, other than a line in the *Telegraph* about Hyperion, we were not aware of any other interest at the time. I even took the trouble to contact Michael Tabor, the horseracing owner, former bookmaker and person most often linked with West Ham whenever there was previous takeover talk surrounding the club. But the feedback

Michael Tabor had lost interest in buying West Ham.

I got was that he wasn't interested. My earlier chat with David Sullivan also ruled him out and I really felt I'd done all my research and established that we were the only interested party in the ballpark.

As my offer in June '05 was only an informal one, there was no need at the time to advise the other West Ham United PLC shareholders of our secret meeting and nothing leaked out to the media about what was said between ourselves, Paul Aldridge and Nick Igoe. They obviously went back and briefed Terry Brown on what was said and from that moment on I knew that he never believed I was capable of putting together a consortium capable of taking over the club.

One of my character traits is stubbornness. The more someone tells me I can't, or won't, do something, the more determined I am to prove them wrong and achieve it. West Ham's knockback had momentarily deflated me but I then set my mind on trying to find the £60m Terry Brown and his fellow directors wanted for the club.

Destination Spain

At the start of July '05, Gary and I, along with the legal lads from Walker Morris, Ben and David, flew out to Spain's Costa Del Sol, where our biggest investor Sasha Shojai lived in a traditional villa in the hills high above Estepona. The place reminded me of 'Big' John Cannon's ranch in the *High Chaparral* TV series of the 70s but thankfully there were no cowboys and indians or gunfights to be seen on our visit.

Sasha had fled the Iran Islamic revolution of 1979, came to settle in the UK and made his money through a petroleum company that employed 25,000 people and had an annual turnover in the billions. He also owned the Mush-Mush Club, a short walk from the luxurious Puerto Banus resort, where some of the world's richest men moor their private yachts. Of all the businessmen I'd met, I knew this guy was in a different league, financially.

He spoke perfect English and from the moment we first met we got on very well. He studied our revised financial projections and was genuinely enthusiastic about coming on board with us. He was ideal, to the point where he was happy to be a silent investor who appeared to have no ego and was happy to stay in the background and leave us to run the club.

We stayed overnight at Sasha's Spanish retreat and after re-evaluating all the figures based on Premier League status, including the value of the Boleyn Ground itself, we came to the conclusion that the share capital of West Ham was probably worth around £50m.

Sasha was happy to remain involved up to the point where West Ham would cost £45m or £50m to buy, of which he said he would put in £30m. The remaining £15m to £20m had to come from other investors, from whom we also needed an increased financial commitment.

The circus comes to town

At the beginning of August I received a call out of the blue from a man called Frank Buchan, who said: "Hi Tony, you don't know me but I'd like to have a chat about the West Ham situation...I have some information for you."

I went to Palms Hotel, Hornchurch to meet Frank – a businessman with an East London accent and a West Ham supporter. He said: "I just wanted to let you know that I'm aware, through a friend of a friend, that there's another guy trying to buy West Ham. His name is Kia Joorabchian."

"Who the hell is he?" I responded.

My reliable informant explained that Iranian-born, British-educated Joorabchian had really good contacts in South American football and was trying to bring everything together in order to buy West Ham. He also revealed that Joorabchian had significant backers, had no wish to join our consortium and was going to offer £60m for the club.

I asked if it was possible for me to speak to Joorabchian and Frank immediately gave me his number. I waited until I got home before making the call. I remember it clearly...walking to the end of my back garden in Brentwood, dialling the number and, after a few seconds, going through to answerphone. I left a message explaining who I was and the reason for calling. I emphasised I'd been working on a project for the best part of two years and how very keen I was that my plan was executed in a certain way with a strong West Ham influence. I suggested that we should meet up to discuss if there was a way in which we could work together.

I was still trying to formulate my own consortium and raise the capital we needed, so I obviously didn't want to go into battle with a rival group. I was very interested to hear his plans and also what we were up against.

I'm 100% certain I dialled the correct number for Joorabchian – I later recognised his voice on the answerphone – but to this day I've never even had a reply from him. It was clear from his lack of response that he had no intention of listening to anything I had to say.

Within days, he and his Media Sports Investments Ltd (MSI) group had emerged from nowhere and suddenly was being widely touted in the media as the potential new owners of West Ham.

On August 18, the BBC quoted Joorabchian's ridiculous claims that he would lavish £100m on new players alone if his takeover bid was successful. The BBC's online report went as follows:

Joorabchian is planning a £200m takeover bid. "There is huge potential there," said the 34-year-old.

"There's no point in buying West Ham unless you are going to invest in turning them into one of the top teams in the country."

Joorabchian was taken for a tour of the stadium when he visited West Ham for preliminary negotiations last month.

However, Joorabchian's £45m valuation of the club's equity is believed to be £15m short of the board's valuation.

"My West Ham project has to be worth around £200m," he added.

"That breaks down as £45m on buying the club, £30m on its debts, another £30m to keep the cash-flow going and around £100m on new players.

"At one point we are going to make a bid, although at the moment we have not done anything.

"The fact that I want to buy a European club is obvious and there is still a possibility it could be another Premiership club other than West Ham."

Joorabchian insists that if any formal takeover is launched, it would not take place this year.

"If there is any bid made, it will only be for next year," he said.

"But if next week the board of directors decides that they want to start to make a bid to take over in January, then we may do that."

It was annoying and frustrating to see a stranger with no West Ham affinity whatsoever make such a dramatic public declaration of intent that would be very difficult, if not impossible, to back up. I'd been beavering away for ages, carefully trying to avoid media exposure until we had everything ready to put to the club, and here was this former car dealer from Kent being acclaimed by the press as the possible saviour of the club. On August 22, Terry Brown wrote to West Ham shareholders informing them of MSI's interest.

I couldn't let Joorabchian's presence derail my efforts, though, and on August 17 I went to Liverpool Street station to meet an Australian called David Lewis, a director of the Santa Clara Group (SCG) based in Balrain, New South Wales, who specialised in financial investments and how to secure them. David was naturally keen to talk because he was also president of the Oz Hammers supporters' club.

He advised me that we would be best served by continuing to maintain a low media profile while at the same time moving towards making a full offer to the club in order to assure them that we had a credible bid on the table in case MSI didn't come up with the goods.

As it happened, West Ham basically told Joorabchian to 'put up or shut up' and on November 24, following months of media speculation, MSI announced they would not be making a bid for the club. As events would prove, though, it wasn't the last we'd hear from them.

Not that the board was under pressure from fans to sell out at this stage. Already relieved at gaining promotion, they were now basking in the glow of the team's unexpected flying start to the 2005-06 Premier League season, which produced only one defeat in the first eight games and saw the Hammers in sixth place at the start of October. The board were so overjoyed by the unexpected start to the campaign, they offered Alan Pardew a new five-year contract with undue haste, although it was the next regime who would be left to pick up most of that hefty tab in the form of a reported £1m pay-off.

At least the brilliant form on the field would theoretically help us to 'sell' the club to potential investors, albeit at a higher premium. Our next move was to revise our Business Plan in the quest to secure the correct level of investment.

Football is littered with well-worn clichés and, as I soon discovered, so too is the world of finance and commerce. I mentioned before about 'getting all our ducks in a row', a phrase often banded around among business people. Another one that seemed to crop up quite regularly in finance-speak was 'don't stick your head above the parapet'. So we decided to keep our head under the radar and let the Joorabchian circus fizzle out. We were confident he wouldn't be able to raise the money and that's just how it panned out.

Terry Brown's rant

By November I felt that we were nearly there and, with Joorabchian out of the picture, I wanted to push on and hopefully bring about an earlier conclusion to the takeover process. After speaking to Sasha and a couple of our other investors, we agreed that I should call Terry Brown to sound him out.

In the meantime, Sue Page, West Ham's commercial manager, had mentioned in passing to the chairman that I was genuinely sorry to have fallen out with the club and how much I had missed not working there since they sacked me, which was all true.

I was on a golf day at the Celtic Manor hotel and golf resort, near Newport in Wales, venue for the 2010 Ryder Cup, when I decided to phone him before I went out onto the course where Monty's Team Europe would beat the Yanks by a point some five years later.

Terry's PA Alison took my call and put me straight through. I assumed that he had only recently spoken to Sue Page about my desire to return to the club in a corporate role and, from the opening tone of his voice, I guessed he was clearly expecting me to ask about the club giving me my old job back. The mood of our conversation soon changed, though, and went like this:

"Hello, Terry, how are you?"

"Yes, I'm fine, Tony."

He then threw in a rather flippant remark when he added: "I hope you're not ringing up to make another bid for the club . . ."

"Funny you should say that, Terry...I am."

Stoney silence, followed by a curt "Huh."

"Look," he said, "you made your offer before and, as I told you, it was far too low."

"OK," I countered, "what I would like you to do, Terry, is tell me what I need to do to be able to come back to you with a proper offer."

He said: "I can tell you right now, I want £60m (for 100% shareholding). I want it paid into a British bank. I want to know who your backers are, proof of funds and a letter proving you actually have the funding. When you've done that, you can come back and talk to me."

"OK, at least I know where I stand," I responded, trying to keep my cool.

Brown then went off on one, an absolute rant, saying: "I don't know why you're trying to do this, Tony, by upsetting the team and Alan Pardew...we're trying to build something here."

I pointed out that I had done nothing of the sort. On the contrary, I had done everything in my power to keep our consortium's bid out of the public eye.

"But you went to Sky TV and told them," he blurted out, struggling to maintain his composure.

I tried to explain that I was put in a very awkward position by my main employers and the *News of the World*.

"Yes, but you did this and you did that," he went on, accusing me of tapping up his corporate clients in the lounges.

I must have listened to a five-minute personal barrage down the phone and he was going off on one to such an extent that I held the receiver a foot from my ear and was actually laughing to myself as he continued to vent his spleen.

He finished the conversation, albeit a very one-sided one, by repeating his demands for a £60m payment, proof of funds, blah, blah, blah, before slamming down the phone.

It pleased me that I'd clearly got under his skin. In fairness, though, I understood where he was coming from. It was his duty to get the best possible deal for himself, the majority 36% stakeholder, and his fellow shareholders and he certainly left me in no doubt that he wouldn't entertain a sale for anything less than £60m. At least I'd finally heard it from the horse's mouth, although the figures somehow went north further down the line.

He could have told me his price at the Tower Hotel if he'd been there but he sent Paul Aldridge and Nick Igoe along instead. What I couldn't understand is why the club were happy to talk to Kia Joorabchian, with his dodgy contacts, mysterious background and no links whatsoever with West Ham, and not someone who played 336 games and scored 146 goals for the club and who bleeds claret and blue.

Main man pulls out

I never thought for one minute that Terry Brown ever believed I was capable of coming up with the kind of money he wanted to vacate the boardroom. He didn't treat me like a serious player throughout the whole takeover process but his arrogance and disrespect simply spurred me on even more.

What his asking price for the shares did, however, was cost us our main benefactor. When I went back to Sasha at the end of November to tell him how far the goalposts had moved, we met in a West End hotel – along with his English advisor - and he gave me the disappointing news that he was withdrawing his interest. I suppose I half saw it coming. Although Sasha had been very enthusiastic and communicative right up to the '05 Play-off Final, he became harder to get hold off after that – even allowing for the fact that he was clearly a very busy man.

He explained that although he could still see the potential in West Ham and recognised they were a successful Premier League club again, he said the total shares were not worth Brown's £60m valuation. He said they were worth £50m top whack.

How correct Sasha was to be more conservative than Terry Brown in his valuation of the club did perhaps not become obvious until the end of the following (2006-07) season, when the team only just managed to avoid relegation on the final day of the season. Sasha might not have known much about football but he quickly realised it was a precarious business to be in.

With the extra investment needed to service the club's estimated £25m debt plus expenditure on new players – albeit reduced from our previous budget of £20m to £10m in light of the good start to the season – and other costs such as legal fees, Sasha had worked out that it was getting on for a total takeover not far short of £100m, with his share of the proposed investment having virtually doubled on the 'rescue package' we'd first discussed with him.

If I could show you the full extent to which we examined all the financial aspects of what the takeover would entail in the most minuscule detail, it would blow your mind...or more likely send you to sleep. Gary had Excel spread sheets, graphs, profit and loss projections, five and 10-year plans coming out of every orifice. And as our journey progressed, many of those projections had to be re-calculated, re-written and then re-submitted for the consortium's benefit countless times. It was bewildering to a layman like me but it had to be put together and presented properly so that accountants and financial experts could make sense of it.

We not only checked out West Ham's annual financial reports with a fine tooth comb, we ordered year-end accounts and background reports on rival bidders like Joorabchian, so we knew what we were up against. We even discreetly checked out our own investors' financial status! Well, you can never be too careful about who you get into bed with! It's all very well a person saying they want to put up a million quid here or two million there but if they don't actually have the financial muscle to deliver on their promise or pledge, then you don't want to waste time finding out they were bullshitting all along. After our amateurish gaffs of the early days, we did everything professionally.

Sasha was a very successful businessman, he'd been brilliant for us throughout 2005, and I couldn't argue with him or change his mind. I understood his decision and if I'd been him I would have pulled out too at that point. He was very apologetic but it left us with a massive financial hole to try and fill. Sasha had been prepared to inject £30m-£40m for a major shareholding, so he was going to be very hard to replace.

17

Proud to be a Hammer

CHRISTMAS 2005 was a time to chill out, clear the head and do a lot more soul-searching. With Sasha gone, we were down to three investors in Russell Bartlett, Kevin Stevens and Mick Villiers but, between them, it amounted to about £15m of funds – if we were lucky. Realistically, we could bank on about £10m of that, so there was a lot of work to be done if we were ever going to meet Terry Brown's £60m asking price.

The next few months were packed with meeting after meeting as I explored every possible avenue in our search for serious investors. We weren't quite dead in the water but I felt like a captain of a ship in the middle of the Atlantic with no rudder or sails. Oh, and there was also a slight hole in the bottom of the boat. I was floating in no man's land, although still passionately believing in what we were trying to do and wouldn't give up on the dream. On the pitch things were going well but the supporters were still suspicious of the board. No change there.

My first assignment of the New Year for Sky was on the TV gantry at Norwich, where I saw West Ham win in the FA Cup thanks to a good goal by Hayden Mullins. Little did I know then that I was watching the start of the team's epic journey to the Cup final for the first time in 26 years.

The first significant business call I made in '06 was to Dave Hahn, a PR agent who I'd known for the best part of 10 years. I must have been a bit short of cash after an expensive Christmas and was looking for work doing personal appearances. He asked me how my West Ham plan was going and suggested I spoke to a friend of his called Chris Hutton, who he described as a very clever man with novel ideas about how to raise money. Chris was a tax specialist who knew the financial world inside out. He sounded just what we needed, so I arranged to meet him and Dave at the Four Seasons Hotel, Canary Wharf on Friday, January 13 – omens didn't bother me.

I got on really well with Chris, who was based in Dublin, from the word go and he offered to give us as much help as possible once he'd spoken to a few of his contacts. We ended our meeting around one o'clock in the afternoon and I was surprised when Chris phoned me at 5.00pm later that day, just as he was about to catch a flight back to Ireland. He said: "I've just had the weirdest phone call on my mobile from the *Sunday People*, saying that I've just had a meeting with the Tony Cottee consortium and that I am the new money man heading their bid to take over West Ham."

Whether someone had been sitting behind us in the Four Seasons, earwigging our conversation, I don't know but that didn't explain how they got his mobile number. Neither Dave nor I had breathed a word of our meeting with Chris to anyone, so it remains a mystery how it leaked to the *Sunday People*, who mentioned our not-so-private meeting in a small piece two days later.

At this point I re-visited our list of potential investors and phoned each one to see if they were still on board or, like Sasha, had got cold feet. I even tried to call Sasha in the hope that he might have had a change of heart but when I did eventually get through to him, in early February, he confirmed what he'd told me before Christmas.

I was pleased to find Russell Bartlett still in very positive mood. Of all our potential investors, he was a constant support, always positive and willing to make himself available.

Mick Villiers and Kevin Stevens indicated they were still interested if the deal was right and, obviously, I kept in close contact with Gary White throughout.

Here I refer again to my diary notes to give you an idea of the lengths I went to as 2006 unfolded:

February 9, Great Portland Street, W1.

Met with Russell Bartlett, Gary White, Chris Hutton and Paul Duffen (who was CEO of a sports media company) to discuss fund-raising options and individual pledges. Paul had worked previously with Chris on private equity and fund-raising ventures and was introduced to us by Chris.

Early in '06 I had to accept the reality that my dream of forming a consortium of West Ham-only supporters had to be abandoned. By then I had exhausted all obvious options. David Sullivan, Michael Tabor and Robbie Cowling, who all had enough money to invest, weren't interested in joining us, so I had to look beyond my idealistic claret and blue world. By hook or by crook I vowed to myself that I was going to raise the money.

March 28, South Mimms Services Hotel, M25.

Met Mark Garwood, a PR agent, again (we'd met up on Feb. 10) to see if he could find me more work. He called before the meeting to say he was bringing along a couple of friends who had ideas. One was an English guy I remember only as Brian but the other proved to be a more significant figure. Haftor Svensson – or 'Haffi' as he became known to us all – was from Iceland.

Haffi had bought the biggest portable TV screen in Europe with the intention of transporting it to the 2006 World Cup tournament coming up in Germany that summer, where he planned to put on events in parks in the big city venues. He thought I might be interested in hosting one or two of these events for him, even though my German is limited to little more than 'Ja'.

When Brian and Mark slipped away to take phone calls, I found myself chatting to Haffi and enthusing about my passion for West Ham with this bearded Icelandic stranger who lived in Cambridgeshire. I explained to him about losing my major backer and he said that he knew quite a few people, both in England and Iceland, who might be interested in hearing my plans. He didn't mention anyone by name and didn't even appear to be overly enthusiastic about my mission, so we all exchanged business cards and left it at that.

March and April, more meetings.

Met with Chris Hutton in London to try and find more investors, including a meeting with some bankers in Piccadilly.

Chris was looking at raising money, firstly through investors and, secondly, through hedge funds, loans and various other ways. He had lots of creative ideas and talked about raising £10m through a tax scheme. Gary attended all these meetings with me and, being an accountant, understood most of it. To be honest, I just went with the flow. As long as it was 'clean' money, I didn't really care where it came from. After many doors slamming in my face before Christmas, Chris' involvement reopened them and I felt re-energised.

With Russell, Chris and Paul Duffen on board, plus the legal lads from Leeds, who were also brilliant, we had formed a formidable team capable of taking our plan to fruition. By now we were meeting serious bankers and city firms who I believed could help us make it happen.

John's gone

April 18, Miami, Florida, USA.

I took a 10-day holiday break in Florida that we'd planned for some time. I felt absolutely knackered when I went to bed after a long flight and awoke the next morning to switch on my mobile and find a text message from a mate, which read: 'Shame about Mr Lyall'. Soon afterwards I received another saying: 'Sorry to hear about John Lyall'.

When I called Dad at home he confirmed the sad news that John had died of a heart attack at his Suffolk home. I wouldn't quite compare it to losing your own father, but it felt like I'd lost the man who had taught me so much about life, and my football career in particular. John had been so instrumental in getting me to West Ham as a kid, bringing me through the youth team and giving me my first team debut at 17, so I owed him a lot.

The previous October, John had been our special guest of honour when the Boys of 86 organised the 1975-80 FA Cup Finals anniversary dinner. It was his last public appearance and his presence made it a very special night, which Galey and I co-hosted. All the ex-players, including legends Sir Trevor Brooking and Billy Bonds, received a fantastic ovation but when John entered the hall the noise soared to another level.

Aside from the team's continuing good league form and the charge towards the FA Cup Final, it was a sad time for Hammers fans. John's mentor, Ron Greenwood, had died a couple of months before him and for the club to lose two great men who were an institution in just a matter of weeks was unbelievable.

Perhaps selfishly, my first thought after having the bad news confirmed by Dad was, 'would I miss the funeral?' I knew we would be in Miami for another nine days but there was no way I was going to miss John's send-off. I owed it John and the Lyall family, who had always been kind to me, to be there.

May 5, John Lyall's funeral, Ipswich.

I drove up to Ipswich for the service of thanksgiving which began at 2pm and, naturally, it was a very emotional day. I saw John's widow Yvonne and son Murray, with his wife Samantha and their boys. I had a lovely cuddle with Yvonne and Murray and I just felt so sad.

It showed the high esteem in which John was held by his peers that Sir Alex Ferguson came down from Cheshire to deliver one of the eulogies. Sir Trevor Brooking also stood up and spoke about John and what he meant to him personally. He said: "The last time I saw John was six months ago, when some bright spark had had the idea to put on a dinner for the 1975 and '80 teams."

When Trevor said that, I knew who the 'bright spark' was. It was me. I'm not saying that to blow smoke up my own arse. The actual idea of bringing those two FA Cup-winning teams together was something I'd pushed for within the Boys of 86 for a couple of years and I was heavily involved in organising it. When Trevor said those words in church, I realised the significance of what we did in putting on such a magical night. I thank God we did it – although I had the original idea, the other Boys of 86 all got behind it and made it happen. John and his family loved the occasion and it will live long in the memory of all those lucky enough to have been there.

Legends John Lyall and Billy Bonds at our FA Cup winners' dinner in 2005. Sadly, it was the last time I saw our former manager.

John had become almost something of a near recluse in his later years, staying away from football and immersing himself in the upkeep of the beautiful farmhouse near Ipswich, where he and Yvonne lived, with Murray as a close neighbour. About six months before the dinner, Galey, Phil Parkes and myself drove there to spend time with our former manager. We had various replica shirts we asked him to sign, which formed part of the auction on the night of the dinner. We only expected to be there an hour or so but, six hours later, we

It was no surprise to see such a large turn-out of former Hammers players and others in January 2008 on the day the Sports Heritage unveiled their blue plaque in honour of John Lyall at Upton Park. Back row, left to right: Alvin Martin, Billy Bonds, Ray Stewart, Alan Devonshire, Bobby Barnes, Phil Parkes, Stuart Slater, Keith McPherson, Tony Gale, Frank McAvennie, Mick McGiven, David Cross. Front: Pat Holland, Sir Trevor Brooking, rocker Rick Wakeman, Martin Peters, Sir Geoff Hurst, Rob Jenkins, myself, Frank Lampard and Terry Venables.

were still soaking up his every word and enjoying his company. When John spoke, you listened but very few men have that aura about them. Martin O'Neill also had that about him. We chipped in every now and again and had a laugh and joke with John but it was great just listening to him talk about football and any other subjects that came up in conversation. He seemed to enjoy the day as much as us three did and I'm just glad we had that time with him before he died.

John Lyall was a huge loss to football, because he still had so much more to offer when he left West Ham in 1989 having given the club 34 years' loyal service.

Icelandics warming to our plan

Before I went to the States, Haffi had phoned to try and find out more details about my plans for West Ham. I put him on to Gary, who furnished him with our full business plan and financial projections, plus West Ham's latest published accounts, while I was away and it was agreed that we would meet soon after my return.

April 28, meeting at Berkeley Square.

Haffi, our new contact from Iceland, was accompanied by a friend and fellow countryman, Jon Olaffson, who, according to Haffi, had some 'serious money' and advised us to speak to him. Jon didn't know who I was and knew nothing about football either, although he understood all the figures we put in front of them. The meeting didn't last particularly long and, due to his lack of football knowledge, Gary and I assumed the amount of money involved in our fund-raising quest would be too much of a risk for Jon. At least it was a good sign that Haffi had brought someone to the table.

May 2, meeting at Campbell Montague International Ltd (CMI).

This was set up by Chris Hutton, who had contact with CMI. Russell, Gary and myself attended on behalf of the consortium, along with two other representatives of CMI, chief executive David Campbell and the rather eccentric Rod Mackenzie. Roger Jones, who worked for a boutique investment bank called Euro-IB Ltd, was also present and his company would prove very significant as the story unfolded.

The main purpose of the meeting was to formulate a strategy and to instruct CMI to act as our exclusive financial advisor whom we had empowered to negotiate with potential financing partners as well as directors/shareholders of the company – in this case West Ham United PLC – we were trying to buy. CMI were effectively middle men.

In order to instruct CMI to work on our behalf, Gary and I needed to form a company, or an 'Investment Vehicle'. There would be no money in it initially – it was simply a shell – but the idea was that we would attract backers and issue shares accordingly as things progressed. We wanted a company title that reflected West Ham's history and after considering and rejecting options such as 'Historic Sports Ltd', 'Vintage Sports Corporation Ltd' and 'Title Sports Corporation Ltd', we eventually settled on '1895 Corporation Ltd', to mark the year in which the club's forebears, Thames Ironworks, were formed.

It emerged that one of the CMI guys knew Terry Brown's brother, Ken, and it was mooted that they would make contact with him, to test the water and try and find out what, if anything, was going on at West Ham.

One thing that came out of our first meeting at CMI which concerned me was the Letter of Engagement they subsequently drew up for us to sign. It mentioned a non-refundable retainer of £60,000 to be paid in full by us to them within 15 days of the date of the agreement. Now people may find it amazing that I'd come this far without paying a penny to anyone for any work undertaken. Gary and I funded all our travel expenses, including flights to Spain to see Sasha, out of our own pockets. Even our solicitors, Ben and David, were working on a 'quid pro quo' basis on the understanding that if our plans bore fruit, the rewards would be there for all further down the line. Gary gave up an unbelievable amount of his spare time in his commitment to the cause because he too believed in it. We didn't have a penny to our name, let alone £60k to pay upfront to a firm of financial advisers we had only just met, for work that might well not produce results.

On top of the £60k retainer, CMI also insisted on a further £20,000 per month fee thereafter until completion of the takeover. And if they happened to complete a deal with West Ham, they stood to benefit by another 4% of the purchase price (or transaction price, as they called it) above £50m – worth an extra £2m to them.

The bankers Euro-IB also informed us they would expect a hefty retainer to conduct work on our behalf – in their case £50k over three months.

And they say footballers are overpaid! I tell you what, some of these financial institutions and the people who run them don't do too badly either, as we've all discovered in recent years following the global banking collapse and subsequent credit crisis.

The only person in our camp who could afford to pay CMI and Euro-IB the upfront payments they were seeking was Russell Bartlett but it wouldn't have been fair to have asked him to cover it. A rock solid West Ham man, Russell was the one who really stood by us all the way. While the two other original potential investors, Mick Villiers and Kevin Stevens, both indicated they could not put up any more than £2.5m, when we had to revise our target to around £5m each, Russell was the one who hung in there with us. As things progressed, he actually offered more than that.

Apart from the retainer aspect – we didn't sign anything with them and they didn't bring anything to the table – I came away from CMI's West End offices thinking we had taken another important step in the right direction, miles away from the distant days when Gary and I were hopelessly out of our depth.

But the 1895 Corporation's plans had to be put on hold due to a very important date in my diary that was simply unmissable.

May 13, FA Cup Final v Liverpool, Millennium Stadium, Cardiff.

West Ham are through to their first FA Cup final since 1980 and, due to my fall-out with the club, I've not got a ticket! And there seemed no way of me getting one until about a week before the game, when Galey mentioned that a contact of his at the FA was looking for someone to do a bit of corporate work before the big game in Cardiff. The function was being held in a marquee on the rugby pitch next door to the stadium, although I'd happily have slept in a tent all night to do the 'gig' once I heard that two

Fans enjoying their day out at the 2006 FA Cup Final.

Dean Ashton celebrates the opening goal at Cardiff.

tickets were included as perks of the job.

I was going to ask my brother Paul if he'd accompany me but he was away, so I called up my best mate John Cornwell instead and he jumped at the chance to claim the other ticket. It felt right being there with John. Way back in 1980, he, my brother and I had gone to Wembley together to see West Ham beat Arsenal, 1-0, in the 1980 FA Cup Final.

I must say that to finish ninth in the Premier League after gaining promotion was a fantastic achievement by Alan Pardew and his players and I really wanted them to end the season with a trophy. God knows, the long-suffering fans had waited long enough for some meaningful silverware since Trevor stooped to head his famous winner past Pat Jennings 26 years earlier.

As the cup run progressed, there was a moment when I wondered, 'is this going to jeopardise our bid in any way? If they beat Liverpool in the final and qualify for the UEFA Cup next season, will Terry Brown be swept away on a wave of euphoria and add another £10m to his asking price?'

It was an unbelievable start to the FA Cup Final and when we went 2-0 up thanks to Jamie Carragher's own goal and Dean Ashton's close-range strike, John and me were hugging each other and jumping for joy. You know the rest...

Djibril Cisse pulled one back and Steven Gerrard lashed home an equaliser after the break before Paul Konchesky's speculative cross put West Ham ahead again.

Stevie G had a really good game and I remember turning to John, five minutes from the end, and saying: 'We're going to win this...unless the ball drops to Gerrard'. Me and my big mouth! Instead of kicking the ball out of play, Lionel Scaloni hoofed his clearance straight to Gerrard, who beat Shaka Hislop with a stunning last-minute long-range strike that forced extra-time.

I still can't believe Marlon Harewood, the semi-final hero, missed that chance in extra-time. Never mind whether or not he was slightly injured, you forget about that in the heat of battle and he should have scored. It was a bad miss.

Paul Konchesky celebrates his goal with Nigel Reo-Coker.

Killer blow: Steve Gerrard's thunderbolt strike denied the Hammers victory.

Pepe Reina saves Anton Ferdinand's tame penalty in the shootout.

Once it went to penalties, I just didn't fancy us. Liverpool had won the 2005 Champions League final on penalties and had more experienced players. Pepe Reina saved from Bobby Zamora, Konchesky and Anton Ferdinand in the shoot-out. Dietmar Hamann, Gerrard and John Arne Riise all scored from the spot for Liverpool, with only veteran Teddy Sheringham finding the net for West Ham.

After the shootout I went downstairs to go back to the corporate area where I'd been working before the game and I bumped into a West Ham fan, who said: "They don't remember losers in the Cup final." I got up on stage with Sky's Jeff Stelling, told him what the man had just said to me and then announced to the audience: "They *will* remember the losers this year."

I know I'm biased, but it was a privilege to be at an FA Cup Final that was played in the true spirit of a proper cup final, with end to end football and six goals before the penalty shootout. It fulfilled every romantic image we used to have as kids, when every Wembley Cup final we watched on the telly seemed to be packed with drama and excitement even when they probably weren't. They were usually just illusions in our mind but what the world saw at Cardiff in '06 was definitely for real. Both sets of fans were magnificent and I was pleased to be there with them among the 74,000. For the first time in ages I felt proud to be a Hammer.

Georgia on my mind

Not much happened during the summer of 2006 by way of progress in finding new investors but it soon became clear that West Ham's success in the previous season – ninth place in the Premier League and unlucky FA Cup runners-up – had significantly boosted the club's value. Again, Gary had to revise the projected figures and when he did it showed an altogether much brighter outlook for the Hammers and its board of directors.

Having decided that we wouldn't be engaging the services of CMI, I came back from holiday in August refreshed and ready to push on and find that elusive backer we so desperately needed. I was totally consumed by the challenge. It had become an obsession.

I took a call from a guy in Switzerland called Robert who I'd first met in 2005. He first checked to see if I was still pressing on with the West Ham bid and then put me in touch with a Ukrainian banker named Michel who was working in Geneva. He was expecting my call and proceeded to tell me that he had a contact in London and another in the country of Georgia, who was worth millions of pounds and might be interested in investing with us.

Acting on Michel's advice, I phoned a guy called Gigram in Georgia and to say it was hard work was an understatement. He spoke very broken English and didn't have a clue about me or who West Ham was. After he'd listened to me talk for a few minutes about my background and plans, I quickly decided this wasn't going anywhere and Gigram wouldn't be the right man for us. It was worth the call, though – we had to follow up every lead.

We spoke to IMG, the 'global leader in sports, entertainment and media', through a contact of theirs called Rory. They were suggesting taking over ticketing and possibly funding against future commercial revenues as a way of financing some of the purchase price.

Chris Hutton kept plugging away, as did bankers Euro-IB, who had examined our projections and thought they might be able to raise what is termed 'non-recourse debt'.

We had another meeting at Euro-IB's Cheapside, London EC2 offices with Roger Jones who introduced us to his CEO, Alexander von Ungern-Sternberg. Alexander talked and looked like a German military officer from one of those classic World War Two films but he was a very intelligent man. He sent an impressive four-page letter to Russell Bartlett detailing various ways in which our £50-60m valuation of the club could be funded – a combination of equity investment, collateralised bank loan, an 'icebreaker' structured investment (tax efficient structured investment for high net worth investors) and a bridge loan to cover any timing gap for the icebreaker funds. I know, this financial jargon didn't mean much to me either at the time, so it was good to be talking to and receiving sound advice from experienced people like Alexander who clearly knew what they were doing.

But I kept coming back to the same thing: 'Where was our big investor? He (or they) must be out there somewhere...'

The look on the faces of Anton Ferdinand and Lionel Scaloni say it all at the end of a rollercoaster FA Cup Final that will live long in the memory.

18

Dagger through my heart

I WAS pleased when Sky sent me to Watford to cover their second game of the season on August 22, because West Ham were the visitors that night. What I didn't like was the ominous news I received soon after my arrival at Vicarage Road.

While standing in the tunnel area before the game, talking to Galey, my mobile rang. It was my friend Terry Creasey with some shock news: "You know the Iranian's back in the picture, don't you?"

"What?"

"Yeah, you know, Joorabchian – he's looking to put another bid in," Terry added.

"Oh, for f*** sake!"

The news felt like a dagger through my heart, the last thing I wanted to hear after working my nuts off for two years. I honestly thought that if Joorabchian was ever going to buy the club it would have been in the summer of 2005, when he burst onto the scene amid a blaze of publicity before disappearing just as quickly once West Ham told him to put up or shut up.

He didn't have the money then and even if he still didn't have enough to buy the club a year later, I knew his reappearance spelt bad news for us. I thought at the time, and still believe to this day, that he was on a massive ego trip. He loved being in the papers and with a top media PR consultant like Phil Hall, former *News of the World* editor, looking after his interests, he was never going to be short of publicity.

Much was about to unfold in the days and weeks ahead. On August 30 I met an Englishman called Jesse Learoyd-Hill, who had done a few player deals and had very good connections in the Middle East, through his father who worked in Dubai. Jesse also spoke Arabic, as I discovered when I called him and left messages on his answering machine.

Two calls change all

Jesse got my number from his friend Haffi, the Icelandic who I'd not heard from since April and was thought to be well out of the picture by now. Jesse didn't promise he would bring money to the table but he said he would speak to Haffi and see if they could come up with something.

The following day, Thursday, August 31, I received two phone calls that would change the course of our plans and have a huge impact on West Ham United.

The first was from Haffi, who rang out of the blue that morning. Even though we hadn't spoken for months, he sounded his usual bubbly self when he said: "Tony, I've got the right people. I've found the big investor."

My initial enthusiasm didn't match his, though. In the back of my mind I recalled the last potential investor he'd introduced me to, Jon Olaffson, who wasn't remotely keen to become involved and turned out to be a waste of time.

"That's good, Haffi, so who is it?" I asked, trying to sound keen.

"Well, when I was younger," he explained, "I used to play football back in Iceland with a guy called 'Siggi'."

Haffi went on to say how Siggi Bjarnason had done really well for himself, having made good money through the fishing industry. He went on to enthuse about how Siggi also had really good connections in Iceland and knew people who had serious money. He offered to arrange for Siggi, me and himself to meet up in London.

"Where will that take place, Haffi?" I asked.

"Landsbanki," he replied, "I'll get back to you when I have confirmed the date."

I'd never heard the name of Iceland's biggest private bank before and was pleased to find that its London offices were in St Botolph Street, a short walk from Liverpool Street station. On a good day, no more than a 25-minute journey from my Shenfield home.

The second call I received on the last day of August was from Sky Sports News whose reporter asked: "Have you heard the news that West Ham have

Kia Joorabchian with Carlos Tevez.

signed Carlos Tevez and Javier Mascherano?"

"Yeah, all right...is this April Fools Day?" I laughed.

Except it was no joke. The two Argentinians, who had starred for their country during the World Cup finals in Germany that summer, really were on their way to Upton Park as the biggest transfer deadline story ever.

It was very quickly revealed that they were effectively owned by Kia Joorabchian who also part-owned Corinthians, the Brazilian league club the Hammers signed the players from. This was the first time most of us in football had heard the term 'third party ownership', although we'd sure hear a lot more about it in

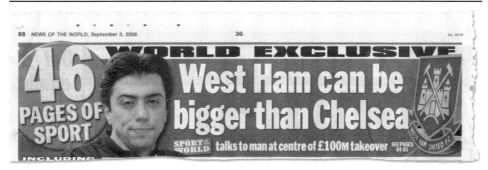

WORLD EXCLUSIVE

West Ham can be bigger than Chelsea

SPORT WORLD talks to man at centre of £100M takeover SEE PAGES 84-85

Joorabchian courted the media with claims he couldn't back up.

the months that followed.

Terry Creasey had been right – Joorabchian was back in town and this time he'd brought two headline-making acts to his media circus.

"Well, yes, they are two world class players and this is fantastic news for the club," I enthused to the SSN reporter live on air, somehow managing to conceal my inner turmoil.

I thought, 'how on earth have West Ham managed to sign two Argentine World Cup stars?' And more importantly, 'why hadn't Manchester United, Chelsea, Arsenal or Liverpool signed them instead?' The players were apparently valued by their club Corinthians at £11.5m (Mascherano) and £7.5m (Tevez) yet, apparently, West Ham were not paying any transfer fees for them. It didn't add up. Everyone in my consortium was baffled by the shock announcement but soon things became much clearer.

On September 1, West Ham released the following announcement to the stock exchange and their shareholders:

Press speculation regarding a possible offer

The Board of West Ham notes today's press speculation concerning a possible bid for the company following the signing of Carlos Tevez and Javier Mascherano on 31 August 2006.

The Board confirms that it has had exploratory discussions in relation to a possible bid but these discussions are at a very early stage and there can be no certainty that an offer for West Ham will be forthcoming. The Board also confirms that there is no contractual link between the signing of the players and the bid discussions.

In accordance with Rule 2.10 of the City Code on Takeovers and Mergers (the 'City Code'), West Ham announces that it has 20,202,352 Ordinary Shares of 25p each in issue.

A further announcement will be made as appropriate.

Deal that didn't add up

Putting aside how I felt from the perspective of trying to buy the club, from a footballing point of view I shared the fans' delight that West Ham had signed two big-name players. It was fantastic, almost on a par with Spurs' coup in signing Argentine 1978 World Cup-winning stars Ossie Ardiles and Ricky Villa.

Even though it's easy to say with hindsight that it was never going to quite go according to plan, I did have reservations from the moment they were

*A shell-shocked Alan Pardew with Carlos Tevez and Javier Mascherano
on the day they signed.*

unveiled to the media at the first press conference amid great fanfare and a blaze of publicity. The fact that neither player could speak English was bound to be a drawback and to pluck two 22-year-olds from their comfort zone in the Brazilian league and drop them into a totally different environment in East London, and expect them to have an immediate impact on the team, was asking a lot.

Although he did his best to sound delighted, you could tell from Alan Pardew's body language at the club's hastily arranged press conference that he had just been told of the new signings by West Ham's most senior executives, as opposed to Tevez and Mascherano being on his wish list.

I subsequently learned from my West Ham sources that the manager only heard very late in the day that the players would be coming to Upton Park. I felt for Pardew a bit on the day, it was clearly an awkward situation for him. There was a shambolic, amateurish feel to proceedings – at one point, I think I saw one of the tea ladies walk past the cameras carrying a tea urn.

Pardew and the two players were joined on the pitch by Miranda, the club's press officer, but surely Terry Brown and Paul Aldridge should have been there too. They should have been revelling in it, basking in the glory of signing two world class players. It was unfair on Pardew that he had to fend off questions from journalists who were bound to ask valid, searching questions that he was clearly unable to answer. As events proved, this really was too good to be true.

Hammers' fans were probably perplexed about the failure of both players to make an immediate impact. Quite apart from their obvious lack of fitness, there are so many aspects of English football that are different to what you find in most other countries. The pace of the game here is more frenetic, which places greater demands upon fitness, and it was understandable that Pardew didn't just throw them both in at the deep end, preferring to ease them in from the bench.

On the other hand, if he had put them in sooner than he did and they had got settled into the team and adapted to the special demands of the English Premier League, perhaps the club might have avoided the need for the last day heroics at Old Trafford that eventually kept them up. It was largely only after Tevez was given a decent run in the side – by then under Alan Curbishley, who had also initially been hesitant in playing him – that things started to improve. Mascherano never did get going at West Ham.

The other effect their sudden arrival had was a destabilising effect on team spirit. Put yourself in the position of the players who had done so well the previous season...ninth in the league and FA Cup Finalists, they clearly punched above their weight and deserved great credit for doing so. Then two foreign superstars turn up out of the blue and receive the acclaim of the supporters and media. The other players are thinking, 'how much money are they getting compared to us lot?' and 'why are they here if our manager doesn't actually seem keen on playing them?'

According to reports, the Argentines were Hammers' biggest earners on £1.75m each per year.

I know that they are all paid very handsomely to do a job for the club and, in an ideal world, should get on with it. But it's human nature. Their noses will have been put out of joint. That's the football dressing room for you, it's just the way it's always been. If you've worked your nuts off for the boss all year and done much to improve the company's profitability, how would you feel if the firm suddenly brought in an outsider, with no previous experience of your working environment, to replace you, and pay them much more money?

The two players whose places were most vulnerable to the threat from the South Americans were holding midfielder Hayden Mullins and striker Marlon Harewood. Hayden was a very popular figure in the dressing room and while Marlon was never my favourite player, the fact is he'd had a very good season in 2005-06.

Bobby Zamora, the other striker who could have made way for Tevez, had arguably done more than any other player the previous season to take West Ham back to the Premier League – don't remind me! For Mullins and Harewood/Zamora to lose their places under those circumstances would not have gone down well among their team-mates, you can be sure of that.

Not surprisingly, team spirit did suffer and they went on an awful run, including an abysmal League Cup defeat at Chesterfield that I covered for Sky. All the good work of the previous season started to unravel and, as well as poor results on the field, we were reading numerous negative stories and hearing a hell of a lot of rumours about all sorts of problems behind the scenes, from compulsive gambling to improper 'sexual liaisons'. I can say no more than that here.

I'm reliably informed that cliques did form – and not because of the Argentines. The different factions could have formed before they arrived.

I've been in split dressing rooms before and they are a recipe for disaster if allowed to fester and get out of control, as appeared to be the case under Pardew in the autumn of '06.

There are generally three camps: the happy ones, who are regulars because they are playing every week; the bunch who hate the manager because they're not in the team; and then there is a middle group, who are in and out of the team and their view of the manager changes according to whether or not they are in the side.

How you deal with the middle group is key and dictates how long a manager will last at a club. Lose those in the middle group to the 'rebel bad boys' and you're in trouble, because then you've got only a third of the squad playing for you.

For whatever reason, I think Pardew 'lost' his middle group of players, so there were two unhappy factions for him to handle, or not in this case.

In this instance the problems weren't only confined to football issues. There were rumours circulating on the internet forums and around the club itself about Alan Pardew's personal life. Personally, I felt the manager, his coaching staff and some of the players got carried away with what they had achieved the previous season and took their eye off the ball. The attitude changed. Some of the players thought they were better than they really were but as they must now realise, football will always kick you up the arse if you take liberties and lose concentration.

It's easily done, I've been there myself. You can believe your own publicity too much. I had to be pulled down a peg or two by John Lyall and one or two of my senior team-mates in my younger days at West Ham, even at the start of our most successful season ever, in 1985-86, when the lads pointed out to me in no uncertain terms that I wasn't working hard enough for the overall good of the team.

That's OK if there is only one or two who are proving a problem but when eight or nine drop their standards, as happened soon after the start of the 2006-07 season, it spells trouble.

19

Breaking the ice

DESPITE West Ham stating on September 1 that the signings of Carlos Tevez and Javier Mascherano "were in no way linked to a possible takeover by their agent Kia Joorabchian's MSI company", it was a futile attempt to blur the truth. The media immediately put two and two together and came up with four.

The Daily Telegraph's David Bond was on the ball when he wrote:

"While the deal was the most eye-catching it was also the most mysterious with neither club prepared to disclose the real sums of money involved or the length of the players' contracts."

The Telegraph also correctly seized upon the issue of third-party ownership well before it came back to bite the club on the backside in April '07. Bond suggested that MSI were effectively 'parking' the two Argentines at Upton Park before moving them on for a big pay day elsewhere (Mascherano left for Liverpool five months later and Tevez joined Manchester United the following summer).

He went on: "The deal is all the more intriguing because the ownership of the players is split three ways, between Corinthians, the club's London-based parent company, MSI, and a group of investment funds.

"*Further questions are certain to be prompted by the fact that MSI last year made a bid to buy West ham for £75m. That bid failed but there is bound to be speculation that the Tevez and Mascherano deal is just the start of a longer-term plan which will eventually see MSI assume control at Upton Park.*

"*Kia Joorabchian, who until recently fronted MSI and ran Corinthians, denies it is part of a takeover plan and insists the deal came about because of the good relationship built up with West Ham chairman Terry Brown during negotiations.*

"*For all the excitement, football authorities here and in Europe will be eyeing the deal nervously amid growing suspicions that some of the world's biggest clubs are operating as a cartel in the ownership of the world's best playing talent.*"

Even Sports Minister Richard Caborn got involved when he called for the football authorities and clubs to show transparency over such transfer dealings.

Who is Kia Joorabchian?

So what of the complex character who became my rival, a man I would come to despise, in the race to buy West Ham in 2006? The day after he had unveiled his two prize assets at Upton Park, Joorabchian was profiled in *The Independent* (Sept 2) by journalist Nick Harris, who tried to shed new light on this mysterious character. This is an extract from Nick's piece under the heading 'Colourful life of car dealer turned oil trader who wants to own Hammers':

If Kia Joorabchian's life story was written as fiction, it would be laughed off as incredible. Yet there seems to be the very real prospect this morning that the Iranian-born, London-based 35-year-old businessman, a university drop-out and one-time car dealer, could soon become the owner of West Ham United, with resources to transform them into major Premiership players.

He acknowledges he has backers with considerable means, but told The Independent yesterday: "I absolutely, categorically deny the money is Russian."

He has been linked persistently to controversial Russian billionaire oligarch Boris Berezovsky, who now resides in London. The pair are "friends", Joorabchian said yesterday, and have known each other since 1999, more of which later. But Joorabchian maintains that Berezovsky is not, and never has been, his backer.

Rather, he says, he has been extremely fortunate to have built up an extensive network of influential business and social contacts during a nomadic and colourful life. He knows Pele. He knows the 'super agent' Pini Zahavi. He got to know powerful people in the oil industry as a trader in his early 20s. He was involved in hedge funds in America when most people still thought that the profitable, high-risk sector had something to do with topiary.

He also got involved in the stock market and, after five years building contacts and experience, decided to chance his arm with his own investment company, American Capital, in the US. AC's first deal saw them buy 85% of one of Russia's most influential newspapers, Kommersant, or rather they thought they had bought it.

The paper, like other planned investments in 'emerging markets', would be restructured and then sold on for profit. "Except we never completed the deal," Joorabchian said. "The vendors agreed to sell it to someone else. We sued, and that's how I met Boris Berezovsky, because we ended up doing a deal, out of court, where he got the paper, and we got a settlement. I've known him ever since, but that was the first and last time I have done business with him. People can try to link us all the time, but I'm telling you there is no financial link."

Joorabchian said that AC branched into hedge funds and became a "boutique investment house". Things went well until 9/11, when the markets "became volatile and I wanted out". He says he sold his company for "between £50m and £60m" and returned to England, to be closer to his sick father. Joorabchian then ran several low-key businesses, including a health spa in Camden, north London, and an investment company dealing with Iran that was not very successful.

It was after a chance meeting with Pele's agent that Pele convinced him to put his money into football, and Brazilian football in particular. Pini Zahavi, another contact, agreed.

In August 2004, he set up a company, Media Sports Investment, with a 'shell' office in central London. He bought Corinthians in Brazil and, with assistance from anonymous backers, spent £50m on club and players, including Tevez. The rest is recent history.

Other journalists greeted Joorabchian's explosive arrival in East London much less enthusiastically. Under the headline 'Football sold out long before West Ham did', *News of the World* columnist and sports writer of the year Martin Samuel began his typically no-holds barred reactionary piece (Sept 3) with:

Shadowy. Murky. Suspicious. Worrying. All adjectives used in the last few days to describe the arrival of Carlos Tevez and Javier Mascherano at Upton Park.

Who gets the fees? Who owns the assets? Whose money bankrolls it all? Will there be a takeover? Is this a Russian carve-up?

The *Daily Telegraph's* Sue Mott also expressed some concern in her piece (Sept 5) under the heading: 'Fever over West Ham hotshots gives cold clues to a mad world':

If companies or individuals,

Joorabchian was given the red carpet treatment by West Ham.

rather than clubs, are allowed to own and operate world class players as though they were bars of gold bullion on legs and if clubs are allowed to be bought by so-called businessmen behind whom lurk a number of unnamed investors, then it leads us merrily on the road to corruption.

There is absolutely no reason to believe that Mr Kia Joorabchian, who is moving and shaking the two Argentines just now, is anything other than a bona-fide operator, despite listing conflicting dates of birth with Companies House, owning several businesses in financial distress and apparently working with someone called Boris who is always described as 'an exiled Russian oligarch'. His purity of motive cannot be doubted from the evidence thus far obtained, especially as he calls the two players in his care, his 'babies'. Bless him.

But if you imagine another, shadier character in this position, only interested in profits, hawking players like living oil barrels all over the world, only anarchy can ensue. We have worried for years about lunatics – i.e. players – running the asylum. Now we face the prospect of the lunatic's agent running the asylum, which is infinitely, dramatically, worse. Mad men achieve mayhem by accident. Sane crooks achieve the same effect by design.

Award-winning journalist Mihir Bose, also writing in the *Telegraph* (Sept 7), appreciated the probable long-term benefits to owning West Ham when he added:

West Ham are attractive not merely because of Tevez and Mascherano, but because of London 2012. In six years the Olympic Games will transform the East End. There will be an Olympic Park, a shopping centre, new housing and a stadium seating 80,000 available to football after 2012.

Much more is now known and has been written about Joorabchian since early September '06, especially his controversial management of the nomadic Carlos Tevez, but the above is just a flavour of the picture painted by the

A rare sight...Carlos Tevez and Javier Mascherano together on the Upton Park turf.

British media at the time we were rivals to buy West Ham.

At the first home game following the capture of the Argentines, Joorabchian was spotted sitting next to Paul Aldridge in the directors' box at Upton Park on the day Hammers drew 1-1 with Aston Villa. Perhaps it was merely the club's polite way of saying 'thanks' for the two gifts that had fallen into their lap.

As David Bond of *The Telegraph* (Sept 14) pointed out:

"Contrary to reports at the time of the transfers, it is believed West Ham do not stand to make anything from the future sales of the players.

"While no transfers fee were paid to Corinthians, the club they left for West Ham, sources say there was a commitment to pay up to £5m to two companies who shared equally the ownership of Macherano's 'economic rights'."

Pini Zahavi certainly wasn't working just for the fun of it either. One paper claimed West Ham had to pay £5m in agents' fees to secure the Argentines.

Red carpet treatment

It annoyed me to see Joorabchian being given the red carpet treatment by the club who gave him exclusive use of their newly-converted directors' suite, a lounge that held around 20 people and was adjacent to the main boardroom area in the Dr Martens Stand. Surrounded by his family and cronies, the man was clearly being courted by the club and this gesture looked for all the world like a sweetener.

That lounge should have been filled by a paying sponsor or one of the club's biggest corporate clients, as indeed it subsequently was. I thought it was poor judgement on the part of the club but the inescapable fact was that Joorabchian has brought two fine players to West Ham and I hadn't. It definitely gave him a big advantage over us and there is no point in denying it, he gave us cause for concern.

September 6, 2006, first meeting at Landsbanki.

Haffi arranged our first meeting at the Landsbanki Corporate Finance offices in London for 2pm that Tuesday. I went with Gary and as well as Haffi and Jesse also being present, the Icelandics were represented by Steinar Kristjansson and a couple of his assistants, one of whom left within about five minutes.

I basically did a presentation telling them what a wonderful investment it would be, selling the virtues of the club and its history, before Gary went through the figures. I also told them that the deal would only go ahead if I was involved. I reiterated the point I'd made from day one: the importance of having someone in the boardroom with a strong West Ham connection who knew what the club was all about. As I said, I'd passed the point of worrying where the actual money was coming from but the club still had to go in the right direction as far as I was concerned, as opposed to them getting in on the back of me before pushing me aside.

This was something Gary and I had spoken about and feared could happen. But what could we do? You can't ask someone to invest serious money in a project and not show your full hand in terms of financial calculations, projected costs and revenues plus background reports on the company you are aiming to purchase. The Icelandics were in full possession of all our figures ahead of our first meeting at Landsbanki. There was always the risk they, or any other potential major investor, would cut me loose once the deal was done but that's the big, bad world of corporate finance. All I could do was ride the waves and hope I got the rewards at the end for all the effort Gary and I had put in.

Apart from all the reports and figures that I've mentioned and which had to be regularly adjusted and re-presented by Gary as the club's fortunes improved on and off the field between 2004 and '06, we even got hold of a confidential Initial Development Assessment report that West Ham had commissioned on the Boleyn Ground and was delivered to them in April '06. The report basically informed the Hammers' board of the true residual land value from both a residential and commercial retail aspect. There were projections of what it was likely to cost to build and sell rows of densely populated houses and/or flats, plus a major foodstore and other retail units in the event the football ground was sold and the club moved to a new stadium.

Given the fact that Terry Brown had accumulated most of his wealth through shrewd property investments since the 60s, he would have immediately grasped the full worth of the land on which the stadium is built and how it could be used to further maximise profit. The same possibilities were no doubt occupying the thoughts of the current owners, David Sullivan and David Gold, when the club declared its intention to move from the Boleyn Ground – home to the club since 1904 – and move into the Olympic Stadium at Stratford from season 2014-15.

So we had all our updated figures, projections and God knows what else and now we also had this dossier to show our potential investors what a prime asset the Boleyn Ground site was – or should I say still is – to a major investor in West Ham. We could hardly have been more thorough in our research and planning, as our new contacts from Iceland would soon discover.

Not that the people we met at that first meeting gave anything away. Like hard-nosed poker players, they listened intently and emotionless to what I had to say, took it all in and said very little. But I think they quickly appreciated West Ham's huge potential. At the end of the first meeting we exchanged email addresses, business cards, then shook hands and agreed to talk again soon once they had fully digested everything.

The Icelandics might not have known too much about West Ham before we walked through their door but they understood the potential financial benefits as well as the glamour associated with owning one of 20 English Premier League clubs. Ownership of a very well-supported London club like West Ham would have raised the profile of Landsbanki, which, as it turned out, was exactly what happened. I think I even mentioned the glamour and raising of profile aspects in my presentation to them, although for Gary and I it was all about securing the investment.

A few hours before our second meeting with the Icelandics, I met a guy called David Bick, who was introduced to me by Chris Hutton. David was a PR man and West Ham supporter who had been closely involved with the Whistle supporters' pressure group created by fans that were critical of Terry Brown following the club's relegation in 2003 and the subsequent sale of many of their top players. In April 2004, the group published a dossier accusing the board of financial incompetence, and asking 180 questions regarding the club's finances. Whistle claimed that around £20m had been pledged to them by anonymous investors willing to buy into the club via a share issue if major lenders – Barclays Bank being the main one – could force Brown to step down.

Keith Harris, the charismatic boss of investment broker Seymour Pierce.

In an unprecedented move where a club sued its own supporters, Brown took legal action against three members of the Whistle group, so David Bick was about as welcome at Upton Park as me. For that reason, he couldn't be seen to represent us in this process but he put me in touch with someone who could.

David was close to Keith Harris, chairman of Seymour Pierce Ltd, who a month earlier had brokered American Randy Lerner's £62m takeover of Aston Villa and Michael Wilde's acquisition of Southampton. Keith was someone I'd met briefly some 10 years earlier when he was chairman of The Football League. A nice bloke, he had made a niche for himself at Seymour Pierce and, basically, if you wanted to buy a football club he was the go-to man. He was later also involved in Thaksin Shinawatra's takeover at Manchester City in 2007.

I should perhaps explain at this point that when a consortium like ours wants to buy a football club, even when you have all the funding and everything else in place, you still need someone to broker the deal, act as a go-between and make it happen. This particularly applies when you are dealing with PLCs, because you have to produce offer documents and it all has to be done properly within FSA regulations. You just can't roll up at a club and plonk £60m in used readies on the chairman's desk!

We'd been advised by others and now David Bick to engage an investment broker with a proven track record like Seymour Pierce, so that's what we did. We were due to meet them for the first time on September 18...four days before we were back 'shopping' at Iceland again.

September 14, 2006, second meeting at Landsbanki.

Haffi remained our go-between with the Icelandics and at this meeting, as well as Steinar Kristjansson and his assistant, Haffi's footballing mate from back home, Siggi Bjarnason, was also there, along with Gary, Jesse and myself. We didn't take Russell Bartlett or Chris Hutton with us at the time because it wasn't relevant – we were still feeling out the Icelandics to see if they really were going to become big investors or just another waste of time.

Siggi mentioned that he had wealthy contacts in Iceland who he thought would be interested. And although Steinar was employed by Landsbanki, there was no suggestion up until that point that the Icelandic bank itself would be investing in us. The way we saw it at the time, there would be three or four individual Icelandic investors forming a mini consortium to become our single major investor in our larger consortium with a 62% shareholding in the club – or an equity investment of about £36m. We envisaged the rest would be made up of Russell Bartlett's 31%, leaving the remaining 7% to be split between myself and other potential shareholders. Joorabchian was being linked with a £60m takeover bid, so the Icelandics and ourselves knew what we were up against.

As Siggi had not been present at the first meeting in the bank, I had to virtually repeat my presentation for his benefit and it was another positive meeting, albeit there was still no emotion shown. When the meeting ended, Gary, Jesse and myself left the bank and sat in a café about 20 yards along the road in St Botolph Street for a de-brief, while Haffi stayed in the meeting room with the other Icelandics to mull over what had been said.

When he joined us at the café about 20 minutes later, he was very excited. He said: "This deal is definitely going to happen...even the chairman is interested." I didn't quite realise it at the time, but he was referring to the chairman of the bank, Bjorgolfur Gudmundsson.

Siggi said he was a West Ham fan and to back up his claims he had tickets for the home UEFA Cup game against Palermo, which Gary and I were also going to that night. But instead of joining us for a lift to the ground, Siggi skipped the match and flew back to Iceland to speak to his friends about what we had been discussing.

It was a really good second meeting at Landsbanki and afterwards I felt excited that something positive would happen soon. Joorabchian's re-appearance spurred us on again. We now knew we had a serious opponent, although, when push came to shove, I still didn't really believe he would come up with all the money he was talking about. In addition to paying £60m for the full shares, he was also boasting to the press about a further £100m injection for new players. Yeah, right. Who did he think he was, Roman Abramovich? Despite his apparent delusions of grandeur, we couldn't treat him lightly. The fact that he had supplied the club with two top quality internationals players seemed to put him in the driving seat.

He was getting plenty of media attention, too, although much of it was far from positive. As we had done from day one, we continued to stay out of the press and remain under the radar. We didn't employ a PR agency to drum up publicity or try and schmooze our way through Fleet Street and Wapping. Maybe we should have.

It became very irritating, while speaking to West Ham fans around this time, to hear them enthuse about Joorabchian and all he was doing and could do for the club. I felt like saying to them, 'if only you knew what *I* am trying to do for our club'. Surely, given that choice, the supporters would rather have had me – West Ham through and through – in the boardroom than someone of his background?

September 18, first meeting at Seymour Pierce

Our next destination was Queen Victoria Street, London, EC4 and the offices of investment brokers Seymour Pierce, where David Bick joined Chris Hutton, Gary and me at a meeting with their charismatic company chairman Keith Harris. By now I could reel off all the virtues of investing in West Ham without needing to refer to notes. Keith promised me that he wouldn't get involved in any deal with West Ham if it didn't include me – he could see how hard I'd worked to get this far and acknowledged that I was the main man putting the deal together.

He mentioned he was a good friend of Terry Brown and would talk to him at the appropriate moment, so that was another positive meeting. We weren't quite there but yet but we were getting close.

September 21, meeting at Euro-IB

All of our existing consortium – Russell, Paul Duffen, Chris, Gary, Rory from IMG and myself, plus our solicitors Ben and David – were there at 9.30am to meet our hosts Alexander von Ungern-Sternberg and Roger Jones while Paul Panayi, our latest recruit, was on conference call in Biarritz, France. Paul, who ran a wealth management company in the City called Howard and Co., came on board relatively late but he had the idea to raise £10m via a SIPP (Self-Invested Personal Pension) equity scheme involving West Ham supporters.

Landsbanki had requested a third meeting with us, scheduled for 1.00pm that afternoon, so it was an important day.

The gathering at Euro-IB was a strategy meeting to finalise our final push, if you like, and I was pleased to find that each consortium member reinforced their commitment to proceed. By mid-September we had assumed a purchase price of £70m, with a further £10m needed to spend on new players in the January '07 transfer window

On behalf of mine and Gary's 1895 Corporation, I had in fact signed the letter of engagement with Euro-IB a couple of days prior to this meeting. I was put under a bit of pressure to sign the agreement that guaranteed

Euro-IB £50k for at least three months' work but I could understand their position.

There was an air of paranoia around at this time as people tried to protect themselves from being cast adrift or gazumped before the last hurdle. Obviously, we were all looking towards a pay day at the end of it all as just reward for all our efforts but as I scanned the room at these 10 people sat around a large boardroom table, without wishing to blow my own trumpet too loudly, it struck me that I'd brought these people together and it hadn't cost a thing in legal fees, just personal travel expenses. We were all in the same boat and assumed that Euro-IB would recoup their guaranteed fee after the deal had been completed with West Ham.

For a while I'd stopped worrying about Joorabchian and never felt as positive or optimistic as I did at the end of this meeting. It was all falling into place, the ducks were almost in a row. We had about £60m in pledges from our consortium members. And we had the so-called boutique investment bank Euro-IB, who were going to raise £30m through non-recourse debt, which left £20m more needed from one big investor to complete the package.

We hoped the Icelandics would be that other investor, the final missing piece in the jigsaw. After grabbing a quick sandwich, we were going to see them next...

20

It's personal

THE first sign of a problem with the Icelandics came at our third meeting, on the morning of September 21. Although they were very keen to get involved with us, they cooled a bit when I mentioned that I had engaged Euro-IB as our investment bank, an agreement I'd signed in all good faith.

But the Icelandics pointed out that they wanted one of their own securities houses, Teather and Greenwood, to handle our deal with West Ham, which was perfectly understandable given that we regarded them as our single biggest investor. We didn't need two investment banks dealing with the club on our behalf but I dug my heels in a bit and said that I wanted Euro-IB to remain involved. The way I left it that day was that Landsbanki would liaise and work together with Euro-IB to try and keep things moving forward.

The following day Keith Harris went to see Terry Brown. We thought that by appointing Seymour Pierce as our investment broker, it would give us a certain credibility that surely even Brown couldn't dismiss. Keith and Terry were old friends anyway, so surely that could only be of further benefit to us...or so I thought.

When Keith reported back to us following his 'sounding out' meeting at Upton Park, the first thing that struck me was the news that the West Ham chairman was now demanding £75m for the 100% shareholding, which came as a surprise. As far as we knew, Joorabchian had offered only £60m. Keith told us that Terry had indicated to him that MSI had offered to buy the club for £70m but he wanted £5m extra from whoever Joorabchian's rival bidder turned out to be.

There was inevitable speculation about who was backing the Joorabchian bid, which was typically shrouded in mystery. As mentioned earlier, the press were quick to link him to Russian oligarch Boris Berezovsky, the 60-year-old London businessman who was Russia's first billionaire. Joorabchian also denied a more far-fetched rumour that Berezovsky's former business partner, Chelsea owner Roman Abramovich, was one of his 'mystery backers'.

Georgian billionaire and Dynamo Tbilisi FC owner Badri Patarkatsishvili was also mentioned in *The Times* as a potential source of cash for Joorabchian, along with an unnamed consortium or individuals from Iran. The other man closely linked to him was Israeli property magnate Eli Papouchado who, as

Israeli to back West Ham bid

Property tycoon behind Red Sea Group will join international consortium stalking the Upton Park club

By Jeff Randall

A CONTROVERSIAL Israeli property magnate, Eli Papouchado, with business interests in Britain, America and the Middle East, is one of the money men backing a possible bid for West Ham United.

Known by friends as "Papo", he is expected to join a group of investors being assembled by Kia Joorabchian, a 35-year-old Anglo-Iranian entrepreneur, who is considering making an offer for the Upton Park club.

Mr Joorabchian burst on to English football's centre stage 10 days ago, when his management company sold two of Argentina's World Cup stars, Carlos Tevez and Javier Mascherano, to West Ham.

The deal was a stunner, not least because only three seasons ago the club had been on the brink of bankruptcy.

But when it emerged that the Hammers had paid no transfer fee - not a penny - for the South American superstars, estimated to be worth £40m, conspiracy theorists went into overdrive. Mr Joorabchian, however, insists that the terms of deal are not linked to any takeover move.

Mr Papouchado founded Red Sea Group in the 1960s. The company's activities include the management of hotel, residential, retail and medical properties in Israel, Europe, the United States and South Africa. It is understood to employ more than 1,000 people worldwide.

In recent years, the business has been increasingly by Mr Papouchado's son, Avner. Four years ago, it took a controlling stake in the Gresham Hotels, an Irish company, and shook up the board before selling out.

The unveiling of Mr Papouchado as one of Mr Joorabchian's financial supporters will intensify speculation that a full bid for West Ham is imminent. Last week, Mr Joorabchian was spotted with the club's chief executive, Paul Aldridge, in a London restaurant.

If Mr Joorabchian decides to press the Go button, Mr Papouchado is expected to play no part in the management of West Ham. His participation would be simply as a passive investor in Mr Joorabchian's consortium.

"Eli wouldn't know West Ham from West Brom," said an associate. "He is not really interested in football."

In order to take full control of West Ham, Mr Joorabchian must make the club's share-holding, and last season played in one of the most thrilling FA Cup finals for years, losing on penalties to Liverpool, after the match had ended 3-3.

With revenues boosted by that cup run and the prospect of further commercial benefits from playing in this season's Uefa Cup, West Ham's finances are healthier than for a long time. Debts are thought to be about £20m, down from more than £70m.

In the bizarre world of football, where the value of money is often detached from reality, putting a price-tag on non-quoted shares is an imprecise process.

Some analysts reckon West Ham could be worth about the same as Aston Villa, which recently changed hands for £60m. Add in the Hammers' debt, and that suggests Mr Joorabchian must offer about £80m.

Double take: Carlos Tevez and Javier Mascherano show off their new shirts after their shock transfer to West Ham, in a deal clouded in secrecy

---

MEDIA

News Corp pays rent on Murdoch's penthouse

By David Litterick in New York

NEWS Corporation is paying $50,000 (£27,000) a month to rent a New York apartment for chairman Rupert Murdoch, even though the media baron was paid more than $25m in salary and bonus last year.

The apartment is understood to be a penthouse in the Trump Park Avenue building, which stands at the bottom of the exclusive Upper East Side near the corner of Central Park.

News Corp said it had been paying $50,000 a month rent, plus around $500 a month in utility and maintenance costs since May.

Mr Murdoch recently sold his apartment in Manhattan's Soho neighbourhood and is renovating another penthouse on the Upper East Side that he bought from Laurence Rockefeller for $44m two years ago.

Patrick McGurn, a corporate-governance expert at Institutional Shareholder Services, a shareholder advisory firm, said he had never heard of a company paying for an executive's personal residence in the city in which the company has its headquarters.

"Does News Corp pay for his primary residence? No. So why would they pay for the replacement residence?" he said. "That just boggles the mind."

News Corp said the New York apartment was akin to a second residence for Mr Murdoch, "While Mr Murdoch's New York home is being renovated, his family is staying at their home in Los Angeles," a company spokesman said.

"Given Mr Murdoch's business requirements in New York, the company decided that for its convenience it would pay for an apartment in New York for Mr Murdoch for the duration of the renovation."

He added that Mr Murdoch will pay taxes on the benefit. Mr Murdoch's total compensation was 10pc up on the previous year and includes a $21m bonus.

---

one of his friends put it, "wouldn't know West Ham from West Brom".

None of which really mattered to the West Ham board of directors, especially Brown, who stood to make around £32m from either deal. He must have been rubbing his hands in glee when he was first contacted, on our behalf, by Keith Harris and was told that there was now a second serious bidder virtually in place and eager to buy the club. For Brown, it must have seemed a long way from the dark days of 2003, when chants of 'Brown Out!' reverberated around Upton Park at many home games and the club's best players were about to be sold off.

Despite his friendship with Brown, Keith didn't reveal the identity of his client at that stage – he was working for us, not West Ham – but the chairman gave us more encouragement when he indicated to Keith that he could guarantee the sale of 84% of the shares – principally the two-thirds controlling interest held by himself and fellow directors Charles Warner and Martin Cearns, along with several lesser shareholders such as David Sullivan, Paul Aldridge and relatives of the main trio of board members. Although the business was nominally a public company, the remaining 16% of shareholders could not have prevented a takeover. Once a buyer obtains more than 90%, the rest of the shares can be compulsorily purchased.

Keith said his hour-long talk with Brown had gone well and he sensed a clear indication that Terry had had enough of all the speculation surrounding the future of the club and was ready to sell if the right offer came in.

But before they ended their meeting the Hammers chairman added a proviso that hit me personally like a sledgehammer. "I take it Tony Cottee is not involved in this," he remarked to the boss of Seymour Pierce.

Keith said he had not mentioned my name in his conversation with Brown and told me later that he did not confirm or deny my involvement when my name came up at the end of their meeting. But Keith made it clear when we spoke after his meeting at West Ham that Terry Brown definitely still had a problem with me.

I thought we'd moved on from the ill feeling he had shown towards me 18 months previously, when I was sacked as a corporate host. Since then I had done nothing to publicly damage or destabilise the club in any way – unlike Joorabchian, who had been spouting off to the press again about how he was going to buy the club and transform it into a European super power.

If anything, I'd ignored – some might say wasted – an opportunity to court support from the fans and potential investors by NOT entering into a public contest with Joorabchian. When the wheels started to come off at West Ham and Alan Pardew 'lost' the dressing room soon after the start of the 2006-07 season, it would have been very easy, and possibly advantageous to me, to undermine the manager, his team and the board of directors. How could they have allowed it to go pear-shaped so soon after such a wonderful season?

West Ham lost eight consecutive games (including the League Cup fiasco at League One Chesterfield), their worst run for 74 years, went seven games without scoring and were on the back pages for all the wrong reasons. At any time during that horrendous run I could have gone to the press and used my wealth of contacts to ignite a media frenzy against the board of directors presiding over yet another shambolic series of events in the club's chequered history. They could hardly deny how badly things had got – even Brown was widely quoted as having described the side beaten 2-1 at Chesterfield as a "pub team".

During this turbulent time I spoke to a number of influential national sports journalists, including Martin Samuel, Paul McCarthy, Rob Shepherd, Lee Horton and Lee Clayton – all West Ham supporters – who were very supportive and kept all my takeover plans under wraps at my request. They knew what I was working on behind the scenes and how close we were to succeeding but they agreed to hold fire until such time as it was right for us to go public. In fact, I made calls to them seeking advice about how to play it, even wondering if it might be in our best interests, tactically, to be more public with our plans, and they told me there was nothing to be gained by trying to wage a public war with Joorabchian.

I could have exploited any one of several moles I had inside the club to heap even more pressure on the board. Did Terry Brown honestly not consider that I had good contacts in and around the club who were regularly updating me with tasty titbits of gossip that the tabloids would have gobbled up had I leaked it to them?

I had a mole at the training ground drip-feeding me information and another one working in the offices at the stadium. I had moles everywhere who would phone up and tell me about meetings going on behind closed doors, with whom, when and where.

At any stage I could have pressed the button and fired nuclear missiles over Green Street E13 to set things off but I continued to believe that it was not in our best interests to do so. Instead, I kept my head down and focused on what I needed to do.

When I'd phoned Terry Brown the previous year and he bawled me out and made it clear he definitely wanted £60m for the club, I went away and came up with a revised plan to raise £60m. Then when told by Keith Harris that he had put the price up to £75m, as he was perfectly entitled to do, I went away again and tried to raise another £15m. But then he insulted me by saying he wanted nothing to do with me or any consortium I was involved in.

Brown had turned it into a personal issue and it was a bitter pill to swallow.

For me, it had become personal with Joorabchian too. It got to the point, in the last quarter of '06, where I had two agendas: a) to take over West Ham; and b), if I couldn't, then I was hell bent on stopping Joorabchian from doing so. Everything I heard about some of the characters he surrounded himself with up in the directors' lounge disgusted me. He'd already given me the hump by not returning my phone call and by now I wanted to stop him buying the club at all costs.

I honestly still believe that West Ham would have imploded within two years if he had taken control of the club with his 'mystery' foreign investors, a foreign players' agent renowned for moving his helpless clients around like pawns in a chess game; the inevitable fashionable foreign manager; and a team packed with foreign imports.

Before the PC brigade get on their high horse, this is not the rant of a xenophobe. In trying to buy the club, my consortium was simply trying to preserve its best traditions, a footballing ethos and culture imbued in generations of players and staff who played or worked under Ron Greenwood and John Lyall for so many years throughout the 60s, 70s and 80s. Call it an old fashioned idealogy, but it still meant something to us. Still does.

As it happened, I didn't need to wage a public war with Joorabchian because the press were already busy digging up plenty of dirt on him. He wasn't exactly being portrayed as the ideal new custodian of West Ham. With his 'flash' demeanour and hangers-on, he was doing a pretty good job of shooting himself in the foot without any help from our camp.

Ultimately, though, Joorabchian wasn't my biggest problem. The fact that Terry Brown still held a grudge against me meant we had to come up with a different strategy as far as my role in the consortium was concerned.

21

Who the f*** is Eggert Magnusson?

IN trying to keep our bid alive and deal with Terry Brown's personal grievance with me, it became clear that my role in the consortium had to be redefined. At our next meeting, on September 25, it was suggested that instead of being the next West Ham United chairman, I could become the club's first football director, forming an important link between the manager and board of directors.

Paul Duffen had emerged from within our group as the ideal candidate to assume the role of chairman. He was perfect for the top job.

Much as it annoyed me, I also had to accept the unanimous view of my fellow consortium members that, for our bid to succeed, I had to adopt a low profile from now on. My name could not appear on the indicative offer document we were poised to present to West Ham, although my presence on the board would still have been guaranteed if we had taken over the club.

We all agreed that we needed the Icelandic investment, which became the last piece in the jigsaw. Euro-IB were instructed to liaise with Landsbanki and hopefully get them to commit as quickly as possible.

In the meantime, amid another flurry of phone calls and emails back and forth, Gary and I also had the matter of dealing with Haffi and Jesse, who, if the deal went ahead, were both rightly anticipating an introductory fee for bringing the Icelandics to the table. There was a snag, however. Because I took a back seat at this delicate stage of negotiations, our original 1895 Corporation Ltd vehicle had to be abandoned, so Gary and myself were no longer in a position to promise them anything by way of commission. This matter could only be dealt with once the club had given an irrevocable undertaking to accept our offer.

I could understand how insecure Haffi and Jesse must have felt, though. I, too, was feeling very vulnerable. It had been my 'baby' since the word go but now I was struggling to stay in control of a runaway train as it approached its long-awaited destination but my growing fears that our bid could be derailed or hijacked at the eleventh hour turned out to be absolutely correct.

Before they showed their hand, the Icelandics emailed us with a request for further information relating to West Ham. Apart from wanting sight of their latest set of accounts for the year-ending May 31, 2006, they asked us to estimate the current valuation of the playing squad and wanted to know what the Boleyn Ground was worth. At the time, we were privately speculating on the possibility of the club moving to the 80,000 Olympic Stadium at Stratford after the 2012 Games, which was naturally also of great interest to our biggest investor.

On Friday, September 29 we received a phone call from Roger Jones at Euro-IB to confirm that the Icelandics were 'in'. Landsbanki had agreed to be part of our consortium and they informed us that a guy called Eggert Magnusson would be their man named on the offer document that Seymour Pierce were preparing to send to West Ham.

What is called an 'Indicative Offer' for West Ham United PLC was sent to Terry Brown on Tuesday, October 3. Subject to due diligence, our basic offer to buy the club was in the range of £65m to £75m.

The four parties named on the indicative offer document, along with their respective background summaries, and how our purchase would be funded, was set out as follows:

R3 Investment Group Limited is a property investment business ultimately owned by Russell Bartlett, a UK businessman and a life-long keen West Ham supporter and box holder. Mr Bartlett has over 30 years' property experience and owns and controls an extensive property portfolio that includes large corporate and central government buildings.

Paul Duffen is CEO of Catalyst Media Group plc (CMG), a media company which he co-founded in 1999 and floated on the AIM market of the London Stock Exchange in May 2000. Under Mr Duffen's leadership, over the past seven years CMG has been very active in the M&A field and has successfully raised over £75m in debt and equity to enable various acquisitions. The main focus of these transactions has been media companies specialising in extracting value from sports rights, specifically motor racing in the USA and horse racing in the UK.

Eggert Magnusson has been prominent in international football for some years and is currently serving on the Executive Committee of UEFA, having been a member of various committees within both UEFA as well as FIFA for the last 15 years. He has been the President of The Football Association of Iceland for the last 17 years. He also serves as a board member of investment bank Straumur–Burdaras and Avion Group.

Howard & Co is an FSA-registered IFA specialising in wealth management for professionals, who have advised in recent years on completed investments amounting to £487m.

In addition to the equity funding being provided by the above, amounting to approximately £40m, the Bidco (our consortium) has received assurance subject to due diligence in respect of additional non-equity funding from:

IMG, the world's premier sports, entertainment and media company in respect of revenues from the club's commercial operations.

Icebreaker Management, in respect of a new sporting future LLP who would make available £10m.

A UK-based bank for non-recourse finance.

A question of trust

Seeing Magnusson named as the Icelandics' proposed representative on the new West Ham board didn't set alarm bells ringing in my head at that stage. It came down to a matter of trust. I'd got to know all of the people in my consortium well over a long period and I had absolute faith in them, whereas the Icelandics had emerged very late in the process. I didn't know them or what their motives were but, as our only remaining option as the major investor, we had to show faith in them. Our brief dealings with them at Landsbanki had been very businesslike, not pally-pally. I was just thrilled that we had reached the stage where Keith Harris had sent our proposal to West Ham. We were nearly there.

Even so, I still had my doubts. Indeed, the previous night I'd met up with a guy called Richie at Liverpool Street station, to try and implement a contingency plan just in case something went wrong with the money men from Iceland. Richie was an East End lad who had put some sponsorship West Ham's way. He was a friend of ex-West Ham player Stuart Slater, who knew Richie had good financial contacts.

During our chat over a drink, Richie mentioned that he had a pal based in the Caribbean who potentially had between £20m and £30m to invest in West Ham. Our conversation didn't really go any further than that.

On the night of October 3, the day our indicative offer was sent to the club, Gary and I went for a meal in Brentwood with Chris Adams, a steel markets broker and corporate box-holder at Upton Park who worked with Dean Carr (son of West Ham Academy Director Tony Carr). Again, Chris appeared very interested and indicated that he could come up with £10m to invest.

The discussions we had with both Richie and Chris were simply off-the-record talks about a possible Plan B option but they were enough to send me to bed that night with a smile on my face. I slept content in the knowledge that we had put in a provisional bid to West Ham while also keeping other investment options open.

We had not received any verbal or written response from the club before the *London Evening Standard* broke the news on October 5 that an unnamed second consortium – a rival to Joorabchian – had made a bid for the Hammers. Ken Dyer's exclusive back page lead story contained no quotes from any of the interested parties and did not mention any of our consortium members by name, although there was a passing reference to 'foreign backers'. Clearly, someone at West Ham had leaked our bid to Ken – yet another West Ham-supporting journalist I'd known well from my earliest playing days who, as far as the club was concerned, became the most trusted of all scribes covering events on and off the field at Upton Park.

On October 6, and with still no further word from Terry Brown, I received a call from Roger Jones to say that there would be a consortium meeting at Landsbanki on October 9 at 10.30am. He then started to begin a string of sentences with the words "Eggert Magnusson has said this" and "Eggert Magnusson has said that." It irritated me so much that I had to interrupt him to ask: 'Roger, I'm not being funny, but who the f*** is Eggert Magnusson?'

"He's the guy who is representing the Icelandics," Roger replied.

I said: "This is MY consortium, it's not Eggert Magnusson's consortium. I don't want to hear you say 'Eggert Magnusson said this and Eggert Magnusson said that' anymore." I lost my rag with Roger, a rather placid guy who was perhaps a bit too laid back at times. I had no problem with Magnusson being named on the offer document as the designated

SPORT

It's a return to London
or bust for Parlour
Page 64 ▶

New consortium in for West Ham

Chelsea hit back after Real chief's Roman jibe

LEO SPALL
Football Correspondent

CHELSEA today hit back at Real Madrid's claims that billionaire owner Roman Abramovich is ready to walk away from them.

The Spanish club's chairman, Ramon Calderon, believes Chelsea's future would be threatened if the Russian leaves.

He said: "You don't know how long those people are going to stay in soccer. If somebody decides to leave, it's going to be a problem."

But Chelsea insist Abramovich is staying with them and has no plans to turn his back on English football.

Communications director Simon Greenberg said: "I would not doubt Roman Abramovich's commitment, not just to Chelsea but to football generally."

Calderon also feels Chelsea are artificially inflating the current transfer market to the detriment of the rest of Europe.

He told BBC Radio Five Live: "It's a problem — it's putting the prices very high. He is paying a lot of money for players but we have no competition with it. In Abramovich's case, he admitted to having lost 220million euros last season. It's very dangerous."

Rivals battle to scupper Kia takeover

EXCLUSIVE
KEN DYER
Football Correspondent

A SECOND consortium is attempting to win the fight to take over West Ham.

Standard Sport can reveal today that rival bidders to Kia Joorabchian are attempting to raise the investment to buy out chairman Terry Brown.

The club are aware of the secret new consortium — who also have foreign backers — and its plans to raise the finance to prevent Joorabchian getting his hands on the club.

West Ham were today continuing to have communication with Joorabchian, the Iranian-born businessman who is heading a consortium — linked to Israeli property magnates — hoping to take over the Premiership club.

The West Ham board of directors gathered yesterday for a regular board meeting with the takeover top of the agenda and decided they would not impose a time limit on the takeover talks. The final figure for the buyout may be around £90million with Brown's stake worth in the region of £20m.

Brown is eager for the matter to be resolved before West Ham's next match, at Portsmouth on Saturday week, but has not given Joorabchian a deadline.

Any proposed takeover deal has been delayed by the recent death of Joorabchian's father.

Religious beliefs meant Joorabchian was precluded from working for 40 days following his father's death.

Manager Alan Pardew also attended the board meeting. As Standard Sport revealed yesterday, the West Ham boss

Under pressure: West Ham chairman Terry Brown is anxious to finalise a deal before the club's next game

denied speculation that he had threatened to walk out if the matter isn't resolved swiftly.

The club issued a statement last night on the issue, with Pardew saying: "I absolutely did not threaten to resign in any shape or form. I have a good working relationship with the board and we are working hard to turn the poor results around."

West Ham have drawn once and lost five in a row since Argentine superstars Carlos Tevez and Javier Mascherano were brought to the club just before the close of the August transfer window.

The players came from Brazilian club Corinthians, who are part owned by investment company Media Sports Investment, for whom 33-year-old Joorabchian

worked. The Iranian played a part in getting the two players to the club.

Meanwhile, West Ham midfielder Lee Bowyer has undergone a groin operation in Germany and is expected to be out of action for three weeks.

LONDON TRANSFER SPECIAL:
Pages 66&67

How the Evening Standard broke the news of our consortium's interest.

representative of the Icelandics but he now appeared to be calling all the shots and that was very hard to take considering I knew nothing about him.

Come the morning of the crucial meeting at Landsbanki and Russell Bartlett called to say he would see me there, as arranged, at 10.30...before adding that he had been asked to go in 'a little bit earlier' to meet Magnusson and the other Icelandics. As the only man in our consortium with serious money to put down (£10m in cash), I had no problem with that. When he added that Keith Harris would also be present, I took it as a positive sign that we were making encouraging progress.

'The consortium is no more'

Whatever was said at that early morning meeting at Landsbanki, the bottom line was the Icelandics had declared their intention to immediately withdraw from our consortium. "The consortium is no more," announced the Austrian voice of Euro-IB's Alexander von Ungern-Sternberg when he emerged from the earlier meeting.

Russell Bartlett came out shortly afterwards and basically said that it would be very difficult for us to proceed with the Icelandics.

I was dumbstruck, in a state of shock as Gary and I boarded the train at Liverpool Street back to Essex. We'd gone from being on the brink of taking over West Ham, to our main investor pulling out without any explanation.

At that stage, all we knew was that they didn't want to be part of our consortium but there was no suggestion that they would go it alone in buying the club.

It left us with a £20m hole to fill, so we turned to Plan B. We very quickly got in touch with Chris Adams and my consortium – with the exception of myself - met him the next day at his office in Canary Wharf. I felt angry with the Icelandics for pulling out and further aggrieved because I couldn't attend the meeting at Chris' office because he was a box-holder at West Ham and we couldn't risk it getting back to Terry Brown that I was still involved in any shape or form.

But my consortium colleagues were correct in wanting to keep me out of sight. Richie phoned to say that someone at the club had found out that we had met for private talks at Liverpool Street a week or so earlier, which resulted in him being ostracised by the club.

I felt emotionally drained but had to hang in there and just hope it would all turn out OK. But on Wednesday, October 11, Magnusson was named in newspapers as the man heading an Icelandic consortium bidding for control of West Ham. What immediately struck me on reading the report was that Magnusson and Keith Harris were the only individuals named, with no mention of the three other parties named on the offer document. And why was it being described as an 'Icelandic consortium'?

I should have smelt a rat but, naively, I believed that it must have got out that one Icelandic individual was named on our offer document and it sounded more interesting to the media to describe it as an Icelandic bid, as opposed to mentioning local businessmen. Foreign owners of English football clubs were becoming increasingly in vogue. Even then, I didn't think Landsbanki had abandoned us to pursue their own takeover. On October 16, Russell Bartlett and Paul Duffen met Keith Harris, who said he was also in the dark about the Icelandics' plans

Hammers open up books for Icelander

KEN DYER
Football Correspondent

WEST HAM'S future took another twist today when the club allowed a second consortium headed by Icelandic businessman Eggert Magnusson access to club accounts.

Club chairman Terry Brown and the board of directors were holding their monthly meeting to discuss the takeover but were not anticipating making a statement. They hope that a decision on the future ownership of the club will be reached by the end of the week.

A consortium headed by Iranian-born businessman Kia Joorabchian, and backed by Israeli property magnate Eli Papouchado, has completed due diligence but has not made a firm bid.

The discovery of what they consider to be around £14 million of extra debt in the form of outstanding transfer monies and performance-related payments for players such as Dean Ashton has been a setback.

West Ham say the liabilities were openly declared in the club's recent set of accounts and they do not view them as debt.

Another problem for Joorabchian, whose long-term strategy is to sell off Upton Park and move to the new Olympic Stadium in Stratford after the 2012 Olympic Games, is that Culture Secretary Tessa Jowell is keen to keep the stadium as an athletics venue.

Even if West Ham did succeed in moving there following the Olympics, it could cost them £100m

Continued on Page 63

and was still awaiting instructions from them. As a friend of Terry Brown's and also our go-between, Keith was right in the thick of it all.

But two days later, Keith's contact David Bick was the first one to hint that the Icelandics might well go it alone when he phoned me while I was down in the West Country. David phoned again that Friday and this time he was more explicit when he told me that he thought the Icelandics were about to put in a bid to buy West Ham.

Regardless of what the men from Iceland were really up to, I continued to press on in a desperate effort to plug the £20m hole they had left. On October 26 I went to see a friend who worked for the investment bank Goldman Sachs, then Chris Hutton and I visited a contact at the Japanese bank Nomura. By now we were effectively trying to form a third consortium, competing against Joorabchian and the Icelandics. And this time I was determined our consortium would be made up entirely of West Ham people.

The final confirmation that the Icelandics had decided to go their own way came in another phone call from David Bick on the morning of Wednesday, October 25. Ironically, I was in the Castle Lounge at West Ham attending a Boys of 86 committee meeting, along with Galey and Phil Parkes, to discuss arrangements for a dinner we had planned for later in the year.

David's words were a hammer blow. I was fuming and struggling to contain my emotions as I paced up and down the corridor. Although there was always the risk that the Icelandics might take all the detailed information we had supplied them with and freeze my consortium out of the equation, it was still a sickening feeling when it happened.

The following night I phoned Siggi, one of the Icelandics we'd met at Landsbanki, who claimed he "didn't really know" what was happening with an Icelandic bid for West Ham. And when I pointedly asked him about his relationship with Eggert Magnusson, he played it down, saying: "I met him about 10 years ago but I haven't spoken to him since." It's fair to say that his reply was unconvincing.

When I met Russell and Paul the following week, they said they had spoken to Keith Harris and Magnusson and pretty much confirmed my worst fears. Russell and Paul remained loyal to me throughout and there was no question of them being part of the Icelandic takeover group. However you try to dress it up, the Icelandics had basically nicked West Ham from under our noses.

At the time, even one of the West Ham board of directors wasn't sure who was and wasn't part of the Icelandic bid. On November 4 I was covering the Colchester United v Cardiff City for Sky and afterwards I sat in the directors' box chatting to Scott Duxbury, the club's commercial and legal director who I'd seen at the ground once or twice but not really spoken to. Scott was at Colchester with agent Barry Neville, whose clients included Alan Pardew and Hammers striker Teddy Sheringham.

Scott intimated that the seven-man board was split on the takeover, with Terry Brown and Paul Aldridge understood to favour the Joorabchian bid while he and finance director Nick Igoe hoped the Icelandics would succeed. Brown and Aldridge, who were on 24-month notice contracts, were both expected to retain their executive roles if the Iranian gained control

FOOTBALL

ICELANDIC MOVE FOR WEST HAM

EXCLUSIVE

By David Bond
Football News Correspondent

WEST HAM have received a formal takeover approach from Eggert Magnusson, the Icelandic businessman and head of the country's football federation, the *Daily Telegraph* can reveal.

Magnusson, who is also a member of the Uefa executive committee, is heading a bid which values the East London club provisionally at £75 million.

If successful, the takeover could bring to an end months of uncertainty over the future ownership of the club.

Magnusson last night confirmed his interest to the *Daily Telegraph*, saying: "We are at the very beginning, we have shown an interest but there is some way to go. We need to see everything before we make a bid.

"But West Ham are a great club with a great history and good reputation. They have a very good manager and great players and are backed by fantastic support.

"I want to stress I am a football man and that this is about football, nothing else."

Magnusson is now waiting to see if the club will give him permission to start examining the club's accounts ahead of making a

formal offer. The emergence of Magnusson's interest raises the prospect of a bidding war for Upton Park although it is believed a rival approach from the Iranian businessman Kia Joorabchian is increasingly doubtful.

With the team struggling on the pitch manager Alan Pardew has called for an end to all the speculation.

Magnusson, 59, has appointed the former Football League chairman Keith Harris, head of the investment bank Seymour Pierce, to oversee the takeover approach.

Harris recently advised Randy Lerner, owner of the Cleveland Browns American Football team, on his £56m acquisition of Aston Villa and Michael Wilde's takeover of Southampton.

It is understood the Magnusson bid also has the support of a large City bank as well as the global sports marketing giant IMG.

Icelandic sources told the *Daily Telegraph* that Magnusson was prepared to put in around £40m of his money with the rest coming from a mix of debt and what is known in the City as "quasi-debt" – a mix of equity and borrowing.

They have also agreed to take on the club's debts of more than £20m giving the bid a total value of about £100m.

Full report: Sport 8

but Duxbury and Igoe would have been out in the cold. "Are you part of the Icelandic consortium?" Duxbury asked me.

I told him I was trying to put together a third consortium and he confirmed that, apart from talk of interest from an American family, which never surfaced, there were no other bidders. He also revealed that Keith Harris and Magnusson had been at the club the previous day, trying to speed up the takeover process.

Even then, I still hadn't quite admitted defeat. I contacted David Lewis in Australia with the purpose of giving him the authority to go out and try and find the extra investment needed to keep our consortium's bid alive.

But on the same day his letter of engagement reached me, the Icelandics were publicly named as Joorabchian's only rival. The *London Evening Standard* broke the news on Tuesday, November 7, stating that, although they had completed due diligence at the club, Joorabchian's group were reportedly put off by the discovery of what they considered to be around £14m of extra debt in the form of outstanding transfer monies and performance-related payments for players such as Dean Ashton.

November 7 also happened to be the date of our final consortium meeting, held at Chris Hutton's office. I walked in holding a copy of the *Standard,* bearing the back page headline 'Hammers open up books for Icelander'. Although the newspaper report didn't come as a shock – we were all resigned to the Icelandics making their own move for the club by then – it still left a bad taste in the mouth after all we had been through.

SPORT | **The Daily Telegraph**

FOOTBALL

East End magnet for Magnusson

EXCLUSIVE

DAVID BOND
FOOTBALL NEWS CORRESPONDENT

EGGERT MAGNUSSON, the latest businessman to be lured by the prospect of buying West Ham, made his fortune from making biscuits and went on to become one of the most influential figures in European football.

Magnusson sold the successful biscuit and bread business, Fron, five years ago. Now the diminutive businessman has his sights set on becoming the latest foreigner to join the growing list of overseas Premiership club owners.

As revealed by the *Daily Telegraph*, Magnusson, 59, is leading a bid to buy West Ham and wants to establish the club as a major Premiership force.

An outline proposal of the offer, which values the club at between £65 million and £75m, is being considered by the West Ham board.

It is understood the club are now weighing up whether to grant Magnusson and his advisers access to the books, a process known as due diligence.

If chairman Terry Brown gives the go-ahead then a formal offer could be launched before the end of the month.

But no takeover runs smoothly. There are many more obstacles to clear before Magnusson is installed as the new chairman at Upton Park.

First, there is the potential for a rival bid from the London based Iranian businessman Kia Joorabchian.

Speculation that he would renew his interest in the club surfaced following the August deadline day transfer of Argentine duo Carlos Tevez and Javier Mascherano.

West Ham issued a statement a day later declaring they were in "exploratory talks" with a possible bidder, understood to be Joorabchian, but since then the bid has gone nowhere.

The team's dismal form on the pitch since the arrival of Mascherano and Tevez has only added to the pressure on the West Ham board to resolve the issue of the club's future ownership.

Manager Alan Pardew last week appealed to the board of directors to issue a "put up or shut up" ultimatum to Joorabchian and it is believed he now has until the start of next week to make his move.

Although Magnusson is far further down the line – a respected City bank has already agreed to help finance the bid and the club's £22m of debts – there is still a major chance it could fail.

Brown and his board of directors are believed to be worried about other figures who may be lurking in the background and want to know exactly who is behind the Icelandic approach before opening their books to the possible buyers.

But where the Magnusson bid enjoys far greater credibility is through the presence of the hugely respected former Football League chairman Keith Harris, head of the City investment bank Seymour Pierce.

Harris, who helped broker Randy Lerner's £56m takeover of Aston Villa as well as Roman Abramovich's £140m purchase of Chelsea in July 2003, is an adviser to the Magnusson team.

On top of that Magnusson is a highly regarded figure, not only in Icelandic business and football circles, but also inside the corridors of power at Uefa, where he has been on the executive committee since 2002.

He became president of the Iceland Football Federation in 1990 before being voted on to Uefa's executive committee 12 years later, where he is now playing a leading role in the development of women's football and is a member of their clubs and leagues working group.

Magnusson has said in the past that, despite being a successful businessman, – he is a director of the Icelandic investment bank Straumur – he sees his involvement in the beautiful game as a privilege.

"Football has always been for me a wonderful opportunity to learn about life," he has said. "Since my childhood, I have been immersed and captivated by football's magnetism.

"I have always had a passion for football and I still enjoy playing several times a week."

Premiership football is hugely popular in Iceland where fans of the English game can watch up to five matches a week live on television.

But the last time an Icelandic businessman got involved with an English club, it was hardly a roaring success.

Gunnar Gislason's seven year reign as chairman of Stoke, which ended in May, resulted in him losing 70 per cent of his investment and the club failing to achieve his aim of reaching the Premiership.

However, according to sources in Iceland, Magnusson is a very different character. One insider described him as a "genuine football lover" with "extensive and powerful" business connections both in Iceland and in London.

The West Ham board now face an almighty dilemma – and the clock is ticking. On the one hand they wish to preserve the unique identity of the club.

On the other they know this could be the optimum moment to cash in. The club announced yesterday that they made a pre-tax profit of £6m and recorded a turnover of £60m during their first season back in the Premiership. They have also reduced their debts significantly.

But they could easily be sucked into a relegation battle this season and any prospective buyer will not want to take on a club apparently bound for the Championship.

Brown, who controls 35 per cent of the shares, stands to make at least £25m from selling up, while there are big profits in it too for the other major shareholders, Charles Warner, who controls about 21 per cent, and Martin Cearns, who owns about nine per cent.

Men of the moment: Eggert Magnusson (right) and manager Alan Pardew with his Argentine imports

▌TIME LINE

JULY 2005 – Kia Joorabchian makes his first approach to buy West Ham. Weeks of talks fail as West Ham decide not to sell

MAY 2006 – First season back in the Premiership ends on a high, finishing ninth and reaching FA Cup Final

AUG 31 2006 – Argentine stars Carlos Tevez and Javier Mascherano sign on four-year contracts. They will share in any future transfer profits with the players' owners

SEPT 1 2006 – A Stock Exchange announcement confirms talks with a possible bidder for the club, understood to be Joorabchian, the man behind the Tevez and Mascherano deal

SEPT 5 2006 – Joorabchian confirms he may make a bid but adds it will be delayed by the death of his father

SEPT 9 2006 – *Daily Telegraph* reveals Israeli property entrepreneur Eli Papouchado is behind Joorabchian's possible £80m bid for the club

SEPT 17 2006 – West Ham suffer third loss in four matches

SEPT 26 2006 · Manager Alan Pardew admits takeover talk is hurting the club

OCT 1 2006 – Sixth defeat in seven matches

OCT 4 2006 – Club's board meet to discuss Pardew's concerns and takeover – they are split on whether to issue an ultimatum to Joorabchian

OCT 5 2006 – Club play down speculation that a second consortium is looking at making a bid for the club

OCT 11 2006 – *Daily Telegraph* reveals Icelandic businessman Eggert Magnusson, head of the country's FA, is leading a £75m bid for West Ham

PREMIERSHIP'S FOREIGN OWNERS: Roman Abramovich (Russia) – Chelsea, Malcolm Glazer (US) – Manchester United, Randy Lerner (US) – Aston Villa, Alexandre Gaydamak (Israel) – Portsmouth, Mohammed Al Fayed (Egypt) – Fulham

22

Cashing in

O N Tuesday, November 21, it was officially confirmed that West Ham had accepted an £85m offer from the Icelanders (who formed a company called WH Holding Ltd) to buy the club for £4.21p per share – a fantastic, irresistible deal for the board of directors and all the other shareholders.

I couldn't understand why they ended up paying some £10m more than Terry Brown's asking price. Unfortunately, as events would subsequently prove, this was the start of a trend for the Icelandics, who were inclined to pay over the odds in their first year in charge at West Ham.

For me, it was the culmination of more than two years' blood, sweat and tears. All our hard work had gone down the drain with no end product or reward to show for it.

I soon obtained a copy of WH Holding's offer document, which detailed everything about the takeover, including a full list of all the beneficiaries from the sale in terms of the shareholders and what they each gained financially from the deal. Some of the amounts were mind-boggling.

Terry Brown made around £31m by cashing in his 36% majority shareholding (7,392,000 shares) and standing down as chairman after 14 years. Charles Warner (4,252,000 shares) netted £17.9m and Martin Cearns (1,844,000 shares) received £7.76m.

Brown, who first joined the board in 1990, two years before succeeding Cearns as chairman in the wake of the much-maligned debenture bond scheme, retained his title of honorary life vice-president and took on a role as a non-executive director. He also managed to agree for the new owners to pay him £492,000 a year for two years and would receive his eight top complimentary tickets for all home games.

Interestingly, David Sullivan was also £4m-plus richer following the takeover, which is what his 985,370 West Ham shares were worth.

Paul Aldridge (55,900 shares) also pocketed more than £235,000 from the sale of his 0.3% shareholding but the MD immediately left the club to make way for the new figurehead, although he returned to the game as CEO at Sheffield Wednesday in 2011.

The 59-year-old Magnusson was identified as the CEO of WH Holding and chairman of West Ham United, the new front man, but most of the purchase was funded by 65-year-old Bjorgolfor Gudmundsson, the chairman of the

Terry Brown welcomes Eggert Magnusson to Upton Park.

non-executive board of Landsbanki.

They were respectively described in the offer document as follows:

Eggert Magnusson is a former owner and chief executive of an import/export and bread and biscuit manufacturing company. He has been president of the FA of Iceland since 1989 and is a former president of Valur Reykjavik (1984-89), one of Iceland's oldest football clubs. He was elected to the UEFA executive committee in April 2002, having been a member of the Licenced Match Agents Panel (1992-94), the Fair Play Committee (1994-96) and the Club Competitions Committee (1996-2002). He has also

Magnusson and BG after the 2006 takeover.

been a member of a number of FIFA committees. Mr Magnusson also serves as a board member of Straumur-Burdaras, an Icelandic investment bank, as well as the logistics firm, Avion Group hf. Both Straumur-Burdaras and Avion Group hf are listed on the Iceland stock exchange.

Bjorgolfor Gudmundsson is an international investor with interests in various sectors, including financial services, international transportation, seafood processing and sales, real estate and publishing. Mr Gudmundsson is the chairman of the non-executive board of Landsbanki, a leading Icelandic bank with operations in 12 countries. Since Mr Gudmundsson became chairman of Landsbanki in 2003, the bank has taken a lead in sponsoring sport in Iceland, particularly football, where it has focused on the development of young players.

Immediately the media began to question how the deal was funded and structured. Under the heading 'Take note of this strange arrangement', *Daily Express* columnist Harry Harris wrote:

"We wanted to know whether the sale of the new shares – 'loan notes' in financial-speak – would pass from the Icelandic consortium to new, as yet unspecified, owners. The response was that, so far, none of the new loan notes had been sold on, but Magnusson has publicly expressed that he is seeking new investors. Magnusson moved to quell fears that the club has been taken over with those loan notes saddling the club with massive debt and interest repayments."

Harris went on to observe from the offer document that:

"WH Holding will pay back the £100m loan notes and the £5m a year interest by means of dividends directly from the East London club's coffers."

Like Harry Harris, I too was searching for answers to questions and one of them was right there in the offer document itself. Among those proposed to be appointed to the WHUFC board was a certain Sighvatar Bjarnason. This led me to believe he was probably the same man I'd only ever known as 'Siggi', the guy who, when I phoned him on the day the news of the Icelandic bid broke, told me he hadn't spoken to Magnusson for 10 years.

The only consolation I could draw from the whole experience was that we had stopped Joorabchian from taking over. I still maintain to this day that had he succeeded in buying West Ham back in 2006, the club would have imploded. As it happened, soon after the takeover was complete, West Ham found themselves in deep trouble with the football authorities as a result of the Carlos Tevez/Javier Mascherano transfers.

The following email, which I sent to all my fellow consortium members on the day the club was sold in November 2006, summed up my thoughts at the time:

Subject: *WHU*

Gentlemen,

Following the news coming out of the club today, I think even the optimist in me has accepted that we have finally been defeated. For 30 months I have been trying to get the club into a situation where it is back to where it belongs (The Premiership) and with the future looking good. It appears that this might now be the case and, if so, we might well have done our job, albeit not with the end product that we were all hoping for.

We can't really lose, because if the Icelanders make a huge success of the club, then we will all be happy; and if they make a complete pigs ear of it, that was because they didn't go in the direction we were telling them to go in! If the latter is the case, then you can expect a call at the relevant time!

At least we prevented Kia from getting it, which was an achievement in itself.

I think there is no doubt that we all made various mistakes and miscalculations as a team and if the club hadn't got promoted last year we would probably be in control now. Hindsight and fate play a big part in life, and in football this has always been the case.

Whilst there are people out there who should hang their heads in shame with the way they have carried on, I can honestly say that everyone reading this email can stand tall and hold their head up high. I am proud to say that you all stood with me through thick and thin and that I can now count you all as friends. You all helped me to chase the dream and for that I would like to thank all of you for the fun, laughter and enjoyment we have had along the way. I have learned more about life in the last 30 months than I did in 20 years as a player (although some would say that's not hard!) and wouldn't swap the experience for anything.

As for me, well, I am taking stock of all that's gone on and taking advice from various quarters. When the time is right, I will put my side of the story but in a positive way that protects all those who have been on my team. Paul Panayi's idea of a Xmas drink is an excellent one and I look forward to hearing where and when it is.

In the meantime, thanks again.

Tony

Although the failure of our bid came as a massive disappointment, the fact remained that I am West Ham through and through and still wanted to be part of the club – not just working in the corporate lounges on match day, but in a more significant commercial role. In this respect, I phoned Scott Duxbury and met him at City Airport where I handed over a 30-page dossier I'd put together as part of our takeover document, detailing how the club could improve its commercial revenues.

Scott Duxbury offered me my old job back at West Ham but I accepted too hastily.

Scott seemed impressed with my ideas and he called me to arrange for us to meet again, on December 4, this time in the Thames Ironworks bar at the ground, where we were joined by commercial manager Sue Page. At the end of our chat Scott offered me my original job back – not the wider commercial role I'd been hoping for but, to be honest, I was so desperate to return to the club I would probably have agreed to put out the rubbish bins.

But when I got home feeling quite delighted and told Dad that I had got my old job back at West Ham, he didn't share my enthusiasm. "Is that all the last two years and more have all been about?" he asked.

He was right, too. I thought about it a bit more that night and started to feel angry. I'd put everything into the takeover bid at the expense of my family. I was too wrapped up in it all and can honestly say that I wasn't a good husband or a good father to my three kids at the time. How could I have put them through all that happened just to resume at West Ham on the same basis as I'd worked before starting our takeover attempt?

The next day I sought the advice of Paul Duffen, who encouraged me to go and see Magnusson in search of the recognition and compensation I knew I deserved for having brought the Icelanders to the negotiating table.

I was also referred to some specialist sporting lawyers and met two of their men at the Hilton Hotel on the M1 near Derby. I spent a couple of hours with them and although they were happy to help me, their fee of £15,000 put me off! They suggested it would be better if my consortium claimed against

Landsbanki and Seymour Pierce, rather than myself as an individual, but none of the other guys wanted to pursue what could have been a long and costly legal case.

That's when I decided to take the direct approach.

23

Cool response from the ice man

D ARKNESS had fallen on the afternoon of Wednesday, December 6, 2006 and in less than four hours the Hammers would face fellow strugglers Wigan Athletic in a Premier League match they desperately needed to win to ease the fear of relegation and mounting pressure on manager Alan Pardew.

Not that beating Wigan was uppermost in my mind on this occasion. The 2006-07 season had turned as miserable as the winter gloom that had descended on the club but I had other more pressing issues on my mind. This time I was returning to Upton Park for a pre-arranged 4.00pm meeting with Eggert Magnusson, the new executive chairman and CEO of West Ham who had been appointed two weeks earlier.

I made the appointment to see Magnusson – via his deputy CEO Scott Duxbury – because I wanted him to help me gain the compensation I felt I was owed for effectively putting him in the highly privileged position he now enjoyed. The way I saw it, Magnusson was in the seat I had dreamed of occupying – as West Ham's new figurehead.

It was too late, though. My burning ambition had melted away under an avalanche of Icelandic money. All £85m of it – £108m if you also take into account the existing debt the new owners inherited as part of their very expensive buy-out.

I went to the ground that day knowing I'd be watching the Wigan game from the stands, like the other 34,000 or so devotees who have claret and blue blood coarsing through their veins.

I had to report to main reception, where a member of security staff would then escort me across to the Bobby Moore Stand. Once I'd reached the top of the stairs in the 'Bobby Upper', it seemed strange not to take my usual right turn – towards the offices where the commercial, media and general admin staff work and where I'd often pop in for a chat on match days. Instead, I walked in the opposite direction, towards the offices occupied by the club's hierarchy at the far end of the corridor. I popped in to say 'hello' to Scott Duxbury before he showed me into Magnusson's office, just a few feet away.

As I entered, the new chairman was not sat behind his main desk, but at a smaller table a few feet away. He stood up and as we shook hands, I said: "Hello, Eggert, congratulations on becoming chairman. I'm pleased for you."

It obviously wasn't said with much sincerity but it seemed the right thing to say considering that I was seeking his help and co-operation.

After a brief exchange of formal pleasantries, it was time to get to the point of my visit. "I need your help," I said, before explaining the background to why I had come to his office. Let's be absolutely clear on this. If my consortium hadn't met the money men at Landsbanki through an Icelandic intermediary, in the hope that they would back our bid to take over the club, they would never have gone near West Ham. Before our meetings with the Icelandics, it's fair to say that they didn't have a clue just how big an opportunity investing in a well-supported Premier League club would be.

By no stretch of the imagination could my first meeting with Magnusson in his office at Upton Park be described as warm but I detected an even cooler response from the balding ice man when I raised the question of compensation due to me from Landsbanki and also Seymour Pierce, who had brokered the takeover deal. His face took on a more serious look when I asked him for help in gaining financial compensation – or what would normally be termed an 'introductory fee'.

I didn't have a specific figure in mind at that stage but I knew that whatever amount I might eventually receive, it would be nowhere near the standard rate of 1% applied to corporate finance deals of this magnitude. After all, 1% cent of the £108m transaction value would have made me an instant millionaire.

After telling Magnusson how much time and effort I'd devoted to our failed takeover bid, and how our meetings with his backers had triggered their acquisition of West Ham, his initial indifferent attitude disappointed me. In impeccable English, he dismissed my request by saying: "I don't know anything about that, it's not my concern."

At that point, my tone also changed. It was inconceivable that he had been unaware of the role I'd played in bringing the potential of buying West Ham to the attention of his fellow countrymen, via meetings, phone conversations and written correspondence between the consortium I'd originally put together and Landsbanki. In fact, Magnusson had himself met the man who, at £10m, would have been our biggest single investor – a successful businessman and lifelong Hammers fan whose company had an executive box at Upton Park – in offices at Landsbanki just eight weeks before the takeover went through.

That's when I told him straight: "Eggert, I'm not being funny, but you wouldn't be sitting in the chairman's seat if it hadn't been for me."

After weeks of disappointment that had manifested itself in anger, I felt a lot better for having got it off my chest. Magnusson just shrugged his shoulders a little and said: "You will have to leave it with me..."

He then changed tack completely. Normally when I meet football people for the first time, they tend to ask about my playing days and some of the greats I played with at Upton Park. Whether Magnusson really did know as much about his Hammers history as he tried to portray in press interviews, I don't know, but he didn't bring up my past association with West Ham and there was no mention of football at all until, quite out of the blue, he asked: "What do you think of Shaun Wright-Phillips?"

Who knows if he even cared what I really thought of the player or whether his surprise question was just a diversionary tactic. His comment came a few weeks before newspaper speculation linking the then England and Chelsea winger with a possible bid from West Ham during the imminent January transfer window.

"Get a goalscorer!" was my advice to him before he showed me out at the end of what must have been a 10-minute meeting.

It's fair to assume that Magnusson probably had other more important things on his mind when we met in his office that afternoon. The dismal defeat West Ham suffered to Wigan a few hours later turned out to be Alan Pardew's last home game in charge, just a few days before Magnusson

Magnusson had that same surprised look when I sought compensation.

sacked him following another bad defeat, this time a 4-0 capitulation at Bolton.

Just a couple of weeks earlier Magnusson and Pardew had been pictured together smiling and shaking hands on the front cover of the home programme for the game against Sheffield United, the first played at Upton Park following the takeover. Prior to kick-off, the new chairman appeared on the pitch waving a claret and blue scarf (even though Spurs was the team he supported as a boy) and was basking in the acclaim of the crowd who appeared to believe they were witnessing the Second Coming.

Fair play to him, he had put in his money to buy 5% of the club but Bjorgolfur Gudmundsson – or 'BG' as he became known – owned the majority 95%. What no-one could dispute was that Magnusson had the biggest ego in town. Seeing

Magnusson revelled in the media spotlight.

this man getting the reward and recognition for other people's efforts was very hard to take.

He could not, however, be accused of indecisiveness. Despite publicly backing Pardew, he soon wielded the axe and appointed Alan Curbishley as his replacement.

Compensation claim

In my quest for compensation I arranged to meet Keith Harris in the early evening of December 14 at Langan's restaurant, which was full of noisy businessman determined to revel in the pre-Christmas festivities and far from the ideal setting for a serious meeting. I asked him outright: "What happened? Why did you end up handling all the due diligence and brokering the deal between the Icelandics and Terry Brown?"

He expressed his sincere apologies and explained that he was put in a "very difficult position". He pointed out that he was governed by Takeover Panel rules and had to be very careful in what he said and did.

But then I reminded Keith of the promise he made to me, not to get involved in any such deal at West Ham unless I was part of it, which is what we agreed the first time we discussed my consortium's plans. Again, he apologised profusely. "I know, I'm sorry the way things turned out," he said, acknowledging how I'd brought him into the proposed deal from the start for which he was financially rewarded.

I asked Keith why the Icelandics went off on their own and his response to this question was significant. He told me: "When I had my meeting with Terry Brown, it had become very clear that he wouldn't do the deal if you were involved."

If that was the case, and because I like Keith and had no reason to doubt what he was telling me, then it would explain the actions of the Icelandics in severing their links with my West Ham consortium and going their own way.

I just couldn't understand why Brown still held such a grudge against me. Did he really not grasp that it was my approach to Landsbanki that ultimately led to his £31m pay day?

Keith's words about what Brown had said hurt. Call me naïve, but it would have been nice for Terry Brown, and Charles Warner and Martin Cearns for that matter, to have picked up the phone and said 'Thanks, Tony, for what you did' but it never happened. They have never acknowledged the part I played in paving the way for that staggering £108m takeover, which is one of the main reasons for writing this book.

At least Keith agreed to help me in my quest for some financial compensation. Early in 2007 Seymour Pierce agreed to pay me a small five-figure sum, which basically covered my expenses accumulated over the previous two years or so, and Keith also put in a word for me with the people at Landsbanki. Early in that New Year I wrote to Arjun Kapur, the corporate finance director at the Icelandic bank, but instead of getting a reply from him, his colleague Steinar Kristjansson wrote back saying that if I was seeking compensation then I should speak to Haffi and Jesse.

I hadn't heard from these two intermediaries for some three months, since our consortium split, so I emailed them both asking if they had been looked after by the bank and, if so, whether I could expect a slice of the money paid to them. The fact that I didn't receive a reply from either man said it all.

All of which made me even more determined to go back to Landsbanki and demand some sort of compensation directly from them. After all, Haffi and Jesse had only introduced me to the bank; they were not part of our consortium or the Icelandic one that eventually gained control of West Ham.

In mid-February I went back to Landsbanki to meet Steinar, who assured me that he would look into my compensation claim. I was a bit sterner on this occasion, suggesting to him that the press were on my case and pushing me to tell my side of the story about how the Icelandics came to power at Upton Park. After a couple of months of more emails back and forth, they finally settled a small five-figure sum that was less than what Seymour Pierce paid me.

It was by no stretch of the imagination a huge compensation settlement and nowhere near the six-figure amount I'd hoped for and deserved. In the

Sir Trevor Brooking tried to calm fans' expectations after the Icelandics took over.

business world, an introductory fee for a deal valued at £108m would be 1% – or £1.08m. Instead, I had to accept a lot less than what a number of the West Ham players in the Icelandic era were paid per week. I wasn't being greedy, just trying to claw back some money to cover my expenses and by way of recognition for all the time and effort I'd committed to the mission.

24

Tevezgate

ALL the many who doubted the integrity of the Carlos Tevez and Javier Mascherano transfers at the time they joined West Ham were proved correct as the club became embroiled in the biggest dispute in its history.

Just after Mascherano left to join Liverpool on loan at the end of the January '07 transfer window, having played just five games for the Hammers, the Premier League launched an inquiry into the Argentinian transfers.

The new owners and Alan Curbishley must have wondered what they had let themselves in for as the storm clouds gathered over Upton Park. I'd heard rumours that the Icelandics' due diligence at the club had not included the signings of Tevez and Mascherano, which, if true, is remarkable given how much they paid for the club. There was also talk that the Icelandics had actually bought the due diligence previously carried out by Joorabchian's group, which seems plausible in the light of how things unfolded.

There were questions openly raised about the legality of the South American signings from the moment they arrived, so why didn't the Icelandics examine the deals with a fine toothcomb, as my consortium would have done, before they took control? For us, it would have been a priority to check and scrutinise the validity of the most talked about double transfer in modern British football history.

The deal that was too good to be true turned out to be just that when it subsequently emerged that Tevez's economic rights were owned by Media Sports Investments and a second company, Just Sports Inc., while Mascherano was jointly owned by Global Soccer Agencies and Mystere Services Ltd. All four companies were represented by Joorabchian and the deal was brokered by MSI, whose president Joorabchian had been until June '06.

Amid the fallout from 'Tevezgate', Terry Brown left the club in early February. I would be lying if I said I didn't take some satisfaction in the abrupt manner of his departure. I thought, 'what goes around comes around', although I'm sure he didn't lose too much sleep over it and he reached an out of court settlement with the club for what he was owed by them.

But in no way did I want West Ham to be relegated and I was delighted when we became the first team to beat Arsenal at The Emirates, with Bobby

Zamora – yes, *him* again! – scoring another crucial winner. It's amazing how Bob kept popping up at important times. He had previously scored a vital goal in our win at Blackburn, when the ball clearly hadn't crossed the line, and it was probably the defining moment of the season. Zamora played a key part in that remarkable run of seven wins in the last nine games, along with goalkeeper Robert Green and young midfielder Mark Noble, but the spotlight was on Tevez, who scored all seven of his goals in the last 10 games.

When the shit hit the fan West Ham admitted to breaching Premier League rules B13 and U18. Rule B13 states that all Premier League clubs should act in good faith, while U18 relates to third party influence. The original report of the Premier League's independent commission was critical of Paul Aldridge, who, the commission alleged, told a "lie" to Premier League chief executive Richard Scudamore about the transfers, although Paul still denies this and was not allowed to give evidence in person.

The club was found guilty of acting improperly and withholding vital documentation over the duo's ownership by offshore companies, a clear breach of Premier League rules. The club was fined a record £5.5m by the independent disciplinary commission.

Yet to the amazement and dismay of all but the most one-eyed West Ham fans, they were not deducted any league points. Not only that, they were allowed to continue playing Tevez, whose dramatic winner at Old Trafford on the final day of the season secured Hammers' top flight status.

Typically, the football authorities mishandled the whole Tevez affair and in failing to deal with the controversy quickly and decisively, it became a huge

Carlos Tevez scores the goal at Old Trafford that made West Ham safe in 2007.

*Tevez, Anton Ferdinand and Mark Noble lead the celebrations
at Old Trafford on 'Survival Sunday'.*

issue that affected not just the Hammers but the other clubs around them in the relegation dogfight. Wigan Athletic chairman Dave Whelan was the most vocal of the anti-West Ham brigade, claiming that four clubs – the 'Gang of Four' as the media described them, Charlton Athletic, Fulham and Sheffield United as well as the Latics – were threatening legal action against the Premier League for not docking the Hammers 10 league points before the season had ended. Such a deduction would have effectively relegated the club. Even a three-point deduction would have sent them down.

No matter how you look at it, West Ham got off lightly. What is the point in having rules if clubs who are in breach of them are not properly punished?

But it didn't end there. Sheffield United, who were 10 points above West Ham at one stage of the run-in before eventually going down with Alan Pardew's Charlton and Watford, successfully won £20m in damages from West Ham in an out of court settlement in March 2009. The Hammers, then still under Icelandic ownership, agreed to pay the Blades £4m a year in compensation for lost Premier League revenue over a five-year period.

The Premier League took steps to outlaw third-party ownership in 2008 but that came as no consolation to the Icelandics or the current owners, who are still bearing the liability of the Tevez controversy today.

I can't help but think it could have been much worse for my club, though, as that whole sorry saga dominated the sports headlines before Joorabchian moved Tevez on to Manchester United in a two-year loan deal in the summer

Magnusson alongside Alan Curbishley and Mervyn Day on the day the two ex-Hammers were appointed in December 2006.

of '07. Writing in the *Daily Express* at the time, John Dillon commented: "West Ham had been deliberately deceitful in concealing the true nature of the deal. If this did not warrant the deduction of points, it is difficult to know what offence would. And I say that as a West Ham supporter of 40 years. West Ham stayed up because of what Tevez did on the pitch – but he was only playing because Brown had signed him by unfair means."

Joorabchian and even the Sheffield United players were talking of suing West Ham at one stage. It was madness. If Joorabchian had succeeded in his bid to buy the club the chances are the Tevez/Mascherano fiasco would never have come to light. And then you have to wonder what other dodgy third party arrangements would have been inflicted on the club and the mess we'd be in now.

In fairness to the Icelandic owners, you had to give them credit for putting their money where their mouth was. Having invested so heavily in buying the club, they then spent a fortune on a number of new players. During the January transfer window Magnusson sanctioned the signings of Luis Boa Morte, Lucas Neill, Matthew Upson, Calum Davenport and Nigel Quashie in a desperate attempt to stave off the looming threat of relegation.

What I would question, though, is the length of those contracts, the wages lavished on the players and the effect it had by inflating the transfer market as well as putting the club's financial future at risk. Of course, they couldn't contemplate relegation but it very nearly happened anyway, despite that January spending spree.

I felt sorry for Curbs, who inherited a nightmare situation that he had to try and deal with against the backdrop of the Tevez affair. The club was constantly in the news for all the wrong reasons...reports of a 'culture of gambling' with players losing up to £50,000 a time to each other on away trips, nightclub brawls and other problems within the camp.

When Curbs somehow stabilised the club by guiding the team to a respectable 10th place finish in a trouble-free 2007-08, it felt totally unnatural to West Ham fans. For once, an entire season without relegation fears and nothing much happening off the field to worry about either. How boring was that!

SATURDAY, MAY 5, 2007

ph

West Ham face legal battle

By Martin Smith

GARY M. PRIOR/GETTY IMAGES

Fall out: Dave Whelan (left) in happier times with West Ham owner Eggert Magnusson

THE four clubs with most to gain if the Premier League's decision to fine West Ham over the Tevez-Mascherano affair were overturned in favour of a points deduction confirmed last night that they were taking legal advice.

Charlton, Fulham, Wigan and Sheffield United surround West Ham at the bottom of the Premiership, and at least three of the quartet would remain in the division if they won any legal action recommended to them by their teams of lawyers.

The four met in central London to discuss the implications of the punishment imposed on West Ham a week ago over the signings of the Argentine pair Carlos Tevez and Javier Mascherano last August. The independent disciplinary commission set up by the Premier League had fined West Ham a record £5.5 million after they admitted breaking rule U18, a regulation relating to third-party influence over the policies of a team, which requires all members of the League to act in good faith.

Along with the majority of member clubs, Charlton, Fulham, Wigan and Sheffield United expected West Ham to receive a points deduction, as they claim the League's regulations call for. A deduction would have effectively relegated the club. "This is a very serious offence West Ham committed," Wigan chairman Dave Whelan said.

The backlash to the decision had been rumbling since it was announced, and last night the week's rhetoric was put into formal words in a statement issued by the four clubs and sent to the Premier League's board of directors.

In it they said: "You should understand we are separately in the process of obtaining legal advice arising out of the terms of the decision. You can expect to hear from us in relation to this in the early part of next week. In the meantime, all our rights in that respect are reserved."

The statement called upon the League to review the case, and carried a veiled threat that they were prepared to take the matter to higher authorities outside the sport.

"The board are given powers under the rules to 'inquire into any suspected or alleged breach of these rules'," the clubs continued. "The FAPL [FA Premier League] have a duty to act in good faith and with reasonable diligence. That duty extends to investigating an alleged breach of the rules where there is some apparently credible evidence of a breach."

With Tevez expected to play a prominent part in West Ham's last two games – against Bolton this afternoon and at Old Trafford next Sunday – from which they need a minimum of three points to avoid relegation by dint of their endeavours on the pitch, the furious four are demanding swift action. Whether Tevez should still be registered with the club is shrouded in confusion.

"Given the potential significance to our clubs of any further serious breach of FAPL rules by West Ham at this point in time, not to investigate immediately would be a breach by the League of their obligation of utmost good faith to us under FAPL rule B13," they said.

The forthright declaration of intent continued: "We require your urgent confirmation that the FAPL will act as set out above in this letter. If we do not receive that confirmation, we will take all such steps as are available to us to enforce and protect our rights, including taking urgent action with a view to convening a meeting of the FAPL and/or bringing proceedings in court under Section 459 of the Companies Act 1985, on the basis that the affairs of the company are being conducted in a manner which is unfairly prejudicial to us."

The Premier League, who have taken legal advice themselves and been told their position is unassailable, will rely on the fact that it was entirely up to the three-man independent commission to decide on the punishment, and that if they had any influence over the decision it would be a conflict of interest.

Their argument runs that the commission had a wide range of sanctions available to them, and that the Premier League rules do not state what the punishment should be for such rule breaches. A Premier League spokesman said last night: "We will study the contents of the letter and respond accordingly."

If West Ham continue the form that has brought them five wins in seven games, the case could go all the way to the High Court. It could be a long, expensive summer.

25

Closure

THERE was a sad postscript to the takeover. I was driving along in June '07 when I received an unexpected mobile phone text. It said something along the lines of: 'Hi Tony, it's Jesse, just wanted to let you know that I've got some bad news regarding Haffi'.

I hadn't spoken to either of the two guys who introduced us to the people at Landsbank since the previous October. I texted back: 'What's the matter – has he had a heart attack?'

Jessie replied: 'No, it's worse than that, he's dead'. Knowing I couldn't continue a conversation of such a serious nature by text, I called Jesse, who told me that his friend had committed suicide the previous day.

It turned out Haffi was in a lot of debt and had been promised a pay-off by Landsbanki as his reward for introducing them to the West Ham deal, or at least the possibility of it via my consortium.

According to Jesse, he and Haffi had both been expecting payment for some considerable time but when the money didn't arrive as expected, poor Haffi couldn't take the stress anymore and hanged himself.

He was a good family man, in his mid-40s, who lived with his wife in Cambridgeshire and had three kids. I couldn't believe it when I heard the news. Haffi taking his own life put my own previous gripes about chasing compensation from the Icelandic bank and Seymour Pierce into perspective.

One thing's for sure, if Haffi and I hadn't met, the Icelandics would never have got the keys to West Ham.

Moving on

There was, however, also a positive legacy to emerge from our consortium. Gary White's firm of accountants did the due diligence on Robbie Cowling's purchase of Colchester United in 2006. Although it wasn't the football club takeover Gary had hoped for, it was a really good experience for him and I was absolutely delighted when, a little further down the line, he was employed by Robbie as the U's finance director. For a period, the Essex club's new stadium became en enclave of Hammers supporters, because Sue Page also left West Ham to become Colchester's commercial manager.

Towards the end of the 2006-07 season, Russell Bartlett called and invited me to his offices in Essex, where he revealed plans to become involved with a football club, if he could find the right one. His involvement in our bid had

West Ham fan Robbie Cowling after his takeover at Colchester.

whetted his appetite and he asked me to put in a call to my old employees at Norwich City to see if there was anything doing, but there was nothing happening there, or at Cardiff City where he had sounded out Peter Ridsdale ahead of the Bluebirds' move to their new stadium.

Russell then surprised me by saying he had turned his attention to Hull City and proceeded to show me stadium redevelopment plans that clearly excited him. He then added that if he could do the deal to buy out owner Adam Pearson, he would appoint another of our consortium members, Paul Duffen, as his new club chairman. Russell and Paul had never met before joining our 'team' but they clicked straight away and for a time they were a winning combination.

I said before that Paul would have been the perfect chairman had we taken

Russell Bartlett (centre) with Premier League chief executive Richard Scudamore.

Paul Duffen in happy times at Hull City. He would have been the
ideal chairman for West Ham.

over at West Ham but the Hammers' loss briefly became Hull City's gain. Lo and behold, it all went through in June '07 – Adam Pearson moved on to Derby County while Russell bought Hull and led the club into its most exciting era ever.

In May 2008, the Tigers won promotion to the Premier League after beating Bristol City in the Play-off Final at Wembley. It was the first time in the club's

Peter Storrie, West Ham's former MD, with Paul Duffen.

then 104-year history that they had played in the top flight of English football.

However, just a few months after the Tigers' second season in the Premier League ended in relegation to the Championship, Russell sold his entire shareholding in the club to the Egyptian Allam family in December 2010.

In their first season in charge at the KC Stadium, I actually flew up to Hull in his private plane from Southend. In fact, we had a consortium reunion in the boardroom at Hull before one home game in '07, which Gary, Paul Panayi and Ben Mansford also attended.

It was a shame that it didn't work out for Paul and Russell, who, like so many other successful businessmen before them, have discovered that football is an industry like no other.

As for me, my experience in trying to buy West Ham didn't deter me from considering other takeover possibilities. Chris Hutton, another of our consortium members, contacted me in 2007 about the possibility of buying QPR but a couple of meetings we had with the club came to nothing and it was eventually bought by Formula One bosses Flavio Briatore and Bernie Ecclestone.

I also spoke to Sasha Shojai, our original backer in the West Ham bid, about approaching Barry Hearn to see if he would sell Leyton Orient. But as far as Barry was concerned, because he holds a long-term lease on the site where, as well as the Matchroom Stadium, he also owns four blocks of flats in each corner of the ground, he would only talk about possibly selling the club but not the equity value of the land itself. For that reason, we immediately withdrew any thought of taking over the O's.

Back at West Ham

After the bitter disappointment of our failed takeover attempt, I was absolutely thrilled at the start of the 2007-08 season when Sky rewarded me with my first contract, having worked for them in the previous six years on an ad-hoc basis.

Throughout 2007 I'd been speaking to Sue Page and Scott Duxbury about the prospect of me returning to West Ham in a corporate role but, due to all the problems that had engulfed the club for the first half of the year, I didn't reach an agreement to return until mid-September.

They wouldn't agree to my request for a full-time role but I signed a one-year contract and, basically, I had to work the lounges pretty much as I had done before but a broader PR role also meant I got involved talking to potential sponsors, conducting stadium tours and liaising with the full-time staff to try and implement some of my ideas.

On my first day back at the Boleyn Ground I found it interesting to see the name XL Airways emblazoned along the roof of the East Stand. One of my suggestions in the 30-page document I'd handed to Scott Duxbury when we met the previous November was for the club to sell advertising space on the roof of the two-tier stand (the one formerly known as the Chicken Run) to an airline company which could be seen by passengers flying over East

London into City Airport and, more importantly, Heathrow.

As it happened, the XL Leisure Group went into administration a year later, in September 2008, but their logo lasted a little longer on the roof of the East Stand than Eggert Magnusson did as chairman of West Ham. The global economy was in meltdown and Iceland was suffering more than most.

My relationship with Magnusson remained frosty and distant. I must have bumped into him at the club three times but apart from a curt handshake, which he accepted without even uttering a word, there was no warmth from him. I didn't expect us to have a life-changing conversation but a simple friendly 'hello' wouldn't have gone amiss.

The global economic collapse would ultimately force the Icelandics out of Upton Park but you would never have guessed there was an economy crisis about to change the world when you saw the ludicrous wages West Ham were paying their players in the early stages of the Magnusson era. Agents told me the Hammers paid way over the top compared to clubs of a similar stature.

Although it pains me to say it, Terry Brown had got the club under control and put the wage bill on a sensible, firm footing before the Icelandics came in and started throwing money around like confetti. One of the rumours that got back to me from a good source was that Magnusson couldn't agree a deal with a player, but when he came back into his office to continue the negotiations he allegedly offered 15 grand a week more than he had before he left the room.

Alan Curbishley had handled all player transfer dealings when he was manager at Charlton and Scott Duxbury had done it at West Ham before the Icelandic takeover. But then Magnusson came in and wanted to handle all player transfers himself, even though he had no previous experience in that field. I guess players and their agents must have seen him coming and exploited his inexperience and naivety for all its worth. It seemed a case of anything goes, which is a recipe for disaster.

Most fans were delighted to see the chairman splashing out huge fees, salaries and long-term contracts on players that would have been unaffordable to previous regimes. Players were turning down moves to bigger Premier League clubs who were in the Champions League to sign for West Ham, even though they were on the brink of dropping into the Championship!

That wasn't good for the business, though, and Magnusson should have realised that the owner, BG, didn't have a bottomless pot of cash to keep throwing at every player he took a shine to.

Magnusson's delusional grasp of football finances revealed itself again in an exclusive interview he gave to the West Ham fans' website kumb.com in March '07. He was quoted as saying: "The average salary of a West Ham supporter who comes to the games here is the second highest in the league – it's just below Chelsea, and I think it's around £60,000 per year."

Following that crucial last-gasp victory at Old Trafford that preserved the club's Premier League status by the thinnest of margins, Magnusson declared he would 'spend big' again that summer. And that's what he did. West Ham went on to sign the likes of Scott Parker, (injury-prone) Kieron Dyer, Craig Bellamy and Julien Faubert. He had also agreed to pay Charlton a £16m fee for Darren Bent but the striker chose Spurs instead.

Magnusson's magical mystery tour, his reckless ego trip, ended on December 13, 2007. He sold his 5% stake to BG and left the club, which struggled to cope with his legacy long after he was fired.

So there I was, at the end of '07, back at West Ham and all three of my main adversaries, Terry Brown, Kia Joorabchian and Eggert Magnusson, were gone.

26

Meltdown

BY the end of 2008 the financial crisis had spread far beyond all the banks and financial institutions and was threatening West Ham's very existence. While Eggert Magnusson had squandered millions on players and landed the Hammers with a crippling wage bill, hardly anyone could have foreseen the dramatic collapse of worldwide financial markets that caused club owner Bjorgolfur Gudmundsson to go bust. I liked BG and always believed he had the best interests of the club at heart but he became one of the worst hit by the almost total collapse of the Icelandic banking system.

My mate Dave Walsh, who worked in the City for the futures trader ICAP, had warned me a year before BG bailed out of Upton Park that the Icelandics were on a slippery slope. He pointed out that they had bought the club on leveraged money and he was convinced they were heading for trouble. He was right.

In October '08 the club tried to play down the effect the banking crash was having on BG but before the end of the year they were forced to concede that the club was up for sale. Gary Jacob, writing for *The Times*, explained:

West Ham's difficulties arose after Gudmundsson lost hundreds of millions of pounds after the collapse of Landsbanki, the Icelandic bank of which he was chairman and a major shareholder, in October. Asgeir Fridgeirsson, the club's vice-chairman, admitted for the first time that the club are seeking a buyer.

"There is a great interest in the club and many interested parties are calling to show interest," Fridgeirsson said.

In reality, West Ham need to be sold by early January to ensure

BG feeling the chill of the global economy collapse.

that transfer funds can be made available to Gianfranco Zola, the manager, to ensure their survival in the top flight this season. They are only a point above the relegation zone, despite a hard-fought 1-1 draw away to Chelsea on Sunday.

Craig Bellamy and Matthew Upson are a target for bigger clubs, but Lucas Neill has said that he wants to sign a new contract before his deal expires this summer. The defender, 30, who earns £70,000 a week, asked for a rise last summer but he is likely to be offered less than half that sum. He turns 31 in March.

What astonished everyone was the news that BG was looking to sell West Ham for £250m – a ludicrous price tag rightly ridiculed in *The Times* by Martin Samuel, who, under the headline 'West Ham's owners are living in a bubble', wrote:

It is heartening to see that recent traumas at Upton Park have not dampened that famous East End sense of humour. Björgólfur Gudmundsson, the West Ham United owner, may be Icelandic by birth, but he has learnt London ways. It has emerged that he is angling for £250m if he is to sell the club. Cor blimey, guv'nor, you're a right card, you are. 'Ere, lads, come and 'ave a listen to this.

To justify the fee, however, prospective purchasers may wish to ask a few questions. Such as, under Gudmundsson's stewardship, have the team improved? No. Have the coaching staff attained new heights? No. Have the club grown in size or stature? No. Are sporting or financial prospects positive? No. At executive level, is the club more efficiently managed? Not particularly. Hey, hey now, gentlemen, don't all dive for that chequebook at once.

What is remarkable is that Gudmundsson actually bought the club for £108m, including debt. So with the prospect of relegation and a serious financial downturn under way, in two years — during which West Ham have become embroiled in the most expensive legal battle in football's history, millions have been frittered away in the transfer market and two managers and one senior executive have been lost — by the calculation of the owners, the worth of the business has risen £142m.

With accounting like that, no wonder they overpaid for Fredrik Ljungberg.

According to court papers submitted by Gudmundsson's lawyers, the valuation is linked to a number of factors, mainly the recent price of £230m obtained for Manchester City when some of the richest men on the planet came calling, which may prove something of a false reading. "West Ham is thought a more valuable club looking at its location in London, its loyal fanbase, more chance of linked real estate projects, proximity to the Olympic village and the fact it owns its ground," the legal statement read.

Yet every one of those factors was also in place when Gudmundsson paid £108m. He has not bought the ground, relocated the club to the capital or unearthed staunch support that did not previously exist. Real estate potential is the same as it ever was — development on the training ground at Chadwell Heath, a plan frozen in the present climate — while the Olympic link is simply irrelevant. So from where is the extra value of £142m, or is Gudmundsson claiming that he underpaid?

It is not football's bubble that has burst, it is the ownership bubble; the belief that all this new money came from men with infallible business brains, foolproof judges of financial markets. The money that is being demanded by Gudmundsson, by Mike Ashley at Newcastle United and by the American owners of Liverpool suggests only one thing: these guys were not as smart as they thought they were.

They believed that they had spotted something that was undervalued when, in fact, it was overvalued. And they won't admit they were wrong. So they ask these inflated fees to prop up their egos, because if they simply tried to get their money back — and still there was no buyer — what would it say about their acumen?

West Ham is a mess that starts at the top and has been for more than a decade. The stewardship of Terence Brown, the former chairman, was calamitous and his successor, Eggert Magnússon, was foolish and wasteful, and any revival under Gudmundsson has been undermined by his parlous financial position after the Icelandic economic crash.

What happens at the club now will be considered to have great meaning for all, as if this is a lesson to be learnt throughout football, but in reality it is only one line of a song being sung from 10 Downing Street to the office of the financial advisers in your local high street. There are people whose business is business; and what they knew about business was nobody's business.

Of course, no-one in their right mind was going to pay £250m for West Ham to satisfy the owner's debts at the height of the credit crunch and in early June 2009 BG had to hand over ownership of the club to an asset management company. Gary Jacob explained the extent of the club's financial plight when he wrote in *The Times* (June 8):

Gudmundsson owed around £100m to Straumur-Burdaras Investment Bank, his main creditor, who have formed an asset management company called CB Holding that will run the club. Straumur own the majority (70%) stake in CB Holding, with the balance made up of Gudmundsson's other creditors.

These other creditors were Byr/MP Banki and Landsbanki, which together were reportedly owed about £16m by Gudmundsson. Straumur claimed to have had a three-year plan to run the club and had planned to recoup the money it was owed when the financial climate improved. Jacob added:

Gudmundsson was given until tomorrow to sell the club after a court hearing in Iceland in March. But buyers have been unwilling to pay a price that was acceptable

Scott Duxbury and Gianfranco Zola.

to Straumur. Gudmundsson, who has lost around £500m in the global financial crisis, has stepped down and Andrew Bernhardt, a Straumur director, has been appointed non-executive chairman.

"I am delighted that an agreement has been reached and look forward to working with CEO Scott Duxbury and his team in the coming years," Bernhardt said. "We have one of the best young management partnerships in Gianfranco Zola and Steve Clarke and the team has evolved with a great mix of experience and young players coming through from the Academy.

Duxbury said that the transfer will bring stability to the club, which has debts of around £45m.

Scott Duxbury was put in a difficult position, fire-fighting to keep the club going on almost a daily basis. CB Holdings – the initials stood for Claret and Blue – held the fort at Upton Park until January 18, 2010, when former Birmingham City owners David Sullivan and David Gold paid a reputed £52.5m for a controlling interest in the club.

The package offered by the pair was preferred to a series of other offers, including interest from Intermarket, a London-based financial services company, who made the highest bid but was unable to prove that it had sufficient money for a takeover. Apparently, an American group, favoured by the banks that were reportedly owed nearly £50m by West Ham, withdrew because its request for exclusive talks was rejected. Tony Fernandes, a Malaysian airline entrepreneur, boss of the revived Lotus F1 team and West Ham supporter, was also a contender.

Although I knew very little about the Fernandes bid, I did have some contact with the main man at Intermarket. In September '09 I received a phone call from Tony Gale, who said that our mutual friend and fellow West Ham ambassador Matthew Lorenzo had been speaking to representatives of Intermarket and he'd formed the opinion that they were the real deal. They claimed to have the necessary finances available, including a £100m transfer budget. All three of us were keen to find out more about these people, so Galey, Matt and myself met Intermarket's owner Dave Byrne, who was joined by a colleague called Ian, in a City wine bar.

Immediately, this set alarm bells ringing in my head. If you are trying to buy a Premier League club, the last place you want to be discussing plans is in a popular, very busy wine bar full of prying eyes and gossips. So I asked if we could go somewhere more discreet and we ended up moving on to Dave's office in Canary Wharf.

The first bit of advice I gave him was to keep their interest in West Ham a private matter – they hadn't been named in the press at that point – until such time as a deal was in place. We didn't quite extract from him the full ins and outs of their business proposal but, basically, Intermarket were the front men for an American-based consortium who were supposedly going to put up the money.

Matt Lorenzo actually flew out to the States with Dave and Ian and while they were there the Americans put pressure on Matt to use his PR contacts to begin spreading the word that they were very much the front-runners to buy West Ham. Matt and the Intermarket guys were still on the other side of

With my fellow former ambassador Galey and the Premier League trophy.

the Atlantic when the *News of the World* splashed the "£100m buy out" plans across its back page. Matt explained on his return that the Yanks had decided to take this tactical approach to let it be known that they were serious players.

At this time, both Galey and myself were working at West Ham in our ambassadorial roles and when we first held talks with Dave Byrne we had our future in mind. If Intermarket had succeeded in buying West Ham, Galey and I were both told that there would have been places for us within the proposed new hierarchy. By now the Icelandics were desperate to find a buyer, or else the club was in serious danger of going under.

In November '09 I briefly met Tony Fernandes, who was at Upton Park to watch a game and spent a while chatting with Galey. I understood Fernandes' bid included money from Asia, where he'd established himself as the successful owner of the budget airline, Air Asia.

The third party interested in West Ham was obviously Sullivan and Gold, who had been business partners for 30 years and were looking to buy

Tony Fernandes moved on to QPR after his West Ham bid fell through.

into another football club after selling out to Carson Yeung at Birmingham in October '09. In the 80s, Gold and Sullivan bought 29% of West Ham for £2m but, shunned by the ruling Cearns family at the time, they sold their shares and moved on to rebuild Birmingham.

In mid-December I drove around the M25 into Surrey, to visit David Gold. Unfortunately, snow prevented me from accessing the driveway leading to his opulent Victorian mansion set in 55 acres, a far cry from the East End of London where he had survived the Blitz, bomb sites, hunger, illness and anti-Semitism in his youth, so we arranged to meet at the head office of Ann Summers, the lingerie and 'adult shop' chain run by his daughter Jacqueline, at Whyteleafe.

I have always enjoyed working for the club and, apart from seeking a wider role with whoever took over, I wanted to protect my position as an ambassador. I felt then, as I still do, that I have a lot to offer West Ham. I spent half an hour with David and made it clear to him how keen I was to remain involved at the club if he and David Sullivan succeeded in their bid.

In the meantime, Intermarket co-founder and director David Byrne told us that they now had Russian backing after their newly-appointed American CEO, New Yorker Jim Bowe, died suddenly of a heart attack in early January. Jim's death came as a big blow to their takeover hopes but when we met Dave again, this time at a London hotel, he was still talking a good game. We also brought along Scott Duxbury, who was obviously eager to talk to anyone who had serious intentions of buying the club.

Rothschild Bank, who were handling the West Ham takeover on behalf of CB Holding, had set a mid-January deadline by which time the club had to be sold or risk sliding even further into the mire and, possibly, administration – and the clock was ticking. Actually, I was talking on the phone to David Byrne for about 15 minutes late on the designated deadline day and it struck me as odd that he was still chatting away to me when surely he should have been speaking to his Russian contacts and trying to finalise a deal.

Anyway, sure enough, I put the phone down and two minutes later, just before the stroke of midnight, Galey rang to say that David Sullivan and David Gold had bought the club, which was valued at around £100m. I was momentarily stunned and could only conclude that Intermarket were never serious bidders.

I don't know why the Tony Fernandes bid failed but after missing out at West Ham he went on to buy Queen's Park Rangers in August 2011 and guided them back to the Premier League at the end of his first season with the West London club.

27

Hammer house of horrors

ON January 19, the day after David Sullivan and David Gold took control, I went to Upton Park and was stopped in the car park by a reporter for Sky Sports News, who wanted my reaction to the takeover. I basically sang the new owners' praises, saying how good it was that they had put their money where their mouth is.

I made the point that Gold had been a lifelong West Ham fan and proud of his East End roots – his family used to live at 442 Green Street, just along the road from the Boleyn Ground, and in the mid-50s he played for the youth team and was offered an apprentice contract by manager Ted Fenton – while Sullivan had always lived in the Essex area and taken a close interest in the club. I didn't praise them up in front of the cameras out of self-interest, I was genuinely pleased that they had bought the club and saved it from an unthinkable fate.

I was at the club's offices in the Bobby Moore Stand with operations director Ben Illingworth when David Sullivan walked into the room. He was on his way to do a round of media interviews elsewhere in the stadium, so there was only enough time for a quick handshake and for me to offer my sincere congratulations and best wishes, for which he said "thanks".

As David left, in walked Karren Brady, who had just been appointed vice-chairman of West Ham. She seemed very surprised to see me and asked: "What are you doing here? I thought you worked for Sky Sports?"

"I do, but I'm also an ambassador for West Ham, I work for the club," I replied, before she turned on her heels and walked out. It wasn't the friendliest first encounter with the woman who was now running the club.

I had to go back to the ground the next day for a meeting with Ian Tompkins, who was basically in charge of the ambassadors. I had another appointment to go to, so I left before the others. But I'd only got as far as Upton Park tube station when my phone rang. It was Michael Kerr, West Ham's director of human resources, to say that Galey, Matt Lorenzo and me were having our contracts terminated with immediate effect.

Ambassadors at work

We had been appointed the club's first ambassadors by Scott Duxbury in July 2009. The wider PR role included me contributing a weekly column to the club's e-zine newsletter and I was there to assist the commercial department whenever possible.

I'd not been an ambassador long before Tony Bellchambers, a good friend and one of the longest-serving commercial staff, asked me to accompany him to an important meeting he was having with a client who had indicated he might not be renewing his executive box. It was a father and son directorship and Tony wanted to take them both out to lunch with one of their all-time favourite West Ham players, who happened to be me.

Before lunch, the club's client had expressed doubts over signing a one-year renewal for their corporate box – but by the time we left there after waffling away for about four hours, they had agreed to a further three-year contract.

That deal was worth just over £100,000 to West Ham but I didn't receive a penny in commission and nor did I expect to. What I earned in a year working as an ambassador, a lot of the first team squad were getting in a week. I was simply doing my mate Tony Bellchambers a favour and it was a brilliant example of how us ambassadors were able to benefit the club.

Galey and I also helped to organise a couple of very successful golf days with the club's corporate clients, who all had a great time. Obviously, the more they enjoyed themselves, the more money they and their businesses were likely to spend with West Ham.

We went on the club's pre-season tour of Beijing. Apart from the Hammers' party, Spurs and Hull City were also staying at the same hotel...along with about 50 of the West Ham Inter-City Firm (ICF) boys! This made things very interesting and, having taken over as Tottenham manager the previous year, Harry Redknapp steered well clear of this notorious group of Hammers fans with a fearsome reputation!

Galey and I were on hand to intervene when one of the ICF boys got the hump with West Ham's assistant manager Steve Clarke and called him a "miserable Scottish c***". The fella reckoned Steve had caused the problem when he failed to stop and sign an autograph for a fan but we quickly smoothed it over. I knew it was time to go to bed, though, when one of the more boisterous ICF lads located the hotel's grand piano and started to belt out the *EastEnders* theme tune at four o'clock in the morning!

But in all seriousness, it was

Gold and Sullivan inherited a financial nightmare at Upton Park.

David Sullivan and David Gold after their takeover in January 2010.

good that Galey and I were there for the supporters to talk to about issues they had with the club, manager or players. They obviously weren't going to be able to have any long or meaningful dialogue with the players or management, so we acted as a useful sounding board. It was all part of our duties.

The Hammers' Italian manager Gianfranco Zola was polite and came over to say 'hello' but there was no inclusion. He didn't invite us to sit down with him and his coaches for a cup of cappuccino, which was a bit disappointing – especially as Galey had put in a really good word for Zola with Scott Duxbury when the board appointed him as Alan Curbishley's successor in September 2008.

HR director Michael Kerr had never rang me once in my previous 18 months back at the club, although I liked him and got on well with him whenever our paths crossed at the ground. He said: "I don't know how to say this, Tony, but the club has asked me to terminate your contract."

I accepted that the new owners had to make major financial cutbacks as soon as they came in and I know that West Ham is much more important than me or any other individual. But I didn't believe the owners or senior management fully understood or appreciated the valuable work Galey and I had been doing for the previous six months. I was disappointed that they didn't even call me in and give me the chance to justify my position, or give me the option of taking, say, a 50% pay cut, which I would have reluctantly accepted.

Mis-management

The scale of the financial mess West Ham were in became crystal clear from the moment the new owners arrived at Upton Park. Here's what Rob Shepherd wrote in the *News of the World* (Jan 23, 2010):

David Sullivan walked into the chairman's suite at Upton Park and realised that behind the plush facade he had inherited a hammer house of horrors.

After an arduous takeover battle, it emerged that only Gold and Sullivan had the hard cash to buy into the club.

More importantly, only they were qualified to take on the challenge of reducing debts which, according to Sullivan, stand at around £110m.

And it hasn't taken him long to start doing some simple maths and flourish a red pen.

Sullivan has been staggered at what he sees as some of the excesses at the club, free spending that has continued despite the fact West Ham have been on the brink since the business empire of ex-owner Bjorgolfur Gudmundsson collapsed 15 months ago.

"We have bought into an incredibly bad situation. At every level the club has been badly run," said Sullivan. "I'll give you one simple example. It is now January and we have still got 21,000 first team shirts in stock at £21 each. Ridiculous.

"No proper decisions have been made. Bad deals have been done. This is the deck of cards we have inherited and it is going to take us time to play those cards."

West Ham's perilous financial position has forced them to take out loans on the promise of the next two years' Premier League television revenue, despite the fact they are far from guaranteed to beat relegation. Also, 70% of a shirt sponsorship with SBOBET has been taken up front to stave off the threat of administration.

Gold claims the club needed to raise £20m by the end of the month, which would have meant the sale of Scott Parker and Matthew Upson and either Rob Green or Carlton Cole.

Some of the deals that have heaped such a heavy financial burden on the club left the new owners barely able to catch their breath.

In summer 2007, Arsene Wenger was willing to off-load Freddie Ljungberg for £1.5m. The player is believed to have asked for £50,000 a week. In the end, they paid Arsenal £3m and gave the Swede near to £80,000 a week. A year later, they realised he was not up to Premier League pace any more, and they paid up his £6m contract. Players such as Kieron Dyer, Craig Bellamy, Lucas Neill and Scott Parker joined on wages which were way out of West Ham's league.

Sullivan was staggered to discover technical director Gianluca Nani was being paid £300,000 a year while two full-time club doctors earned a combined salary of £400,000.

Sullivan's view is that if the physios need any help, then players will be sent to a specialist. The doctors will go and so will Nani. Nani's track record in recruiting players has, for the most part, been disastrous. Last January, he lured German Under-21 international Savio Nsereko to England for a fee touted at £9m. The player wasn't up to it and has slipped back to Italy for next to nothing.

Sullivan's verdict on the squad is damning. He said: "We have an unbelievably unbalanced team. It doesn't take a genius to see we have more midfielders than we know what do with."

On the coaching front, Sullivan is astonished that, given the club's plight, it still opted to hand Gianfranco Zola a new deal so soon into his managerial career on a salary of £1.9m. Assistant Steve Clarke is on £1.2m, thought to be double the salary of Manchester United's No 2, Mike Phelan.

Sullivan will also wonder why several new company cars were recently acquired, including an Aston Martin on a £1,500 a month lease.

Having brought Birmingham from the brink, Sullivan has a proven track record of putting football clubs back on track, even if it is painful. As it stands the plan is simple. Sullivan said: "The short term situation is survival. The long term situation is our dreams."

One of the first casualties under the new regime was Scott Duxbury, who left the club within a couple of weeks of the new owners taking over. I'd always got on well with Scott – who joined Watford in 2012 after Zola was appointed Hornets' manager – but his position at Upton Park was always going to be taken over by Karren Brady once Sullivan and Gold took control at the top.

Banter with Karren Brady

I've had further communication with Karren since our initial, frosty meeting on the day the new owners arrived. We had a meeting in her office at Upton Park for about 15 minutes and she listened to the points I've made here about my assets as a club ambassador. She seemed to appreciate where I was coming from and agreed to consider a new redefined role for me.

Karren Brady can give as good as she gets.

We next met at the club's end-of-season dinner at The Grosvenor Hotel in May 2011 – the night it all kicked off after Demba Ba refused to sign an autograph. I'll never forget compere Ben Shephard's lovely line when he appealed for calm and said: "Gentleman, will you please sit on your chairs and not throw them!"

Karren told me that evening that she didn't like comments I'd made in an interview with BBC Radio 5 Live the previous day about her 'hiring and firing managers', in which I'd also questioned the clumsy way Zola and Avram Grant had been dismissed. She explained that it wasn't her role at West Ham to appoint and sack managers, which was fair enough, and I responded by saying that I was only doing my job by giving an opinion when asked for it.

And then, tongue in cheek, I asked her: "So you never had lunch with Avram Grant at Langans, then?"

I think she quite enjoys banter and a good finger-wagging debate!

In fact, the club did subsequently offer me a small commercial role but it wasn't really what I was looking for, nor, in my opinion, was the fee they were offering fair for the work involved. I still hope we can work something out in the future, though.

Sullivan and Gold's first 18 months in charge were always going to be a difficult, turbulent period – I'll reflect later on their appointment and sacking of the hopeless Grant – that culminated in relegation from the Premier League in May 2011.

To be fair, though, the following season in the Championship was much better for various reasons. The owners retreated further from the media spotlight, Sam Allardyce did all that was expected of him as the new manager and the long-suffering supporters were finally rewarded with a day they will never forget.

28

Wonderful Wembley

I WAS just 14-years-old when West Ham last won a trophy at Wembley. Wearing my claret and blue Doc Martens boots and scarf, my brother Paul, best mate John Cornwell and myself stood on the terraces at the tunnel end and went wild with delight as Trevor Brooking stooped to steer home our winner in the FA Cup Final against Arsenal in May 1980.

It's a day I and many thousands of other West Ham fans will never forget and the same has to be said of the 2012 Championship Play-off Final victory over Blackpool. Feeling full of nervous energy and anticipation, I awoke at about 3.30 on the morning of the game – even though I wouldn't be leaving my home in Leigh-on-Sea until about 7.00am, before the hour's drive to Surrey where I had to pick up my two boys.

We were back in Essex for about half-past nine and then dropped off at Rochford station. We met up with my friend Dave Walsh and his two sons at Shenfield before continuing on our way to Liverpool Street, where the West Ham fans really began to make their presence felt. The noise coming from the Hamilton Hall pub was deafening – it was only about 11.45 but I think some of the lads had been in there since six that morning!

We boarded the Metropolitan Line tube to Wembley Park, where I met my brother Paul and brother-in-law Andy Laver and gave them their match tickets. When the iconic Wembley Arch came into view beyond a sea of claret and blue shirts, hats and scarves, the excitement became even more intense and there was a feeling that this was going to be our day.

The walk down Wembley Way brought back memories of the 1981 League Cup Final, the last time the club reached a major final at the national

Matt and Billy and their friend James Walsh on their way to the 2012 Play-off Final.

Trevor Brooking's winner against Arsenal in the 1980 FA Cup Final.

**I was stood behind this goal when Ray Stewart calmly slotted home
our equaliser in the 1981 League Cup Final.**

stadium. I attended that occasion as a fan, although by then I was also attached to the club as an associate schoolboy player. I actually signed as an apprentice two months later.

I remember standing on the terraces behind the goal at the end where Ray Stewart calmly stepped up to stroke his last-minute penalty equaliser past Liverpool's Ray Clemence. We all knew Ray wouldn't miss – he very rarely did – and it was amazing to think that just a few months later I was jogging alongside him and the other first team stars in pre-season training at Chadwell Heath.

I relished those Wembley visits in 1980 and '81 and in 2012 I was thrilled to be among the crowd again as they made their way to the 'New Wembley' in eager anticipation and with nerves jangling. It was great posing with fellow supporters as their friends took pictures on their iPhones and I enjoyed soaking up the special atmosphere with them before making our way into the stadium. Our group watched the game from a 20-seater hospitality box, along with other West Ham-supporting families.

The result ensured that manager Sam Allardyce made good on his promise to take the Hammers back into the top flight after his team narrowly missed out on automatic promotion (along with Reading and Southampton) at the end of the regular season. We became the first team since Leicester City in 1996 to bounce straight back to the Premier League through the play-offs, following the semi-final victory over Cardiff City.

Allardyce's side had led at the break through a Carlton Cole strike in the 35th minute but after Thomas Ince – son of former Hammers midfielder Paul – levelled shortly after the restart, the match became increasingly stretched and ragged. Both teams wasted good opportunities to score but it was the Hammers who grabbed what proved to be the decisive third when the unmarked Ricardo Vaz Te, a January signing from Barnsley, drilled the ball into the net from 12 yards.

Ricardo Vaz Te latches onto the loose ball to fire West Ham back into the Premier League.

Julien Faubert, George McCartney and Mark Noble celebrate with match-winner Vaz Te.

It was lovely to see the kids' happy, smiling faces as the two West Ham goals went in, and again as the final whistle blew. The Championship Play-off winners' trophy was presented to the players just in front of our box – another moment to savour from a great day.

Afterwards I went downstairs to a restaurant where I met Galey, Phil Parkes and a few other friends. There were broad smiles and happy people wherever I looked.

The fans were still celebrating promotion when we reached Liverpool Street on our return journey. It was impossible not to get caught up in the emotion of it all. West Ham fans don't get to enjoy many great days out like this, so we naturally milk every moment.

Even if we hadn't won, it would still have been a memorable day. Although it was vital to clinch that coveted Premier League place and it was important for the manager, players, staff and, of course, the club itself, it was, above all, an occasion for the fans.

It belonged to the many people who have had to struggle through the economic recession in recent years, many of them losing their jobs or hoping and praying they can hang on to them. There's not a lot to cheer in the world today, so after waiting 31 years since they were last able to enjoy that magical

Great scenes that no Hammers fans who were at Wembley in 2012 will ever forget.

Wembley experience, they fully deserved this wonderful day out.

Although we had to suffer Chelsea winning the Champions League Final that evening, their victory over Bayern Munich couldn't spoil the party. My two boys said: "Thanks for a great day, Dad," and their enjoyment of it gave me as much pleasure as the result itself. Having brainwashed them into supporting the Hammers from birth, I felt vindicated for inflicting upon them a life of suffering that all West Ham fans take in their stride!

Hopefully there was a new generation of young fans there on May 19, 2012 who will now declare their undying allegiance to the claret and blue flag and support their father's team, keeping their family tradition alive for generations to come.

Sam Allardyce did all that he was asked to do when he got the Hammers promoted at the first attempt.

29

Managing West Ham

I T'S incredible to think that when Terry Brown sacked Harry Redknapp in May 2001, West Ham had only had eight managers in its 106-year history. While many clubs, led by the likes of Newcastle, Chelsea and Tottenham, hired and fired their managers willy-nilly, the Hammers had a reputation for backing their men over a sustained period.

But in the decade that followed Harry's departure we've seen six full-time and one caretaker manager occupy the Upton Park 'hotseat' in much shorter spells. Let's take a critical look at each of them individually...

GLENN ROEDER (June 2001-September 2003)

After Harry Redknapp's surprise dismissal, I remember thinking how I wanted his replacement to be a 'West Ham man' who understood the best traditions of the club and would uphold those principles for playing bright, attacking football. In an ideal world, I've always thought it would be nice for the manager to have either played or supported the club. We accept that we're not up there with the Manchester Uniteds and Liverpools in terms of achievements and silverware won, but West Ham is a special club and, for

Glenn Roeder was a good coach but unsuited to the manager's role.

Roeder with goalkeeper David James, one of his best signings.

me, it's our fans that make it unique. So when Harry was fired, I just wanted someone to come in who understood the Hammers' ethos.

At the time, I recall asking the long-serving former skipper and team-mate Alvin Martin if he would be applying for the job, despite the difficulties he faced in his first managerial role at Southend United. Alan Devonshire, who had proved himself at non-league level and was a huge fans' favourite at Upton Park, was another I thought should have been considered by the board. Alan Curbishley, who had done such a solid job at Charlton Athletic over a long period, had to be another prime candidate.

So I was astonished when they gave the job to Glenn Roeder, who had been given a coaching role in the youth academy by Redknapp as a favour. Although I like Glenn as a person, I just didn't think he was the right man for the club. He hadn't had much

The volatile Paolo Di Canio didn't show too often north of Watford.

success at lower league level with Gillingham and Watford and I thought West Ham was too big a job for him.

He did well to secure a seventh-place finish in his first season but you always felt the writing was on the wall from early on in 2002-03. For us to be relegated with the quality squad he had at his disposal was incredible.

What happened to Glenn towards the end of his second year in charge, when he collapsed at the ground suffering the effects of a low-grade brain tumour, was horrific for him and his family and I wouldn't wish their ordeal on my worst enemy. But the fact is, the team was doomed before Glenn was taken ill. Indeed, it was the late intervention of Trevor Brooking, who took seven points from the last three games, that gave West Ham a lifeline that they just couldn't quite grasp. Even if they had won their final game at Birmingham instead of drawing it, the Hammers would still have gone down with 44 points on goal-difference, instead of Sam Allardyce's Bolton. I doubt that a Premier League side will ever be relegated again after recording that many points.

I didn't know what was going on in the dressing room at the time but it appeared that a number of the players didn't fully respect Glenn as their manager, although a manager has to earn respect.

Trevor made it clear that he would only fill in as an interim caretaker appointment, which was a great shame because he fitted my ideal West Ham manager template perfectly. We all know him as a placid man, a true gent and ambassador of the game with an unblemished career for club and country, but from what I gather he went in there and basically told the players he wasn't going to take any bullshit from them. He galvanised the team and got them playing for him and the West Ham shirt again. I'd love to have seen him take the job full-time but I don't think he wanted the aggro and circus that goes with football management.

Trevor Brooking was only prepared to fill in as caretaker manager.

Alan Pardew looking lost for answers in his early days at Upton Park.

It was a poor decision by the board to appoint Glenn in the first place and an even bigger mistake to bring him back at the start of the 2003-04 season, only to sack him four games into the new campaign.

ALAN PARDEW (September 2003-December 2006)

Once again, Trevor Brooking plugged the gap before Roeder's replacement, Alan Pardew, could be extricated from his duties at Reading in September '03. I mentioned earlier in the book about how Pards and myself fell out over my comment in *Hammers News Magazine* that someone with claret and blue blood in his veins should have been top of the board's wish list. As well as Alvin Martin and Alan Devonshire, by then Iain Dowie had also emerged as a possible contender for the job following the success of his first managerial stint with Oldham Athletic.

Having said that, I think most people quite rightly look back on Alan Pardew's time at Upton Park with huge affection at what he achieved. Those three big occasions at Cardiff in successive years – the two play-off finals and

Pards after the 2005 Play-off Final win over Preston.

the FA Cup Final – will never be forgotten by those who were there. We should have won the 2006 FA Cup, without a doubt.

What people do tend to forget, though, is how poor the general standard of football was in his two seasons in the Championship. When his team scraped into the play-offs and went on to snatch promotion in May '05, a result that had a huge bearing on my own ambitions to shake things up at West Ham, Pardew perhaps proved the old adage that it's better to be a lucky manager than a very good one. That was certainly true of him leading up to the final against Preston. They were awful at times. And lucky.

But all credit to him. To bring in the decent players he did and finish ninth the following season was a fine achievement. The trouble was, he and a number of his players got carried away with their success and there was too much going on off the field, although I did feel sorry for him over the Tevez/Macherano affair, because he didn't ask for those players to be parachuted in.

I've not spoken to him about his mixed time at West Ham, although we've briefly chatted since then and we get on fine. I think he will admit that he learned some important lessons in his 27 months with the club which has stood him in good stead at Charlton Athletic, Southampton and Newcastle United.

When you look back at what he did in his first full season at Newcastle, a job that has always been considered a poisoned chalice, I have to say that I have nothing but admiration and praise for the job he has done on Tyneside. He was the Premier League's Manager of the Year in 2011-12 and deservedly so.

ALAN CURBISHLEY (December 2006-September 2008)

I thought he was a good 'let's steady the ship' appointment. Curbs is a nice man, I get on well with him, and he was the right man for the task.

I still don't quite know how he managed to keep them up, but to win seven games out of the last nine was remarkable – even allowing for the good fortune we had in facing a weakened Man United team at Old Trafford on

Alan Curbishley and expensive signing Luis Boa Morte face the media at Chadwell Heath.

'Survival Sunday'.

Regardless of how much of an impact the Tevez business had on events, we were very fortunate not to go down that season.

People will rightly question a number of the signings the club made during Curbs' tenure but I wonder how much of an influence he had on transfers, and to what extent it was the work of Eggert Magnusson. I suspect the latter's ego had more than a little to do with all the money that was wasted on players who failed to deliver...Boa Morte? Quashie? Ljungberg? Dyer? Faubert? Horrendous, expensive signings – not just in transfers fees, but exorbitant wages and contracts that cost the club many millions over years.

Curbs' first full season in charge (2007-08) showed what he was all about as a manager. Organisation, pragmatism...and mid-table. It seemed unreal for West Ham fans to reach the stage where there were about four games left to play and we were in no danger of being relegated.

With Curbs, he did what it said on the tin. He brought great stability to Charlton – no mean feat at any football club – and they are a fine club with a marvellous heritage, but they are not West Ham, where expectations are much higher. In recent years, after Charlton dropped out of the Championship and into League One, I've often had a laugh with Addicks' fans when I ask: 'Wouldn't you rather have Curbs back and be mid-table in the Premier League?' Sometimes us supporters should be careful what we wish for.

I understood why he resigned not long into the 2008-09 season, after he'd been undermined by the club's decision to sell Anton Ferdinand and George McCartney to Sunderland over his head. To get around £14m for those two defenders was good business for West Ham at the time, especially given the financial straits they were in, but no manager would put up with that kind of interference at boardroom level. He successfully sued the club for breach of contract and was proven right.

Who's the little blond kid receiving the award from Curbs on his return to Upton Park with Birmingham?

Gianfranco Zola tried to entertain the fans the 'West Ham way'.

GIANFRANCO ZOLA (September 2008-May 2010)

My first choice to replace Alan Curbishley was Slaven Bilic, who I'd played with during my second spell as a West Ham player. He knew and understood the club and was clearly looking for his first Premier League job after doing well as the national manager of Croatia since 2006. I reckon he would have walked to Upton Park.

Instead, Gianfranco Zola emerged top of an uninspired shortlist and became our first foreign manager. I wasn't in favour of a foreign appointment but at least Bilic had a West Ham background, whereas Zola was a Chelsea man, just like his assistant Steve Clarke, who earned a good reputation as a coach under Jose Mourinho.

But Gianfranco's desire for his team to play entertaining football was welcomed by the fans and the players mainly responded well to him. He got the best out of Carlton Cole, who became an England international, and Zola lifted the team from near the foot of the table to a ninth-place finish at the end of his first season.

Alas, he became the most high profile casualty of the takeover in January 2010. Once David Sullivan and David Gold came in it very quickly became obvious that

Slaven Bilic was my preferred choice to replace Curbs.

Chelsea old boys Steve Clarke and Gianfranco Zola.

Gianfranco's days were numbered and no-one was surprised when he was sacked as soon as the season finished in May, with the team just one place and five points above the drop zone.

Given more time, he could have become a successful West Ham manager – the players seemed to believe in him and showed him great loyalty right to the end – but he was there at the wrong time.

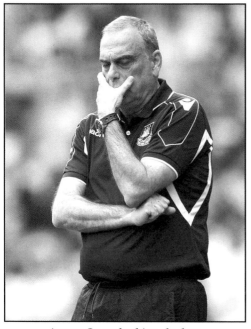

Avram Grant looking clueless.

AVRAM GRANT
(June 2010-May 2011)

The worst appointment in West Ham's history – that's how I'd describe the hopeless Israeli Avram Grant. I know Chelsea reached the 2008 Champions League Final under him but they had some very strong characters in the dressing room at that time and the team pretty much ran itself. It was Jose Mourinho's team.

Grant took cash-strapped Portsmouth out of the Premier League in 2010 and even if you discount their nine-point reduction, Pompey would still have been relegated.

He is the most boring man on earth to listen to and there is no way he would have inspired me to play for him. Whereas the players clearly had respect for Zola, they appeared to have none for Grant and results indicated as much. As a manager, you've either got to have a big personality or gain the players' respect by what you have achieved as a player or a coach. Zola had

Grant thought he was on his way after the Arsenal game and threw his scarf into the crowd.

a brilliant career with Chelsea but what had Grant done in the game? He had nothing going for him.

The disastrous but all too predictable year under Grant had echoes of the Roeder fiasco. How did a team with England internationals Robert Green,

Footballer of the Year Scott Parker did his best to keep West Ham up.

Matt Upson, Scott Parker (voted Footballer-of-the-Year) and Carlton Cole down its spine, plus other promising young players around them, get relegated?

Grant himself seemed to accept that he wouldn't be around to see the season out when he threw his West Ham scarf into the ground after the Arsenal home game. There were strong rumours that Martin O'Neill – available since resigning at Aston Villa the previous August – was being lined up as his replacement and everyone thought Grant was a dead man walking. Having said that, I felt sorry for him at the manner of his treatment from the board, who undermined him in the same way they did Zola. Grant was a poor manager but he didn't deserve that.

One of the most frustrating and upsetting things for me is that West Ham gave up the chance of getting one of the best managers of his era during the winter of 2010-11. Having played under Martin O'Neill for three years at Leicester, I knew what a difference he would have made at

Upton Park. When you talk about the best managers to have worked in the Premier League over the past 15 years, you would have to put him right up there with the likes of Sir Alex Ferguson, Jose Mourinho and Arsene Wenger.

I knew that Martin was itching to get back into Premier League football but I also know that as soon as he saw that news of his likely appointment had somehow been leaked to the press, on the morning of the Arsenal game with Grant still in situ, he would shun West Ham's interest on principle.

Martin didn't go into specifics about what happened when we spoke briefly at the Football Writers' Dinner in May 2011, but he did tell me he was disappointed not to get the chance to manage what was "a great football club." The Hammers' loss was Sunderland's gain in December 2011 and I was gutted West Ham never got the manager it deserved.

I can only assume that by sacking the uninspiring Avram Grant after one year in the job, which culminated in a rock bottom finish, seven points adrift of the 17th-placed team, the joint owners realised their costly mistake in appointing him.

SAM ALLARDYCE (June 2011-)

At the time of the Martin O'Neill debacle in January 2011, the other name that cropped up as a possible alternative to Grant was Sam Allardyce, who is one of a small group of managers who have taken charge of more than 300 Premier League games. Once Grant had gone at the end of that season, I thought 'Big Sam' was the right appointment. We needed a strong manager to come in and sort out the dressing room and crack heads together, and he was just the man to do it.

I'm good friends with Sam's assistant Neil McDonald, a former team-mate of mine at Everton, and I was pleased to see them arrive. Just before the start of their first season at Upton Park, I instigated a dinner date with Sam

Big Sam restored harmony to the dressing room.

through 'Macca', and the two of them joined Galey, Alan Devonshire and myself for a meal and a few beers one night in Canary Wharf.

With more than 1,000 games for West Ham between us and knowing the supporters' expectations, we wanted to grill Sam ourselves about what he had planned and to gently remind him about West Ham's tradition for encouraging entertaining, attacking football. We expressed our concerns about his reputation for advocating a more direct approach.

But as he quite openly asked in response: 'What is West Ham's way? Is it to play good football and get relegated?'

I tried to explain to Sam and Macca that if they could put together a successful West Ham team, whatever the stadium capacity it would never be enough. Whether Sam took what we said on board, I don't know, but I'm sure he understands the importance of having the media on board and how it works. Apart from Galey and myself at Sky, half of Fleet Street (or Wapping) are West Ham fans, so good PR is useful. Anyway, it was nice to have the chance to spend a bit of time with the new manager. If I go down the training ground now, I feel welcome again, but that hadn't been the case since Curbs left.

I understand that some of the fans have questioned Sam's style of play and how he wants to do things, but when you think back to his eight years at Bolton Wanderers, he struck a good balance. As well as the direct approach of, say, Kevin Davies, one of the best headers of a ball, he also brought in more cultured international players such as Jay-Jay Okocha, Ivan Campo, Fernando Hierro and Youri Djorkaeff. Bolton became an established Premier League team under Sam and I'm sure he will look to further develop things at Upton Park in a similar way.

His job was to stabilise the club and get us promoted and to do that in such dramatic style via the 2012 Play-off Final, in his first season, was a great achievement. Strong leadership was also required in the dressing room and on the pitch, and Sam achieved that with the signing of Kevin Nolan, who played under him at both Bolton and Newcastle.

The dressing room is now harmonious under Sam, the players clearly respect him and, most importantly, they are playing for him. It's not always easy to play free-flowing football in the Championship, although I realise Swansea and Norwich managed to do it successfully, but I believe Sam is relishing the challenge of proving his doubters wrong by re-establishing West

*Me alongside Neil McDonald in training at Everton, with Pat Nevin (left)
and Stuart McCall either side of us.*

Kevin Nolan about to score West Ham's first goal of the 2012-13
Premier League season, against Aston Villa.

Ham in the Premier League while also playing decent football.

In a way, the Play-off final vindicated Sam's philosophy. Blackpool were the most creative side and enjoyed more possession, but West Ham won the game 2-1 and that, at the end of the day, is the statistic that matters most.

It's all about striking the right balance. Everyone, from the owners and the manager down, wants to see their team win playing attacking, entertaining football but no West Ham fan is going to complain if we play badly and beat Spurs 1-0, are they? It comes down to what Martin O'Neill has always said: football is a results business.

30

Looking forward

HAVING looked at past events on and off the field at West Ham, now let's try and visualise where the club will be in 10 years' time. Of course, the most burning issue of all surrounds the Hammers' future home.

On the same day that David Sullivan took over West Ham in January 2010, he made it clear in his press conference that one of the factors which attracted the new regime to Upton Park was their vision of the club's future at the Olympic Stadium (OS) built for the 2012 London Games. This came as little or no surprise. The Icelandics had previously been keen on moving to Stratford, my consortium also examined the implications of such a move and even going as far back as the Terry Brown era, the board did its homework on a potential relocation a few miles across East London.

It must have been obvious to the people who first talked about bidding for the London Games, well before construction began in 2008, that there would have to be a viable legacy beyond the wonderful, uplifting festival of sport we all enjoyed in the summer of 2012. It was never going to be sustainable as an athletics venue alone, so football was always going to be the long-term solution to an expensive problem. But the big question was, how could the 80,000 stadium, centrepiece for the Olympics and Paralympics, be converted to make it football-friendly for spectators?

This was a question successfully answered by Manchester City when they moved from their old Maine Road home to the City of Manchester Stadium that hosted the 2002 Commonwealth Games and which was scaled down from 80,000 to 50,000 for City's benefit. But the original construction in Stratford, though superb for athletics, was not designed with a football club in mind.

The biggest problem is the running track, because it means the seats are too far away from the proposed football pitch, especially at each end of the arena. And as Britain is set to host the 2017 World Athletics Championships, it means the track will have to remain in place until at least three years after West Ham are looking to move in there. Numerous clubs have played in stadiums with an athletics track around the playing area but none of the supporters of those clubs have been happy with it – just ask the Brighton fans who had to suffer the dreaded Withdean Stadium.

It's not just fans who are adversely affected by the poor atmosphere that exists at grounds where the pitch is a bus ride from the spectators. When things are going well, West Ham players are visibly lifted by the vocal support of the home crowd and a 'bouncing' Upton Park has been an intimidating place for many visiting teams down the years. Players won't want to perform in a huge, soul-less stadium in which the fans won't be heard.

I know from speaking to people at West Ham that the club is confident and very hopeful of overcoming all the viewing obstacles, so that it won't be an issue. If they are able to install retractable seats on the running track, fans will be able to get much closer to the action – and this has to happen for the Olympic Stadium to be an acceptable alternative to the 35,000-capacity Boleyn Ground.

Another big question mark surrounds future ownership of the Olympic Stadium, which seems likely to remain in the hands of the government or the local Newham Council. The worst thing that could happen to West Ham is for David Sullivan and David Gold to sell the Boleyn Ground – reckoned to be worth somewhere in the region of £30m-to-£35m – and move into a stadium where the club merely becomes a tenant. Without their biggest fixed asset, how would the club be able to borrow money to finance major player transfers in the future? This is an obvious question the two Davids will have to face if, and when, the move happens and depending on the terms of the OS occupancy.

I also wonder if the club will be able to secure stadium naming rights – the Bobby Moore Stadium? – and build corporate boxes, which don't currently exist at the OS?

If all the solutions to the existing problems can be found, then I am all in favour of the club moving to Stratford. West Ham needs to become bigger

The Olympic Park and Stadium – a great venue for athletics but it needs to be adapted for football.

and they must follow the example set by Arsenal, who switched from their 36,000-capacity Highbury home to reap the benefits of the 60,000 Emirates stadium.

Geographically, Stratford makes perfect sense and the infrastructure is ideal. Wherever West Ham fans are based in and around the capital, or even for those travelling much longer distances, the E20 location provides easy commuter access thanks to main rail links, with ample parking within the Olympic Park itself. The same can't be said for Upton Park, which is a pig of a place to get to and from on match days and car parking around the ground is almost non-existent for those who don't wish to arrive three or four hours before kick-off.

I want to see West Ham transform their facilities in the same way Arsenal have. If we are going to progress and eventually compete for a Champions League place, then the only way to do so is through increased ticket sales, which in turn would boost other revenue streams from merchandise, corporate facilities and catering. Or at least it should do.

I don't go along with those traditionalists in the anti-OS camp who question the severing of historic links and whether we even need a 60,000 stadium. If West Ham were successful, 60,000 seats wouldn't be enough. The stadium

How the Olympic Stadium at Stratford looked during the 2012 London Games.

David Gold, Karren Brady and David Sullivan outside the venue they hope will become West Ham's new home.

would be sold out for the biggest Premier League games and by reducing ticket prices, even adopting the 'kids for a quid' scheme for the less attractive games, supporting the Hammers will become much more affordable to those who have been priced out. If we can get the average man in the street and his kids coming to games again, this, in turn, will generate new, young supporters for generations to come.

I love the Boleyn Ground for all the treasured memories it holds for me as a supporter and former player and none of us privileged to have been there will ever forget the European nights under the lights and all the countless other special times we've enjoyed. But we have to move on. Do any Arsenal fans honestly look back now and yearn for the marble halls of Highbury?

The decision as to whether West Ham should leave its spiritual home in Green Street for the Olympic Stadium will be the biggest ever taken in the club's history. It could be so good. But get it wrong and there will be serious repercussions.

The current owners must understand that, although they have put in their own money to keep the club running, they are only custodians of the club. West Ham United belongs to the fans.

Looking ahead 10 years, I'd like to think West Ham will be in the hands of good owners with the club's best interests at heart. I hope we will be enjoying a decade of unbroken membership to the Premier League and getting ever closer to a serious crack at qualifying for the Champions League – at least challenging for fourth place. If Tottenham, with their 36,000 White Hart Lane stadium capacity and more or less the same infrastructure as the Hammers, can recently reach the Champions League, then why shouldn't we?

Winning the FA Cup for the first time since 1980 must also be a realistic aim. The two things I most want to see in football before I die is for West Ham to win the FA Cup for the fourth time and England to win the World Cup again. I was barely one when Bobby Moore lifted the Jules Rimet trophy in 1966!

The foundations have to be put in place and that is what the next few years are all about. We have no divine right to be in the Premier League and you wouldn't bet your mortgage on us not dropping out of the top flight again in the next decade. But I'd like to think that in 2022, we won't be looking back on two more relegations and all the carnage and upheaval that will have caused.

I'd love to see us playing in a 60,000 purpose-built football stadium, trying to qualify for the Champions League and dreaming of classic nights under the lights against the likes of Barcelona and Real Madrid.

I can dream, can't I?

English football

SO that's the future of West Ham taken care of, but what does the future hold for football in general? I dusted off my crystal ball again and imagined what we might expect to find in 2022...

Premier League

It will remain as strong and vibrant as it is now for as long as Sky TV continue to invest in it to at least the extent they do today. The Premier League brand has grown much stronger since its formation at the start of the 1992-93 season and it can only keep going from strength to strength.

The latest deal between The Premier League and Sky, agreed in the summer of 2012 and effective for three years from season 2013-14, is worth £3bn – a massive 71% increase. Premier League chief executive Peter Scudamore called for the 20 clubs to spend the additional incomes on stadiums and infrastructure rather than on players but I doubt that his words will be heeded in most cases.

With future competition from the likes of BT, ESPN and the Arabic Al-Jazeera channel, I can only see the rights to live Premier League games continue to rocket in the years ahead. I'll go as far as to say it won't be long before we see the first Premier League player paid half-a-million pounds a week.

And to those out there who blame Sky for the explosion in players' wages, let me make it clear: The company doesn't tell the clubs HOW to spend the millions they receive in television revenue. If clubs want to shell out big money on players and agents, instead of improving their facilities or reducing ticket prices, that's down to them.

One change I would like to see in the Premier League is the introduction of an end-of-season play-off involving the teams placed fourth, fifth, sixth and seventh, just like they do in the Championship where the race for the third promotion place always produces a thrilling climax to every season.

But the reward for the winners of my Premier League play-off would be the final Champions League spot. At the moment the top three qualify automatically for the group stages of the following season's major European club competition, with the fourth-placed side having to contest the Champions League qualifiers.

So, under the system I'm proposing, the team that finishes seventh in the Premier League could, by winning both their play-off semi-final and

Wembley final, make it into the Champions League the following season. What a dramatic finale this would guarantee us every season.

I'd also love to see Scottish giants Celtic and Rangers (their recent troubles aside) join the English Premier League to add further spice. But instead of being admitted direct to England's top flight, they should have to battle their way up from the Championship – and what a boost it would be to England's second tier clubs to have hordes of Glaswegians flooding south. Think of the extra gates money...and beer sales!

I believe the withdrawal of Celtic and Rangers would also boost the Scottish Premier League, where the rest have virtually been chasing third spot in a two-horse title race for many years. The likes of Hearts, Hibs and Aberdeen, etc, would have a genuine, unprecedented chance of qualifying for the Champions League group stage.

The Scottish clubs would obviously face a reduction in gate revenue if the 'big two' left their domestic league but there's no reason why the problem can't be alleviated by allowing Celtic and Rangers to continue to contest the two main Scottish cup competitions.

FA Cup

It saddens me the way the tradition and prestige of the FA Cup, the world's biggest cup competition, has been steadily eroded in recent years. So how do we revive the glory days when giant-killers dreamed of those special occasions their players and fans will never forget? Well, how about avoiding all-Premier League ties in the third round by introducing a seeding system to guarantee glamour games? Instead of Manchester United v Manchester City, let's see Man U verses MK Dons, or City versus Chesterfield.

To ease fixture congestion, I'd do away with replays – all games to be decided by a penalty shootout if the teams can't be separated after 90 minutes and extra-time.

The first big issue I have with the FA Cup is the FA's decision to stage the semi-finals, as well as the final, at Wembley to boost their coffers. They have to revert to neutral major Premier League grounds, such as Old Trafford, The Emirates or Villa Park, which would restore more prestige to the final itself.

I also found it a complete joke when, for the first time in May 2012, the FA Cup Final was played on the same day as Premier League fixtures, plus other games throughout The Football League. Whenever the FA Cup is played, and I'd prefer to see it scheduled for 3.00pm on a Sunday, there should be no other games played on that day and, what's more, it should be the final game of the English domestic season.

League Cup

I hope the English League Cup is retained, because it's now an accepted way for the bigger clubs to blood youngsters in competitive games. Arsenal led the way in this but their Premier League rivals have also reaped the benefits in giving more experience to their younger players whose league appearances are limited.

Winter break

To further enhance the credibility of the FA Cup I'd introduce a much talked about winter break for Premier League clubs only. The Christmas / New Year period is traditionally a boom time for the clubs and fans enjoy these festive fixtures, so I'd leave well alone there. But after the New Year's Day league game, Premier League clubs should take, say, an 18-day break in which they were not allowed to organise lucrative overseas friendlies or play any other games.

They would then resume at the end of January with the third round of the FA Cup, which would be even more eagerly awaited than normal because of the near three-week lay-off.

The Football League

The need for regionalisation in Leagues One and Two is obvious. It's complete madness in these very tough economic times that Carlisle United are still travelling to the other end of the country to play Yeovil Town, and vice-versa, when you think of what the clubs and their supporters have to shell out in hotel bills and travel costs.

I'd like to see an amalgamation of League One and Two and then split the new division into League One North and League One South sections. The top team in each new section would be automatically promoted to the Championship, with the third promoted club being the winner of the play-offs involving the second and third-placed teams in League One North and League One South.

As well as greatly reducing travel costs that few clubs can afford and increasing the number of local derbies, the new structure would bring all 48 teams in the bottom two leagues that step closer to the Championship.

They successfully introduced regionalisation at Conference level and it's time the bottom two tiers of The Football League followed suit. It has to happen before long. How many league clubs have been in administration over the past decade or so? We have a great pyramid system in English football and we must take steps to protect it and help the member clubs.

International football

There are so many international fixtures today, the honour of representing your country and even the World Cup itself has been diluted. If you asked the younger pros at Europe's top clubs if they would rather play in the World Cup final or the Champions League Final, I have a horrible feeling that most of them would say the latter.

I mean, we now have players turning out for England in a totally meaningless friendly in August before they have even played a Premier League game. I can understand warm-up games before the finals of the World Cup and European Championship tournament but not meaningless friendlies in August.

There are too many also-rans in the World Cup – 32 teams in the final is too many. When I was a kid, the two major occasions in the football calendar were the World Cup Final and the FA Cup Final. Now the Champions League and the Premier League take priority in the eyes of players and fans alike.

European football

The top European clubs have become so powerful since the advent of the Champions League that I can visualise the day when the Champions League will be extended and be run on a proper league basis.

I can envisage, say, 16 teams playing regularly on a Wednesday night, with only the bottom side dropping out at the end of the season.

For me, the Europa League is a waste of time and badly in need of impetus. The best thing UEFA can do is to give the winners a passport to the Champions League the following season – that would give the Europa League fixtures a much needed edge and provide greater motivation for clubs, managers and players.

I'd also like to see UEFA's secondary cup competition revert to a knockout tournament, as it used to be in the days of the Cup Winners' Cup and, before that, the Fairs Cup. Actually, I'd go further by re-naming it the Europa Cup and seed the winners of the final straight through to the following season's Champions League group stages.

Video technology

I've been crying out for the football authorities to use video technology for years and it has to happen before many more perfectly good goals are wrongly disallowed. Most famously, Frank Lampard's legitimate 'goal' for England against Germany in the 2010 World Cup finals.

Goalline technology would have confirmed that Frank Lampard's shot against Germany in the 2010 World Cup was a perfectly good goal.

And that infamous 'goal' by Pedro Mendes for Spurs that should have been the winner against Manchester United in time added on at Old Trafford in January 2005, when retreating keeper Roy Carroll fumbled the ball and it dropped at least a yard behind the goalline.

I was on 'live' commentary for Sky that night and, even from high up on the TV gantry some 50 yards from the incident, I shouted "goal!" as soon as I saw the ball hit Carroll's chest, loop over him and bounce way beyond the line. I think everyone inside the ground realised it was goal – all except the referee and his assistants.

There is probably at least one high profile incident a season affecting the outcome of matches and that can't be allowed to continue. With so much TV income and other revenues at stake in the game today, it's imperative that officials get the big decisions right as often as possible. They are human, of course, and will always make mistakes but their errors must be minimised and the only way to do this is by the introduction of modern video technology.

Those who are against the use of cameras to determine whether the ball has fully crossed the goalline argue that if a system is introduced in the Premier League, then it must also be adopted by The Football League for the three English divisions below the top flight, which may be too costly to implement across those 72 clubs.

That's nonsense. The Premier League is such a huge global brand today, technology can justifiably be used in England's elite division alone. Those who run the Premier League should be innovators, showing UEFA and FIFA the way forward, not waiting for the 'suits' in Geneva to finally get off their backsides and do something to make it happen. If the rest of the world isn't ready to embrace the best available technology, then that's up to them. The Premier League should grasp the nettle themselves and make it mandatory.

Two models have recently been used in experiments to find the best goalline technology but that's still not gone far enough in addressing an important issue. The infamous Lampard incident happened more than two years ago; the Mendes winner chalked off at Old Trafford was five years earlier. It's time every Premier League club was equipped with goalline cameras, with Football League clubs to follow suit as quickly as possible. After all, what price a bad decision in the Championship that could deny a team promotion to 'The Promised Land'?

Technology will also help match officials. They are already under immense pressure and referees are all in favour of cameras positioned on the goalline to assist them in making the correct decisions. Did the ball cross the line, or not? It's a simple matter of fact that cameras would confirm one way or the other.

What referees don't want is technology brought in to check contentious offside and penalty decisions and I appreciate their view. If we had that, there would be too many breaks in the game and there would be no point in having referees – you might as well have a man sat up in the stand blowing a whistle. Referees are often unfairly slaughtered by fans, players, managers and media when they get it wrong, so let's help them as much as we can

Referees and their assistants get a rough time from players and managers but nothing's new. Here Alan Devonshire and I protest about the tightness of our shorts in 1985!

without undermining them.

I'm not saying Frank Lampard's 39th minute disallowed goal against Germany that bounced a foot behind the chalk would have changed the outcome of the second round game in Bloemfontein that ended in a 4-1 defeat. But at 2-1 down, it would have brought England level and who knows what would have happened?

The linesman was doing his job in that he was in line with the most advanced player, Lampard, but he could not keep pace with the ball to adjudge if it had crossed the line. Not his fault. He can only give what he sees. That's precisely the point. He could not see it.

The cameras did, and pinpointed the ball's position accurately without the loss of time. A fourth official would have taken a split-second to inform the referee, perhaps by pressing a button that activates a beep on the referee's watch or a wristband. So why are cameras not allowed to decide? This is the question the football governing bodies must address without delay.

In rugby and cricket cameras are deployed successfully in support of the referee to determine the validity of decisions. Tennis and cricket also use the 'Hawkeye' system to support umpires and line judges. By denying football teams that possibility, FIFA are perpetrating injustice for no apparent good and it's time Sepp Blatter and friends woke up to this fact.

The trouble with Twitter

I STRUGGLE to get my head around the social networking phenomenon that has swept the world in recent years. While I have occasionally read comments by fans posted on internet forums, I don't use Twitter or Facebook and can't for the life of me understand why anyone would wish to know what I'm doing at any given time of the day or night. Or why I would want to tell anyone, especially total strangers, what I'm up to! But some players clearly do.

In the era I played in, we understood that any problems inside the dressing room or within the club had to remain private and were not for public consumption. I can only imagine what people would make of the things we got up to 25 years ago if iPhones and You Tube had been around then but dirty linen was never to be washed in public. It was an unwritten law.

I accept that the world has moved on but players have to be careful not to embarrass their clubs or their team-mates by saying the wrong thing.

Rio Ferdinand and Joey Barton have gained a reputation as the most prolific 'tweeters' and I can appreciate how their 'followers' may find it interesting to keep up to date with their thoughts and activities off the field. It can also be good to get information from the horse's mouth rather than read what a player has supposed to have told a reporter and wonder if what you read in print is in fact true.

While the press have been known to twist quotes and misrepresent the interviewee (shock horror!), I do believe that clubs wrap their players up in far too much cotton wool these days. Journalists used to be welcome at the training ground and the players would happily spend time chatting to a scribe before driving home. We'd give our home telephone number to the most trusted journos and there was a mutual trust that simply doesn't exist today.

Nowadays, you can't do a one-to-one interview with a player without having to go through the hassle of getting the permission of the club's media department. This suggests the clubs have little trust in their players, although I know how controlling some managers can be. During my time with Leicester, I once agreed to do an innocuous family spread in *Hello!* magazine without first asking the manager's permission. When Martin O'Neill found out about it, he fined me pretty much half of what I was paid by the publisher. And I was in my mid-30s by then!

On the other hand, clubs will argue that media representatives have occasionally abused their privileged access. A classic example was the incident involving West Ham stars John Hartson and Eyal Berkovic at the Hammers' Chadwell Heath training ground, where TV cameras captured the Welsh striker booting the Israeli midfielder in the head – and then, much to manager Harry Redknapp's dismay, broadcast the fracas to the rest of the world. Trust is a two-way street.

Not that today's players should be caught off-guard by the press. Tony Carr, West Ham's academy director, told me that all of his youth squad undergo media training in which they are put in front of cameras and coached how to handle certain questions in a typical interview situation.

Twitter has given the modern player control over his own words but it has also served as a reminder that players can be their own worst enemies. Some have already fallen foul of this freedom of speech, by arguing with fans, questioning the manager and becoming embroiled in racist issues sparked by thoughtless comments on their mobile phone or home computer. We've all sent a text in the heat of the moment, or maybe after a few too many drinks, that we've lived to regret, so players need to be more careful and think before they tweet.

For me, Twitter is a potential minefield players can, and should, avoid. In the final analysis, the old rules still apply in the modern world: players should do all their talking on the pitch.

31

That's life

A S I reflect on the past 11 years since I hung up my boots, I know it's been a rollercoaster period in my life. In my ideal world, I'd now be nice and comfortable in financial terms, never having to work again, and I'd be West Ham manager, looking to get them into the Champions League at the end of this season. That's the fantasy vision.

But the reality is somewhat different. I'm not in a particularly good financial position – I missed out on the mega-money today's players earn and good luck to them. Although I'm jealous of what the average players are paid, the good ones deserve every penny they get.

It's no problem having to work either. I love my role with Sky, it's the next best thing to playing or managing and keeps me closely involved with the game I still have a passion for. I've thoroughly enjoyed the last 11 years with Sky and hope to remain part of their team for many years to come.

I have to admit, my catastrophic short spell at Barnet will, barring a miracle, preclude me from ever managing a professional club again. I'm glad I gave it a shot, though. At least I can say I've been a manager and done a bit of coaching. I saw the other side of football and it made me appreciate all the more how lucky I'd been to play at the top flight for the majority of my career, with West Ham, Everton and Leicester City. With the experience and knowledge I have today, I know I'd make a much better manager now than I was back then. I simply wasn't ready for it when the chance came along.

To be honest, I'm not sure I want a way back into management anyway. Why would I want to give up my good job with Sky, where I'm well paid for what I do, to re-enter a profession where the average 'life expectancy' of a football manager is about 12 months? There would be no chance of me getting my dream job at one of the three clubs I've just mentioned, so why take a risky job with a League Two or Conference club where I'd get probably half the money, 25 times the aggro and have to work 10 times harder than I do now?

Proud father

Personally, my life has been a bit traumatic recently. It was very sad that my marriage to Lorraine effectively broke up in 2007, which resulted in us getting divorced in 2009. After what I've gone through, I wouldn't wish divorce on my worst enemy, because it's one of the hardest things you can

With Chloe in 2012. My daughter is much brainier than me and studying hard at university.

go through.

While I wouldn't want to blame the break-up of my marriage on my single-minded pursuit of our West Ham takeover bid – there were quite obviously things that were wrong in our personal relationship anyway, but it's probably fair to say that it didn't help. It's also very difficult when a player retires from professional football (as covered in more depth in chapter 8), not only for the ex-players but the wives and partners and their children, too. I think it's fair to say that, on reflection, my marriage was doomed from the moment I retired from the game.

Where I'm especially lucky is that I have three beautiful children. Chloe is 20 now and is someone I'm very proud of. She's currently studying philosophy and criminology at Northampton University but please don't ask me to explain what that involves! She tells me she might like to eventually work as a psychiatrist or in the CSI department of the police force.

I've tried to help Chloe as much as possible where boyfriends are concerned, like any good father would do. When her first boyfriend declared he was a Tottenham fan, I told her it wouldn't last. The second one was also a Spurs supporter and I said exactly the same thing – and was proved correct

again! Eventually, to my great approval, she brought home a West Ham fan and she received my full blessing! As always, though, your kids seem to have the last laugh, as her current beau is a Chelsea fan and Chloe has stated that the Blues are now her team. Oh well, I did try.

I'm also very proud of my 14-year-old twin boys, Matt and Billy, who live with their mum in Surrey. It's been particularly hard for them over the past five years but often you find that children handle things better than the adults. I try to give them as much of my time as possible and make them part of my busy life schedule. After four years away from the game, I'm delighted that

My boys, Matt and Billy, in 2008.

they have both resumed playing football for a local team at weekends. One achievement I am very pleased about is the fact that – unlike their sister – I've managed to groom them into being massive West Ham fans despite the club's trials and tribulations.

Over the last couple of years, I have taken the boys on holiday to Florida, Tenerife, Scotland and skiing in Switzerland. Just the three of us go and we have special quality time doing the sort of things boys want to do. We've really enjoyed our little trips and hopefully there are lots more to come, although I have a feeling that once the beer and girls kicks in, Dad will become surplus to requirements!

The twins getting muddy in 2009.

The blonde beauty

What has been great for me is that, towards the end of 2008, I met a lovely girl called Karen Gillmore who has been a real shining light in my life.

It's been difficult trying to split my time between where we live in Leigh-on-Sea, Essex and the boys' home in Surrey whilst working unsociable hours. My role with Sky obviously involves a lot of weekend and midweek trips up and down the motorways of England to cover games, while my after-dinner work is usually evenings only. Karen works full-time for Chase Bureau Accountants in Southend, so at times we can be like ships that pass

With the lovely Karen, who has been such a rock in my life.

in the night but there is no doubt that she has been a real rock in my life.

It was thanks to Galey that Karen and I first met. My former West Ham team-mate recommended Chase Bureau to me back in 2004 and I'd go there as a client to meet the boss, John Symons, who would guide me through my, at times, lack of funds and help to re-shape my finances during and after my divorce.

There was always a friendly atmosphere whenever you walked into reception at their seafront offices, with a bevy of happy, smiling beauties ready to greet you. One of them happened to be Karen and it was after my divorce that I started to notice this very friendly blonde beauty a little more!

One day, while I was having lunch with John in Southend High Street, Karen walked past our table and I started to probe him about his eye-catching receptionist. He told me he'd known this lovely girl for around 30 years, that she was single and had a 14-year-old son called Sam.

John gave me her mobile phone number but before I had the chance to call her, in October 2008 I co-hosted a function with Galey at The Boatyard restaurant in Leigh-on-Sea, where our guests were Billy Bonds and Phil Parkes. John had a table at the function and he told me Karen would be coming along with her friends.

Karen had always had her blonde hair straight whenever I'd seen her at work but on this occasion she decided to change the style, which, being the fashion expert I am, was enough to confuse me! I didn't want to find myself talking to the wrong girl, so I literally had to ask John: "Is that Karen who works on reception?" He confirmed it was.

Anyway, once the show got underway, Galey repeatedly had to tell two noisy blondes at the bar to 'shut up' – and one of them was Karen, who was paying absolutely no attention to the West Ham stories being told by me and the three other lads, which was quite amusing in itself.

With Karen's son, Sam Gillmore, on the sand in Dubai in 2012.

I was flying to Dubai the following morning but before the night at The Boatyard ended I plucked up the courage to ask Karen out. I called her when I got back to England, took her out one night and things went from there. I'm pleased to say we moved in together (with Sam) early in 2011 and, touch wood, things have been really good for us and hopefully we will enjoy many more happy years together.

Family issues

One thing that did hit me and my family hard was the divorce of my parents, Carole and Clive, at the end of 1999. It came as a bolt out of the blue because Mum and Dad had always portrayed the ultimate happy couple, which just goes to show that you never know what is really going on.

I couldn't believe it when Mum told me that Dad had apparently been having an affair with Margaret, one of the ladies he worked with at the office and who was well known to all of us. As it turned out, Dad and Margaret have now been married for eight years or so and they seem very happy.

On the downside, the break-up of our parents' marriage has caused friction between Dad and my brother Paul and sister Jo, who both took it very badly and have so far been unable to forgive him. Mum, Paul and Jo all worked at the same office as Margaret and Dad, so I can understand how difficult it's been for them to come to terms with what happened. It's a great shame and I just hope that one day their wounds will fully heal. That's life. I know we're not the only family to have suffered the pain of divorce and have to deal with all the other problems that go on in the world.

Despite this unfortunate family split, I try and spend as much time as I can with my Mum, brother and sister. I have a fantastic relationship with Mum, who's now retired and lives not far from us at South Woodham Ferrers. She has always been there for me and we had some fabulous times during my football career where both my parents followed me all around the world. It's

The four ladies in my life – Mum, sister Jo, girlfriend Karen and daughter Chloe.

With brother Paul, sister Jo and Mum.

been difficult for Mum since the break-up but I admire her for the way she has tried to get on with her life. She has always been there when I've needed her these last few years.

Jo is a fantastic housewife with five lovely kids, Elle, Daisy, Lili, Arthur and William, and lives near Mum in North Fambridge. Both Jo and her husband Andy always amaze me in that, despite all that's going on in their house, there is always such a loving family atmosphere whenever we visit. It's often noisy but always entertaining! Since I've met Karen we have seen quite a bit of the Lavers, as her and Jo get on so well and we have had a few memorable nights recently. I'm probably closer to my sister now than I've ever been, which is nice.

Paul is based up in Wolverhampton with his wife Jane, daughter Amber and son Callum and works as an insurance broker in Birmingham. They moved to the West Midlands a few years ago to be near Jane's family, who had health problems. Although I know Paul probably misses living in the county where he was brought up, I'm pleased to say that Callum is a fully-fledged Hammer despite his Black Country accent! With my sons and nephews all supporting West Ham, the fifth generation of Cottee Hammers is going strong.

Special bond

The special bond I have with Dad still exists to this day. He played a big part in setting me on the right path in football and life itself and I have a lot to thank him for. He gave me confidence and self-belief but he also knew how to keep my feet on the ground and was never afraid to voice an opinion even if he knew I wouldn't necessarily agree with it or wish to hear it. He was at once my biggest fan and harshest critic but I wouldn't have had it any other way.

He tells me he wasn't a bad player himself in his younger days, a prolific striker for East Ham Schoolboys and a good finisher. There's no photographic or video evidence, so I have to take his word for it. Like vintage wine, I think he actually becomes a better footballer with each passing year, developing from a good amateur player into a top amateur player – well, in his own mind anyway! It's still a standing joke between us that he played for East Ham and I played for West Ham!

I'm just relieved he's still here with us after suffering heart trouble back in 2009, at the age of 70. I first noticed a decline in his health that July, when we went on a golfing trip to Scotland. Although the course was only slightly hilly, he had to stop playing after four holes and go and sit down.

Dad kept himself very fit even after he retired, always doing press-ups and sit-ups until his late 60s. His only health complaint was the cartilage trouble that forced him to give up playing Sunday morning football some years earlier.

But later in 2009, he was taken into hospital. The arteries leading to his heart had become blocked and he had to undergo a quadruple bypass operation and have a new valve inserted. It was a massive op' and at one stage it was touch and go – I can't speak highly enough of the wonderful medical staff at the new heart unit in Basildon Hospital who took such great care of Dad.

He was on the slow road to recovery when, in July 2010, he was taken ill while I was away on a golf trip with Karen in Portugal to play in the Sir Bobby Robson charity tournament. We were at dinner one night when we received a text from Margaret to say that Dad had collapsed and been taken into hospital. We flew back home the next morning, went straight to the hospital and this time he had to have a pacemaker fitted to regulate his heartbeat.

He has to take things much easier these days but at least he is in good health again. He officially announced his retirement from golf in the summer of 2012 and there's a funny postscript to this courtesy of my old strike-partner

With my three and Dad on Father's Day in 2011.

Dad and I dressed up in claret and blue top hat and tails for the 2008 Epsom Derby,
where we were supporting the horse owned by West Ham fan Russell Trew and
named after Alan Devonshire. The 100/1 shot came 13th of 16 runners.

Frank McAvennie. All the players I played with met and knew Dad and wherever I go the first question I'm always asked is 'how's Dad?'

When Frankie Mac enquired about Dad's health after the pacemaker had been fitted, I had to tell him that he was fine but he might struggle to play golf again. To which Frank quipped: "He was never any f****** good at it anyway, so what's the difference?"

Dad's a man of leisure these days and enjoying retirement. He still has his flutters on the horses each week and has now bought a two-year-old greyhound that he's named 'Billymatt' – after my two boys – that will run at Romford dogs, which will give him a bit of interest. I've got a 10% share in it, so I hope it does the business for me too! The funny thing is, despite all the serious stuff he's had done to his heart, all he ever moans about are his dodgy knees.

Beaten by a caterpillar

So what else have I been up to apart from growing old as an ex-professional footballer? I don't know whether the thought of turning 40 in July 2005 had anything to do with it or it was a mid-life crisis thing, but I very foolishly decided to run the London Marathon for the first time that year.

More than 30,000 people pounded the streets on the 26.2-mile challenge from Greenwich to The Mall. Paula Radcliffe won the women's race in 2hrs 17mins 41secs, more than five minutes ahead of second place – even though she famously made an unexpected stop to take a pee by the side of the road. Toilet break? I felt I needed a heart bypass and both lungs replaced after struggling across the finish line some three hours behind Radcliffe – in 5hrs 20mins to be more accurate.

I'd like to say I enjoyed it but I'd be lying – I nearly f****** killed myself! I should have listened to my body when, during my first training run in January, I pulled my groin muscle and had to rest for five weeks. I was back on the road in February but trained only once a week. The furthest I ever ran before the marathon was 15 miles, and then only just the once, so in terms of preparation for the big one I was never going to run throughout the full 26-plus miles.

I'd agreed for BBC Radio 5Live to interview me at the 19-mile marker, which was ridiculously optimistic of me. As I trudged through Canary Wharf a radio interviewer started jogging alongside me and as soon as I finished answering her questions I made the mistake of stopping to catch my breath. My legs were killing me but

I just about had the energy to hold up my medal for running the 2005 London Marathon.

it wasn't the wisest thing to do. In the end I jogged a few hundred yards, then walked the next couple of hundred, and so on. I was determined not to pull a muscle in my legs or collapse into a heap and die, so I walked the last six miles.

At one point I suffered the humility of being overtaken by a caterpillar. Then a cow went past and people dressed up as chickens just piled on the embarrassment. "Come on, Cottee, you w*****!" shouted some sympathetic soul who recognised me in my West Ham replica shirt with the famous number six on the back.

When my ordeal was finally over, I just sat down on the kerb and felt my body shake for half an hour. It didn't seem worth all the pain I endured at the time but I knew the £8,500 I raised for the Bobby Moore Fund for Cancer Research was in a very good cause. Just don't ask me to do it again!

Seriously, though, the BMF is close to my heart, because my Granddad died of cancer and I've tried to help Stephanie Moore as much as I can by attending golf days, quizzes and other events for the charity and its aims to raise awareness of bowel cancer.

One of the clowns

Since 2011 I've also been a patron of the Clowns in the Sky charity, who supply soft toys for seriously ill children. I visit hospital wards with the toys on a trolley and give them to the kids. It's heartrending at times but I enjoy doing it.

I did a 21-mile bike ride around the Essex towns of Orsett, Grays and

Bulphan for Clowns in the Sky back in May 2012. Very similar to the London Marathon, my preparations were virtually non-existent and there was a price to pay for this. I'd had far too many drinks at a function the night before the race and when I awoke I was horrified to discover my mountain bike in the garage was covered in cobwebs, there was no oil on the chain and it had two flat tyres!

I had to get it from Leigh-on-Sea to the starting point of the race at Grays. I tried to put it in the back of the car but it wouldn't fit, so I had no option but to remove the roof from my convertible. Which would have been fine if it hadn't started to rain. I drove the 10 miles and lost count of the people who had disbelieving looks for a madmen speeding through the streets of Essex with a bike on the back seat of his open-roof car and rain lashing down!

The inevitable question...

As well as my work for Sky, I keep busy writing a weekly West Ham-related column for the *East London Advertiser* paper throughout the football season. I'm also contracted to do PR work for Rudridge, who are basically a groundwork and civil engineering company run by friends of mine called Alan and Rob and we have a fantastic relationship. I help them to organise hospitality events, where I meet and greet their clients and we have had some wonderful days over the last five years.

It's also been good that I've been able to help out Lyme Regis FC, one of the most prominent clubs on the Dorset non-league scene, in my role as Honorary President in which I've been able to help with fund-raising to finance improved facilities at their lovely little coastal ground. Philip Evans, who has always been closely involved with Lyme as a player and later as chairman, published my first book back in 1995 and now he's published this one, too. Ironically, Philip was once the MD of the local newspaper group I now write for.

My life is good at the moment and seemingly heading in the right direction with both my personal and professional lives in a good place. With the magic 50th birthday milestone rapidly approaching, I'm enjoying everything that life is throwing at me again and I believe that things will only get better in the future.

One of the things I have done lots of since my retirement is the after-dinner work with Galey, who has unfortunately developed into one of my best mates! We have a lot of fun hosting shows and doing other bits and pieces, and inevitably we end up with a question-and-answer session. You can almost guarantee that at one stage during the evening one bight spark will put up his hand and ask me: "Weren't you involved in a consortium...?"